What People Are Sayi

The Ruling Ide

Ari Ofengenden's *The Ruling Ideas* is a tour de force of intellectual history and cultural critique. His very clear writing and astonishing scholarly range provides surprises on just about every page. The book also has the rare quality of actually being accessible to beginners while also being worthwhile to the more deeply bookish among us. It is almost as if Slavoj Žižek were turned into a more readably patient explainer: the same dazzling connections between low and high culture but written in a way that is even more approachable. I learned a great deal from this book and I suspect most everyone will as well. Greater self-awareness of how what we think got into our heads is humbling. Yet it is also exhilarating in that it helps connect us to the larger and more durable meanings that we need for the long run of this life.

David Blacker, author of *What's Left of the World* and *The Falling Rate of Learning*

This is a powerful deconstruction of the ideas that serve to legitimate the power of the ruling classes. In direct, clear and understandable language, it argues for a new vision of values, inspired by critics of the system from Jean-Jacques Rousseau and Friedrich Engels to Tolstoy and Gandhi.

Michael Löwy, author of *Écosocialism: A radical alternative to the capitalist ecological catastrophe*

Contrary to the many attempts to declare ideology critique as outdated, Ari Ofengenden beautifully demonstrates that it is very alive and kicking. The way he deconstructs permeating ideologies like, for example, liberal individualism, neo-

Nietzscheanism, the alienating commandment of enjoyment and short-term pleasures, consumer market infantilization is not only intellectually inspiring, but also accessible, suspenseful, and entertaining. Ideology critique is not just about dismantling ruling ideologies, but also about looking for various sources of resistance, be it in ancient and modern philosophies, in different religions or in Marxism. Indeed, we need a new kind of revolution that addresses both the heating of the biosphere and the challenges of the high-tech mode of production.

Jan Rehmann, author of *Theories of Ideology. The Powers of Alienation and Subjection*

The importance of Ofengenden's book is that it makes readers more conscious not only of their own ideas but of the larger social functions performed by those ideas. It teaches us how and why ruling ideas – sometimes called "common sense" – reflect the ideas and goals of rulers.

Richard D. Wolff, author of *Democracy at Work: A Cure for Capitalism*

The Ruling Ideas is an invaluable analysis of how the broader culture of ideas, values, knowledge, and institutions function pedagogically to shape our sense of self, others, and the larger world in a deeply iniquitous and unjust economic, political, and social order. For too long, matters of consciousness, ideology, and how we are shaped as agents and citizens has escaped serious analysis of power and the looming reach of dominant neoliberal societies. Ari Ofengenden provides a brilliant book for understanding how education has become central not just to matters of individual and collective identity but to politics itself.

Henry Giroux, author of *On Critical Pedagogy*

The Ruling Ideas

How They Ruin Society and Make You Miserable

The Ruling Ideas

How They Ruin Society and Make You Miserable

Ari Ofengenden

Winchester, UK
Washington, USA

JOHN HUNT PUBLISHING

First published by Zero Books, 2022
Zero Books is an imprint of John Hunt Publishing Ltd., No. 3 East St., Alresford,
Hampshire SO24 9EE, UK
office@jhpbooks.com
www.johnhuntpublishing.com
www.zero-books.net

For distributor details and how to order please visit the 'Ordering' section on our website.

ISBN: 978 1 78904 959 6
978 1 78904 960 2 (ebook)
Library of Congress Control Number: 2021942241

A CIP catalogue record for this book is available from the British Library.

Design: Stuart Davies

UK: Printed and bound by CPI Group (UK) Ltd, Croydon, CR0 4YY
Printed in North America by CPI GPS partners

We operate a distinctive and ethical publishing philosophy in
all areas of our business, from our global network of authors to
production and worldwide distribution.

Contents

Also by the Author

Abraham Shlonsky: An Introduction to His Poetry ISBN 987-3-11-
035061-8
Liberalization and Culture in Contemporary Israel ISBN
9781498570367

Acknowledgments

Through the years, many people have had to suffer hearing of my discomfort with ruling ideas, and their pushing back against my critique has helped me think more deeply about it. Maybe the first ideas that I saw as ruling were national ideas. I bugged everyone with my critique from the early 1990s, especially my parents and friends. I would like to thank my parents, Malka and Uri, for their patience and support. I want to thank Tzofit, my partner, for endless discussions on false universality and naturalization and for reading the whole book and working with me on the chapters. My sister Noa as well as Yaniv Kasher for holding long discussions of nationalism, liberalism, colonialism, nationalism and family values. Finally my sons, Emile and Michel, who both patiently listened to my critique of mainstream culture in the US and also brought home the ways in which we are all inculcated into ruling ideas from an early age.

Introduction

Whether you grew up in a liberal Western democracy or in a dictatorship, whether you got a religious education or a secular one, whether you are American or Chinese or Indian, what you come to believe about yourself and the world is not of your choosing. Strangely, you are a captive to thoughts and feelings that others have instilled in you. You may feel joy buying things or playing golf, drinking coffee, or going on a Haig pilgrimage. You may believe that your nation is the greatest, that you are part of a chosen people, that your God is the greatest, you may believe in a disciplined self or in no self, or that genders are fluid, or in inclusion of the disabled, or compassion for animals or that going into space will solve humanity's problems. You may admire entrepreneurs, small business and celebrities or be proud of the welfare state. You may put health above all else or like traveling abroad or praying. Your attitude toward these things was not really your choice.

Though uncomfortable to hear, many of these beliefs were foisted upon you just like your mother tongue when you were young. Many of them are constantly being reinforced today by friends and relatives or curated by algorithms that suggest for you what video to watch and which people to be friends with, and ultimately what to buy, what to think and what to feel.

This book will help you start on a journey to discover what you really want to believe and how you want to be. It is explicitly conceived as a guide, a way out of a world we are made to believe in and even "love" though it oppresses us. This is not an easy journey since we strongly identify and enjoy what was in fact forced on us from an early age and what we are pressured to believe by friends, educators, our surroundings and media. We come to love what we arbitrarily and involuntary were coerced to be. Our beliefs, desires and the way we think present

1

themselves as natural, common sense, self-evident; we feel we just want to fulfill these beliefs, to succeed in what society tells us we should be. This is because we are under pressure all the time. These desires and beliefs were not only forced on us in the past, but are also subtly forced on us in the present. Most of our conversations with people around us reaffirm our ideas and preexisting values. Listen to your friends; underneath what they tell you about a certain film they liked or someone that was mean to them, aren't they saying, "Don't you find that what I believe is true?" or "Don't you find that what I desire is good?" and we are usually expected to validate them with "Yes! What you find good, I find good" and "Yes! What you believe, I believe." When we see a post by a friend on social media, does not this friend want us to "like" this post? That is, to reaffirm that the holiday on the beach is worthy of envy, that that picture of the cat is cute.

As we grow up we look for self-confirmation in the news and novels that we read, the churches and temples that we visit, and the associations that we go to. The type of interaction that will reaffirm, approve, endorse, validate, restate and reassert what we already believe. The novels, newspapers and posts that we read, the films that we see all have the same message: "What you already know, what you already believe is right."

Take action films, for instance. Are they not an eternal repetition of the same ideas and themes? Superheroes, pirates, cowboys, spies and policemen have been doing the same things in the same way since *The Great Train Robbery* appeared in 1903. These films extol the virtue of the rugged individualist hero who, possessed by special gifts and virtues, defeats transcendent evil against all odds. Newspapers, like the *New York Times* or *The Economist*, might bring new events and happenings but rarely new perspectives. *The Economist* and the *New York Times* were filter bubbles long before the term existed. They force reality to confirm their predictable formats and their expected take of things. Algorithm-based media (YouTube, Facebook, Snapchat, etc.) of course go even further, filtering not only according to a large group (liberal middle- to upper-class Americans – like the *New York Times*) but everything not "engaging" for much smaller groups or to you personally. Eighty percent of what people see on YouTube, for instance, are videos suggested by YouTube; this process is so opaque that unlike mass media, one does not even know which and how many people share this reality. Virtual reality will carry this process to the extreme. People will literally inhabit idiosyncratic little bubble worlds with a few giant corporations presiding over them.

It seems that all your communications and interactions are set to reaffirm existing ideas or promote needs and desires that you do not necessarily have. How can one find a way out? How can we know what we want to be? This book attempts to set off on the path of challenge instead of affirmation. It tries to find a way out of a worldview and habits that were taught by parents, schools, Hollywood, social media, friends and spouses. It calls on you to reeducate yourself, to be your own parent, teacher and entertainer. It offers ways for achieving intellectual independence.

What is crucial for this book, however, are not the ways of thought and ideas that you got when you were child, but the way in which certain ideas are reinforced now and keep you from changing. Why do I stress the power of current ideas? Because in contrast to many who would like to tell you that you are fixed, that you have a "nature," humans are flexible creatures; their brains' most essential feature is neuroplasticity; they are able to acquire new thoughts, skills and memories and to reinvent themselves constantly. We all experience many changes in what we believe and in how we act. Many of these changes happen throughout life such as when we move to a new school, new country or new culture, when we find love, when we start working. The actual reason that we believe the same things throughout most of our adult lives is that we are bombarded by these same ideas throughout our lives.

These ideas are not represented as a consistent ideology. They crop up in various ways and in different media, in newspapers, films, social media, musical videos, fiction and nonfiction books. Most importantly, these ideas are usually not represented to us as partisan, or as having interests behind them. They are presented through the medium of what is conceived of as the innocent pleasures of entertainment in our films, television and YouTube clips, in what we take to be neutral reporting on the state of the world, in our newspapers and video clips and in our favorite science and other nonfiction books. Though these ideas are presented through enticing, fun or inspirational experiences, they ultimately cause all of us great suffering as well as being harmful to the world. Undermining them is painful but will ultimately make your life more meaningful. This book will free you from ideas such as individualism, big men and villains, the work ethic, the Enlightenment, knowledge, the glorious past, the dystopian future, God, nation, and family.

One can compare being under the pressure of these ideas to wearing a bizarre set of glasses or an intrusive kind of augmented reality, or to liken them to the refrain of a song that one keeps humming obsessively. The glasses hide certain things from you; the obsessive song does not let you hear the world around you. Even slightly undermining these ideas opens you both to the world and also to discovering new ideas. Challenging ruling ideas can change your mood from being a clenched fist to being open to yourself and to the world. So instead of continuing in the abstract, let's start with one classic idea – the idea of the special individual.

Chapter One

Individualism Part I

We Are All Special

In a famous scene from Monty Python's *Life of Brian*, Brian wakes up in the early morning, yawns and opens his window. Outside a huge crowd surprises him and shouts: "Look! There He is! The Chosen One has woken!" Brian, who still lives with his mother, is in trouble for having all of these followers as well as for sleeping with a "welsh tart." His mother tries to disperse the crowd, but they convince her to have Brian talk with them. He comes to the window. The crowd shouts:

FOLLOWERS: A blessing! A blessing! A blessing!...

BRIAN: No. No, please! Please! Please, listen. I've got one or two things to say.

FOLLOWERS: Tell us. Tell us both of them.

BRIAN: Look. You've got it all wrong. You don't need to follow me. You don't need to follow anybody! You've got to think for yourselves. You're all individuals!

FOLLOWERS: Yes, we're all individuals!

BRIAN: You're all different!

FOLLOWERS: Yes, we are all different!

DENNIS: I'm not.

ARTHUR: Shhhh.

FOLLOWERS: Shh. Shhhh. Shh.

BRIAN: You've all got to work it out for yourselves!

FOLLOWERS: Yes! We've got to work it out for ourselves!

BRIAN: Exactly!

FOLLOWERS: Tell us more!

BRIAN: No! That's the point! Don't let anyone tell you what to do!

5

At this point, Brian's mother pulls him away from the window and he can no longer give advice to the crowd. The scene is funny, we laugh at Brian the reluctant leader, we laugh at the crowd that does not seem to understand the paradox of shouting together "We are all individuals!" But the scene is much deeper than that. Of course, this is a light parody of Christianity. We laugh at the absurdity of it all, and the scene juxtaposes our own liberal individualist values with the foolishness of mass following.

The scene, however, inadvertently shows us the paradox of our own ideology. This reveals itself most pointedly when Brian says "you are all different" and everybody answers "Yes, we are all different!" except Dennis, who says "I'm not." Dennis is truly different while all the people who chant "Yes, we are all different" are not. Is not, however, the whole scene an exaggeration of the situation in contemporary society? Teachers and parents tell ALL children that they are all different, individual and special, and all of these children internalize these same beliefs.

Social theorist Louis Althusser used a helpful term to describe what teachers and parents are essentially doing – interpellation. Children are being interpellated as special individuals. Althusser conceived of production of individualism as a kind of scene but one that is different from the film. In Althusser's scene, you are walking in the street and a policeman is calling "Hey, you." You turn around slowly and say "Who me?" At that moment you have been interpellated as an individual by the policeman, in a way the language of the policeman has singled you out, made you into a singular being.[1] This, of course, sounds absurd. Were you not an individual before the policeman called you? In fact, Althusser is using this as a metaphor and model. It is those in authority who call us into being.

Psychoanalyst Jacques Lacan remarked that before a child is born, a place for it is prepared by his parents. One can obviously see parents or a single parent and those around them busily preparing for the child. They may discuss possible names, prepare rooms and toys, etc. The child is born into a socially constructed place.[2] If that place will put great stress on, for example, family, nation or tribe, then the person might well think of himself as a collective being. Asian culture, for example, traditionally stresses family obligation more than individual self-actualization. If that place stresses a certain kind of individuality – for example, individualistic hedonism – then the person will become this as well.

The scene from *Life of Brian*, however, is in some ways more instructive than Althusser's policeman scene, since it shows us the results of interpellation for a whole society. What does it mean for a large group of people to believe that they are all different? In fact, if you look at people's beliefs, they are radically nonindividual. Millions, in the West at least, shout, "We are all different" while in fact believing and pursuing the same things. For most people a humbler but truer approach to themselves would be to say, "I mainly believe and do as the people around me believe and do. I usually desire what I am taught to desire."

We can turn the tables on Brian, and ask why we look toward the individual and individualism as the answer to difficult questions of existence. We can examine these questions from the nonindividual perspective of ancient Christianity, or a modern nonindividualist ideology like Marxism, or from the perspective of biology. Indeed, why would the answers for the great pressing biological concerns such as death, or social concerns such as status anxiety or suffering caused by working life be so different for different individuals? Are not death and the frustrations of work mostly the same for most of humanity? Why does our reaction to them need to be so different? We are so used to Brian's message, so inundated with it throughout our lives, that we don't realize how strange it is. Perhaps we can see how strange this idea of each one working it out himself or herself is if we look back and examine how this idea was invented and why.

The Entrepreneur on the Frontier

Most historians agree that the idea of the modern individual was born in Renaissance Italy. The nineteenth-century Renaissance historian Jacob Burckhardt wrote succinctly:

> In the Middle Ages, man was conscious of himself only as a member of a race, people, party, family, or corporation – only through some general category. In Italy this veil [under which the Middle Ages lay dreaming] first melted into thin air; an *objective* treatment and consideration of the state and of all the things of this world became possible. The subjective side at the same time asserted itself with corresponding emphasis; man became a singular and unique individual and recognized himself as such...The Italians of the fourteenth century know little of false modesty or of hypocrisy in any shape; not one of them was afraid of singularity, of being and seeming unlike his neighbors.[3]

Some historians today argue against Burckhardt and see the charismatic individuals of the Renaissance as profoundly constituted by their surrounding institutions of family, religion and state. Still this does not make the idea that individualism started there any less powerful. The new idea of the exceptional individual was first articulated around arts and crafts and not just in Italy. In the Middle Ages craftsmen and artists were anonymous. Nobody knows who designed or built the great cathedrals of the Middle Ages, but by the sixteenth century we have artists of truly global renown like Michelangelo, De Vinci, Raphael and, in the north, Albrecht Dürer.

Dürer, for example, appears, almost, to be our contemporary. He ticks all the boxes for the entrepreneur. He is the first to use the technology of printmaking for art, and the first to make himself a brand name by signing all his works and by designing a logo, and the first to commercialize his own self-love and narcissism. You can see the logo and his narcissism in his most famous painting below.

By now we are used to all these, but both logo and narcissism were innovative and strange in the sixteenth century. More than anything else Dürer is special, unlike anyone who came before him. His ostentatious and commercialized self-love, his affirmation of everything about himself and his world seems to inaugurate the celebrity-entrepreneur. This masterpiece in which he poses in the generic pose of Christ (at that time only pictures of Christ had a full frontal view) only serves to paradoxically show just how far from the humbleness required of Christianity he was. His great visual metaphor is his long hair and fur coat. Long hair by definition falls into a unique pattern in contrast to monks' or soldiers' short hair signifying anonymity. Though he might seem to be looking outward at us, he is in fact feeling the felt of his coat. His gaze is inward, a new subjectivity and solitude is born here, the idea of the innovative genius.

Three years after Dürer painted his famous painting in 1500, Hernán Cortés, a new kind of individual, the colonial entrepreneur, destroyer of worlds for profit, sets sail to the New World. Using 600 men he conquered the Aztec empire against an army comprising hundreds of thousands of warriors. Through cunning and ruthlessness he takes Moctezuma as hostage in his own palace and begins the work of dismantling Moctezuma's empire and ruling it single- handedly. The description of what he has done spreads all over Europe due to the recent invention of the printing press, serving as a kind of how-to manual of conquering other peoples in the New World. The conquistadors represent a new kind of individualism. Often going against the orders of the king, manipulating both their own soldiers and the natives, their individualism is closely allied with the aggressiveness of pursuing new worlds in search of wealth.

This kind of image of the individual is still central in our culture. We see it every time an entrepreneur looks to "strike it rich" in the new frontier, whether this frontier can be the new England of 1650, the gold rush of 1848, the scramble for Africa of the 1880s, the internet rush of the 1990s, the social media rush of the 2000s, and the currently evolving frontiers of space, virtual reality, psychopharmacology and artificial intelligence.

The frontier of space and its commercialization provides a good example. Commercialization of space began with the launch of AT&T satellite Telstar in 1962, and continues with the countless commercial satellites currently in space. The commercialization of space will accelerate in the 2020s and

2030s with other services like tourism (Blue Origin), space advertising (Tesla Roadster through Space X), asteroid mining and more. Though international regulations articulate that space belongs to the whole humanity, it is very likely that space will be colonized and commercialized in similar ways that the New World has been. At the fetishized center of the drama stand individuals like Elon Musk, who will make the human species interplanetary and will "die on Mars."

In the field of virtual reality, we also see a similar rhetoric in which Mark Zuckerberg promises to take us to new worlds. In all of these fields the type of individual to do this was created in the 1500s. Modern day conquistadors working on behalf of giant corporations and governments will use outer space and the brain to make themselves inordinately powerful, giving trinkets and beads to the "natives," that is, us. On the obverse, "dark" side of the special individual stand most of humanity that are treated like infants. In fact, already today for the small pleasures of social approval ("likes," photos from friends, etc.) most people give away virtually all information about themselves (who their friends are, what they like, what they hate, their political views, where they are) and willingly subject themselves to behavior modification. This has already begun with the ubiquity of the surveillance business model that took off in the early 2000s.

Nevertheless, the business model of selling both information and attention to advertisers is not what captivates our imagination; it is not emotionally effective as a ruling idea. What all articles both good and bad are about are those tycoons, the business giants posturing on the frontier. The theme of the individual on the frontier of a new world connects a tech billionaire with a 10-year-old child, it brings them both to the same childish imaginary level. They both just want to have adventurous fun. From the point of view of the business model an individual is conceptualized as having two parts.

On the surface he or she is interpellated as a child who enjoys games and immersive social experience, but more deeply she is someone with valuable behavioral data to be collected and sold to third parties.

It is important to dwell a bit on the infantile surface of the individual today as it is the necessary counterpart to the special individual. Treating people like children to be sold "fun" activities has a long pedigree. While in the past only black men were called "boy" by their masters, today everybody self-identifies willingly as a child. The capitalist conquistador constructs us all as childish natives. The symptoms of narcissistic childishness are all around us. Fifty-year-old men playing *World of Warcraft* or *Grand Theft Auto,* blockbusters like *Spider-Man, Iron Man, Star Wars, Avengers, Jurassic World, Catwoman, Transformers,* etc. Adult fiction readers who only read *Lord of the Rings* or *Harry Potter.* The introduction of games and edutainment into classrooms, the surge in Botox for women and hair color for men. The way attractive men and beautiful women are called "cute" in the US, the countless young adults who return to live with their parents after college, the marrying age that has gone steadily up beyond 30. A new individual is created by marketing that seeks to infantilize adults so they can be sold the mostly superfluous consumer goods, games and digital gadgets for which there is no real need but the one created by corporations that need to sell. Consumer goods advertise themselves as an escape from the burdens of responsible adulthood, film series appeal to our infantile wish "to tell me the same story again."

It is hard to take infantilization seriously since it seems harmless, and yet society pays for it dearly as it means the death of citizenship or any kind of civic mindedness. Infantilization, however, has not just been the result of marketing and the advertising industry. This industry would have never succeeded in transforming human beings in its image if not for the puerile direction that leftist politics took in the 1960s in France and the US. Another important layer of today's individualism is in fact rooted there and with the generation that undertook this transformation.

Swinging Individuals

Born after World War Two, baby boomers in Western countries grew up at a time of unprecedented economic growth, almost twice as rapid as the prewar period. Their parents' lives were quickly transformed by higher wages, increased consumption and a developed system of social benefits. Though largely materially secure, by the late 1960s this generation was dissatisfied and angry with the societies and states that it belonged to. First and foremost was the war in Vietnam that the US, the most powerful country in the world, was waging against the poorest peasants of South Asia.

However, and perhaps even more importantly than the war in Vietnam, this generation experienced the culture and society that they grew up into as repressive. It is telling that the strikes and social revolution that were May 1968 began as male and female students protested about being unable to visit each other's dormitories. May 1968 was a leftist political attempt at transforming society and political power in France, and yet at the same time it had an even stronger cultural undercurrent – that this transformation itself entails a freer expression of desire and pleasure. Very telling are the leftist slogans and graffiti used at those times. They are found among classic Marxist sentiments such as "The boss needs you, you don't need him" or "A single nonrevolutionary weekend is infinitely more bloody than a month of permanent revolution." "Run, comrade, the old world is behind you!" We find much that is related to freeing desire, imagination, interest and pleasure such as "It is forbidden to forbid," "Enjoy without hindrance," "Boredom is counterrevolutionary," "We want nothing of a world in which the certainty of not dying from hunger comes in exchange for the risk of dying from boredom," "Live without dead time – enjoy without chains," "In a society that has abolished all adventures, the only adventure left is to abolish society," "Motions kill emotions," "Happiness is a new idea," "I find my orgasms among the paving stones," "The prospect of finding pleasure tomorrow will never compensate for today's boredom," "Workers of the world, have fun!," "The bourgeoisie has no other pleasure but to degrade all pleasures." The slogans signal something new and different than winning power for the workers. There is a new relationship to pleasure that is at stake.

It is difficult to objectively describe this new sensibility and its accompanying philosophy in any objectivity since we are its direct inheritors. It is like trying to distance oneself from oneself. Any knowledgeable writers writing today on social and historical affairs cannot separate themselves from the legacy of 1968 with any kind of detachment, precisely because most of the powerful intellectual tools in the service of everyone doing any kind of intellectual work in the humanities or social sciences come from what has come to be called the "thought of 68." The philosophy and thought of these days was both prolific and has yet to be matched in sophistication and intellectual power. In 1966, for example, Foucault published *The Order of Things*, Lacan *Ecrits*, Althusser *Reading Capital* and Benveniste *Problems in General Linguistics*.

To provide a caricature of the thought of '68, one can say that it saw society, knowledge, history and language as determined largely by structures that are invisible and unconscious but that crucially structure thinking, writing and behavior. At the same time, however, those structures repress or structure desire, pleasure and creativity; in a sense they repress individuality itself. The great metaphor for these structures was language. For Lacan the unconscious is structured like a language, while Foucault has shown the way in which scientific thinking in different fields is ruled by consistent episteme or discourses that are applied to reality. Thinkers of the era stressed the relatively enduring linguistic, symbolic, ideational structures and the way that individuals largely passively partake or are constructed by them. While these structures enable one to do certain things (speak a language, write a scientific article, etc.) they are repressive and limit the horizon of other ways of thinking and being.

Though these thinkers have stressed that other forms of organization are necessary, they have not spent any time articulating these new ways of organization. The lesson for most of those reading their work was a new yearning to extricate oneself from these structures. For example, after reading Foucault one definitely feels a need to extricate oneself from repressive institutions such as schools, hospitals, prisons, etc. This is true even though Foucault constantly stressed that these institutions create powers and abilities in individuals as well as contain them. Lacan's register of the symbolic and imaginary, man's dependence on socially conditioned symbolic language and man's idealization of his sense of self, are also structures that prevent someone from attaining the truth of their self and their situation.

Highlighting the repressive social and ideational structure was a call to free oneself from them, a new appeal for what can be called neo-individualism. This neo-individualism in France was articulated at a time that still had a strong presence of collective institutions such as unions and political parties and collective ideologies such as Marxism. However, a clear sign of the future was the way in which intellectuals have distanced themselves from any kind of party politics and the fact that the events of '68 did not achieve much politically – the left was crushed in the 1969 elections. One can say that libertarian individualism centered on desire as a behavioral and cognitive tendency is precisely one of its most enduring legacies.

In the US neo-individualism was much clearer from the

start, and its effects more far reaching. In contrast to Europe, both collective institutions as well as leftist ideology were significantly weaker. There was relatively little connection between rebelling students and workers. Indeed, in contrast to a massive general strike in France of 16 million workers, no significant alliances between students and workers took place in the US. The whole movement was largely confined to middle and middle-upper classes. The initial political focus of what became the New Left was desegregation of the South and critique of the Vietnam war; the cultural focus was an attempt to experiment in living differently than the consensus culture of the post-World War II period.

The seminal document of the New Left, the Port Huron Statement, reveals a strangely timid agenda mostly couched in terms of participatory democracy and enlargement of the public sector that is supposed to counter the many ills of America (racism, militarism, etc.). The New Left essentially distinguished itself from the Old Left by an explicit distancing and negation of the institute of the vanguard party. The reigning view was that having political activity organized around a small disciplined party led to an authoritarian regime in the Soviet Union. The students of *Students for Demorcatic Society* had no intention of forming a revolutionary party nor of making the United States communist or even socialist.

At the same time, discontent went beyond critiques of imperialism and segregation and toward everyday life. The culture around them seemed repressive, conformist and artificial – "plastic" is a word used in *The Graduate,* a classic film of the period. The movement was complex and multifarious and included a whole palette of different demands to transform society. However, it is clear, especially in the US, that one of its ultimate legacies was to overthrow a repressive "consensus" culture largely in the name of relatively simple enjoyments.

In a dynamic that we see repeatedly, out of the diverse

demands and pressures that political movements made, the most important are violently repressed (e.g., substantive equality). The ones that threaten existing power structures of capitalism to a lesser degree may be incorporated. For example, by the time of the March on Washington in 1963, organizers distanced themselves from both socialist and communist groups in order to appear less radical; even with this distancing the demand they made for an increase in the minimum wage was rejected. The lasting effect of the march has been the Civil Rights Act of 1964, an act that outlaws discrimination in voting, hotels, employment, federally funded programs and activities, etc. Typically for groups demanding change, the focus shifts from greater redistribution of wealth to equality of opportunity, from a higher minimum wage to the intangibles of discrimination. Similarly, out of the immaterial demands of the sixties to switch to a freer, interconnected, enjoyment, spiritual and less materialistic style of living, the only demand that was accepted was the right to enjoy.

The demand for pleasure and enjoyment arose from very specific circumstances in the US. The roots of this demand lay in the students' situation in the late 1960s. The culture and society that post-war generation students grew up in was suddenly experienced as repressive. This expressed itself specifically in their living situation in college. In the 1960s, college administration acted as in loco parentis "in place of the parent." Women were subject to curfew at 10 p.m. and dormitories were strictly separated according to sex. Administrators also restricted freedom of speech prohibiting student organizations that addressed "off-campus" topics. Students were expected to lead a largely docile, apolitical as well as restrictive existence. Their extracurricular life was formed mostly through sports and dances, "games" as one of them called it. As we will see repeatedly, infantilization is one of the most successful strategies of control and depoliticization. Yet students experienced these pleasures as stale and became suddenly aware that they are strategies of social control. Sexuality, being one of the most highly controlled of human activities, and at the same time arguably the most pleasurable, became the focus of attempts to overthrow a repressive culture. To orient themselves on the question of why a new relationship to sexuality was needed, students, activists, hippies and others were aided by a transformed version of psychoanalysis.

Psychoanalysis, in both France and the US, was transformed from its conservative, largely bourgeois outlook to a gospel of sexual freedom. Originally psychoanalysis can be thought of as a kind of worldview mixing conservatism and an Enlightenment belief in reason. Freud was a conservative since he saw human nature as essentially bad; both aggression and sexuality needed repression first in the family setting and then in society as a whole. However, he did recognize that this repression itself, though necessary, is the cause of suffering and mental illness. His procedure, psychoanalytic therapy, was essentially a rational and yet experiential examination of the process of repression itself. The rationality part of it was what made him an Enlightenment figure. In the sixties, Freud's basic doctrine was fundamentally adopted and transformed.

The most important figure in this transformation has been Wilhelm Reich, member of the second generation of psychoanalysts, whose book *Mass Psychology of Fascism* was actually thrown by students at the police in '68 Paris and Berlin. Reich's key theoretical move was to posit pro-social desires underneath those of Freud's. For Reich, the aggressive and violent character of many of our sexual and nonsexual urges is not natural but a result of a primary repression. For Reich the human psyche is composed of three layers. The first is the superficial liberal level – that is, the level of politeness and tolerance that hides and represses the second layer, the aggressive Freudian unconscious, but beneath this layer is the biological core of man that under favorable social conditions "is an honest, industrious, cooperative animal capable of love and also of rational hatred."[4] Liberalism represents the first layer, the second layer (the repressed) is represented by fascism, while genuine revolution represents the deepest layer. Interestingly, fascism for Reich is simply a human character structure that is based on the sexual repression of human beings in a patriarchal family structure. Already with Freud the father is a threatening and law-giving figure. As a defense the child identifies and internalizes the father figure. While for Freud this is a necessary step in the moral education of children, for Reich this kind of family is the first "cell" of a fascist society. Life in the traditional family prepares you for a fascist society. The mentality and everyday life experience that it produces is conducive for all the ills associated with historical fascism.

For American college students of the 1960s, Reich's explanation offered an important link between traditional family life in America on the one hand and racism and militarism on the other. Growing up in white-only segregated suburbs and schools with professional fathers and stay-at-home mothers, they observed the way in which their family reproduced racism and sexism. At the center of the process lies accepting authority through suppression of natural sexuality. This suppression makes the child obedient and inhibited, shy and afraid of authority and thus "adjusted" and "good" in the authoritarian meaning of the word. More importantly, suppression is the basis of individualistic ideology since it precludes pleasurable connection with others. Sex negativity creates an internal drama of repression instead of social cooperation. It perversely causes individuals to be incapsulated in their families and then to project feelings and attitudes from that family toward the state and its leaders. The emotional core of fascism, of homeland, blood and nation, are the ideas of mother, father and family. Inhibiting sexual curiosity has the added "benefit" of inhibiting curiosity in general and the critical faculties in particular.

Sexual repression according to Reich creates a docile person adjusted to authoritarianism and willing to submit to it in spite of exploitation and degradation. This person is unlikely to challenge the supremacy of the father of the family or the nation. If this person is male and becomes a married man in difficult economic times, he is likely to be susceptible to sexual anxiety, that is, open to believing that Jews or other migrants are raping German women. Reich was one of the first theorists to identify that economic insecurity can evoke a deeper sexual anxiety about masculinity. For Reich, the socialist, men and women are faced with an alternative to fascism – to identify with socially vital work on an international scale as an alternative orientation to being atomized, while believing in their own particularity and specialness and in turn identifying with leaders and big men.

Reich's analysis together with the dissemination of the sex research of Alfred Kinsey and Masters and Johnson was very influential in the 1960s. Free love, as it was called, became a political project of asserting freedom from both church and state regulation of sexuality, as well as a political project of sexual transformation. The political thinking of the time was of throwing off the burden of repression, both internal and external. Institutions such as family, school and state and their internalized representations have wronged us in the past and present, and we need to unshackle ourselves and learn to express our more authentic selves. Though the more sophisticated writing of the sixties included the insight that institutions are as much enablers as they are coercive and repressive (e.g., Foucault) and that human beings speak through the social institution of language that repressed their original desire (e.g., Lacan), still, for most, the major lesson of the sixties often became a personal attempt at undermining repressive ideologies and structures. People became highly sensitive to the normalizing and repressive characteristics of the family, the school, the church, the factory, the museum, the hospital, the psychiatry ward, the army, the police, the state and of language itself. While many in the past were frustrated with institutions, their relationship was both positive and negative. In the sixties, negative aspects were highlighted. It is as if the institutional critique of modernism that went against the museum, against reason, against the institution of language has suddenly reached a mass audience. Or as if people have suddenly internalized the lessons of sociology and anthropology that claim that humans are irreparably formed by their institutions and once they have understood this they become intolerably confining.

It is telling that both in France and in the US most of the activities connected with the sixties assumed an active distance from party politics. Reading the biographies of intellectuals of the time, it is striking how a key biographical move is to leave those parties. Participation in institutions and organizations seems corrosive and inauthentic. People gradually switched from collective engagement in the transformation of society to conception and practices of personal expression and personal freedom. This transition expressed itself in the realm of culture as well as politics and presented a break in what was a 100-year-old practice.

From the middle of the nineteenth century until roughly the middle of the twentieth, most producers of ideas, art, music and literature were part of groups. These groups articulated themselves around ideas often explicitly written up in manifestos. Thus in art we have Impressionism, Expressionism, Fauvism, Futurism, Cubism and Surrealism. Music too was idea-driven collective practice and had impressionism, expressionism and modernism. In the realm of politics, Liberalism, Abolitionism, Marxism, Anarchism and Fascism were invented. It is safe to say that most isms in politics, art or music originated at that time.

The shift away from collective ideas and practice as well as from political commitment was already underway in the early 1950s when one of the most important and essentially collective art forms of the twentieth century, film, was reconfigured around the individual artist. The director was suddenly and somewhat arbitrarily chosen to represent an essentially collective endeavor. François Truffaut's 1954 essay "A certain tendency in French cinema" criticized literary adaptation of classics in French films, and called for politics of the author in which the vision of individuals is to be expressed in films. André Bazin, influenced from the catholic doctrine of personalism, went against earlier Marxist approaches to the construction of reality in film and stressed that films should represent the director's personal vision.

In the themes and subject matter of mainstream European art films themselves, one could see a transition away from collective preoccupations. A good case in point is the transition away from preoccupation with social justice in Italy's most celebrated directors of the late fifties and early sixties. In 1957 Fellini directed *Nights of Cabiria*, a story of the difficult and violent life of a prostitute who is cheated and crossed by lovers who are after her money. Though she experiences betrayal and violence she does not give up hope of finding love. In 1962 Pier Paolo Pasolini filmed *Mama Roma*, a story of a prostitute and mother who tries to start a new life selling vegetables and looking after her 16-year-old son, Ettore, as best she can. Ettore stops going to school when he finds out his mother is a prostitute, and then steals a radio in a hospital, gets caught and is sent to prison. In prison he is restrained in an isolation room and then dies from the cold, invoking the death of Jesus on the cross. These films, though innovative in style, depict working-class lives in which people are victims of their social circumstances. In 1961 Fellini directed another masterpiece, *La Dolce Vita*, a film that follows a journalist's erotic involvement with the rich and famous. The final effect on the viewer of the film is to feel the decadence and meaninglessness of pleasure in high society. In the space of four years, Fellini moves from depicting a working-class prostitute trying to find love to the nihilism of the high bourgeoisie. Pasolini, a communist, shoots *The Gospel According to St. Matthew* (1964) after *Mama Roma*, and then turns to a series of films based on mythology or world classics, including *Oedipus Rex* (1967), *Medea* (1969), *Decameron* (1971) and *Canterbury Tales* (1972), ending his short-lived career with another masterpiece, *Salo, or the 120 Days of Sodom* (1975), based on Marquis de Sade. None of the later films of either Pasolini or other important European auteurs are realistic, and the working class rarely makes an appearance in them. In the sixties, the most prestigious films were modernist in terms of their form and style. In terms of their understanding of humans, they drew their inspiration from psychoanalysis and existentialism, both highly individualistic and largely apolitical or even conservative doctrines.

To understand the transition, one would do well to use another 1960s thinker, Abraham Maslow. In 1954 Maslow argued in his book *Motivation and Personality* that human needs are organized according to a hierarchy, first physical needs, then safety, love/belonging, esteem and finally authenticity and self-fulfillment. When lower needs are fulfilled, higher needs articulate themselves.[5] It is characteristic that this kind of positive psychology articulated itself at a time when a mass of population suddenly became highly secured in their basic needs and could then articulate new emotional needs. As Tocqueville asserted, revolutionary change can happen when things get better and expectations suddenly inflate. Among the most pressing emotional needs of the time was authenticity.

Authenticity was conceptualized through Heidegger's philosophy, which was mainly mediated through Jean Paul Sartre's *Being and Nothingness*. This philosophy saw society as making man inauthentic, a force that prevents man from being himself through chatter and superficial socializing. In order to be authentic, one must face one's own death, one must live death in the present, not as something external that breaks life but as something that is internal to life itself. Internalizing death offers the possibility of an escape from rigidly following conventional behavior. Sartre elaborated on the possibilities of escaping from conventional behavior. His concept of bad faith describes the way we try to convince and lie to ourselves that our behavior (let's say our choice of work) is the only possibility that we have, that no other possibilities exist for us, when in fact we are free to pursue other choices. Bad faith is a kind of self-deception that precludes us from other more authentic possibilities. One does not have to participate in oppressive social structures.

Nevertheless, one can raise several objections to this doctrine. It may well be self-deception to think that you can extricate yourself as an individual from oppressive social structures without building alternative institutions. It is doubtful as well that consciousness of death allows one to transcend society. The contemplation of death, for example, in ancient Egypt or medieval Christianity or in post-humanism today is deeply mediated by culture and institutions; there is nothing particularly individual about it. Wanting to get mummified or alternatively burned or cryogenically frozen has everything to do with your society. In fact, the birth of the science of society, of sociology, was demonstrated by Emile Durkheim by showing precisely that suicide, one's very personal death, is highly influenced by social conditions.

The attempts to find an institutionally free authentic self through sexuality as described earlier, or through death, simply did not work. Though there have been a variety of experiments in alternative communities and institutions, ultimately many talented people in the sixties defected from many social institutions without building lasting new ones. With no real deep social or ideational collaboration with other people, suspended between sexuality and death, both falsely conceived of as pre-social and pre-cultural, men and women have little with which to orient themselves. With no orientation from ideas or groups, they look up like children to those they believe are big men.

Chapter Two

Individualism Part II

Big Man

The big man idea is a central ruling idea in our culture. In fact, most of our everyday culture is organized around what we see as larger than life people (usually rich males of Western European origins). An alien who visited our supermarkets, watched our mainstream films, attended our sporting events and read our newspapers would quickly conclude that our whole culture is organized around four great entrepreneurs, a president or prime minster, five Hollywood actors, and perhaps five sports celebrities. It would seem that most of our public communication is about these people. At the time I am writing they would be Mark Zuckerberg, Jeff Bezos, Bill Gates, Elon Musk, Brad Pitt (especially in supermarkets), Angelina Jolie, Tom Cruise, Johnny Depp, Cristiano Ronaldo, LeBron James and Lionel Messi. One can add or take down a few but the coverage that this handful of individuals gets is overwhelming. In a way, humanity does not really exist; only they do. Nor is their coverage only lowbrow. Ostensibly serious in-depth journalism in both the *New York Times* and the *Wall Street Journal* will detail the irrelevant lifestyle choices of Jeff Bezos. Most of the time we accept that this is the way it should be. When questioned, one may claim that these people are super-talented and gifted, singlehandedly they have created tremendous value and that their decisions affect millions. Or that the idea of the big man defends individuals from becoming uniform cells of the state. I will deal with these arguments toward the end of this chapter. For now, we can concentrate on the historical reasons that the idea of the big man became so powerful.

The story begins with how those who are most powerful

now (industrialists, financiers, entrepreneurs, etc.) have had, in the past, to break through an impossibly oppressive system designed to keep everyone in their place and nobility and clergy on top. A system that in one form or another existed for at least 10,000 years. When looking back at the Middle Ages, for example, it is not difficult to see how immobile and unequal that society was. Social mobility was largely foreign to that world. Radical differences between people were seen as natural. One's power and legitimacy stemmed either from God or from one's family. If one did not participate in the work of God or be fortunate to be born into a powerful noble family, there was little to aspire to.

It is important to stress that ruling ideas of the Middle Ages die an extremely slow death and sometimes make a limited comeback. A quick look around the world, from the British royal family to the royal family of Saudi Arabia, shows that royalty still plays a role in legitimizing authority. It took a sequence of a full 200 years carried by the energy of American, French, Russian and Chinese revolutions as well as decolonization struggles to weaken its hold on humanity. It still has a pronounced hold on people's imagination in popular films, television series and even high art.

When we look for queens and kings or warring nobility in our culture, they are everywhere to be found: *The Hobbit, Narnia, Thor, Superman, Star Wars, Game of Thrones* and of course a great portion of all Disney films, including *Snow White and the Seven Dwarfs, Cinderella, Sleeping Beauty, Aristocats, Frozen, Mulan, The Lion King, Beauty and the Beast, The Princess and the Frog, Tangled*, etc. In these films, we are quite characteristically called to identify with the "good" nobility against the "bad" nobility. Many of these films end with the "rightful" king or queen restoring order. The exploitative nature of all nobility is never acknowledged, a toiling peasant or serf is never to be seen, though without them nobody would have survived much less live in luxury. Seemingly harmless entertainment, it nevertheless forces our heads to look "above" us, it uses often brilliant rhetoric in order to convince us that these people are worthy of our admiration and identification, and it obfuscates looking deeply and truthfully at the lives of people around and "below" us.

In tandem with royalty is the way in which God, both in the past and in our present, is used to buttress authority and legitimacy everywhere in the world, most prominently in Russia, Turkey, the US, Iran, Brazil, Saudi Arabia and Poland. The idea of God, of course, has been used both in liberation from authority (Moses, Martin Luther, Thomas Müntzer, Martin Luther King, Liberation Theology, etc.), and to legitimize authority and inequality between man and woman, nobleman and slave, rich and poor. Those who argue for the progressivism of the idea of God say that it always allows one to appeal to a higher authority, that the cults of leaders or earthly politics are a kind of idolatry. Martin Luther, for example, appealed to the authority of the Bible in order to challenge the hierarchy and domination of the Catholic Church. More radically, Thomas Müntzer even challenged scripture, saying that ultimately God manifests himself in the book of nature or within the soul of man and thus we can intuit God on our own through the experience of ourselves and the natural world.

Nevertheless, for an overwhelming majority of people, both the idea of God itself and knowing what he wants from us depends on intermediaries like priests, imams and rabbis or on the Bible or Koran and other holy texts. This already in itself creates a hierarchy. Texts and other people are deemed above you. Having God, priest or Bible above you alienates and projects responsibility from yourself and people around you to a personalized moral force. It may feel relaxing to say that God has a plan for you, that a great daddy in the sky is looking after you, but in truth – as we know from a history of war, slavery, famine and sickness – there is no plan. It is ludicrous to claim that it's part of some overall plan to have 40 million people die in World War One whose causes are obscure and still debated by historians. A child crosses the road and gets killed by a passing vehicle. Accidental deaths also happen every day and ascribing them to a Godly design that we with our small minds cannot understand is simply a transparent defense against their utter meaninglessness.

Sometimes philosophers and theologians invented what is known as the God of the philosophers. Either a depersonalized abstract pantheism or a God that is weak and fragile and exists only on the cross or in the face of the Other. This is a weak evasion. The very reason that regular people believe in God in the first place is to compensate for the pain and dislocation of their lives with someone benign yet powerful who is watching over and caring for them. Elites on the other hand always use God to legitimize their authority, to bring an aura of glory and splendor to their institutions, an air of this-is-the-natural-way-of-the-cosmos to societal order that is in their favor. The God of philosophers is shared only by philosophers; it is inconsequential in all respects.

Many things don't really exist: unicorns, cyclops, minotaurs, dragons, chimeras, krakens, hydras and sphinxes. Fictional characters like James Bond, Jack Sparrow and Homer Simpson don't really exist either. Yet they do have many effects on the world. People might want to become spies or pirates. A handyman who helped us with various jobs at our house robbed a bank and went to jail for five years because he was enamored of Tony Montana, the hero of *Scarface*. Things that don't really exist have very real effects. But if something both does not really exist and has bad effects, then it should be done away with. God both does not exist and is used to make you cooperate with authority.

Yet at the same time, though ideas of God and nobility

are useful for old elites, it is difficult for these ideas to do the legitimization work they have done so effectively in the past. Today, sources of legitimacy and authority cannot rely solely on nobility and God. American presidents, Saudi Arabian princes and Muslim prime ministers need to legitimate themselves through talk of jobs and economic growth, through health and education, and increasingly through their policies on the environment. Just invoking the will of God will not do. Nor are the tremendous forces released by technology and science since the nineteenth century related in any meaningful way to royalty or religion. Industrial production, atomic energy, space technology, design DNA, information revolution, pharmacology, brain interventions and bio-materials all have nothing to do with royalty or God and in fact are ultimately incompatible with the traditionalist worldview. Though they are deeply encouraged by elites and nothing is guaranteed, there seems to be a limit to how much the ruling ideas of the Middle Ages can make a comeback.

These ideas began to be attacked precisely by the idea of the special individual, the big man. Through a complex process of the Protestant Reformation, the idea took hold among merchants, artists, administers, lawyers and artisans that power and wealth should come from talent and hard work, not from being born into noble family. Both talent and hard work were essentially a new kind of values, values that replaced courage (nobility) and piety (clergy). In a culture with a largely fixed social hierarchy, talent and hard work did not really open new avenues. The feelings associated with talent, for example pride, were explicitly frowned upon in traditional Christian culture. Work, predominantly agriculture, was often considered a curse (e.g., in the sweat of thy face shalt thou eat bread, Genesis 3:19). Working ensured survival; it was not something that created novelty and value.

Talent and hard work of the individual were once

revolutionary ideas. They formed the ideational battering ram that toppled the castles of the feudal order. By approximately the second half of the nineteenth century, however, they began to be used against demands for economic equality rather than to fight privileges of nobility and church. In response to various demands set by socialists, communists and anarchists, individualism, hard work and talent transitioned from an idea whose purpose was to promote recognition in people who are not nobles or priests to an idea that is used to justify the inequality between industrialist and worker. The workers and the poor simply did not work hard enough or were not talented enough to become rich. Thus, we see a transition from an idea designed to justify rising powers of middle classes to an idea that is used to keep down those who are under them. These ideas are called upon to do two very different things.

Here we can already see something curious about the ruling ideas, the way they can shift their function depending on context. Ideas like individualism, hard work and talent become fundamentally different when they are used to fight the clergy and nobility than when they are pressed to legitimize economic inequality. The function of ideas changes as those who use them first challenge authority and then represent authority themselves.

The clearest case of these ideas representing authority in the US was in the way that elites traditionally thought that in their society inequalities were based on merit alone. Inherited wealth was played down and inequality based on race and gender was thought natural and biologically based. From that point onward, inequality was often legitimated through talent, hard work and uniqueness of the individual. Almost any depiction of industry "greats" from Ford to Musk by mainstream media includes precisely this mixture of relating their talents and hard work, coupled with their unique individuality. Newspapers like the *Wall Street Journal* have been diligently reporting idiosyncrasies of billionaires for more than 130 years. In the late nineteenth century, for example, we get to know the breakfast rituals, vacation habits and even favorite horses of the DuPonts, the Vanderbilts and the Rockefellers, just like a couple of years ago the media focused on Mark Zuckerberg's gray shirts and the lizard-eating Jeff Bezos. If nothing politically radical has transformed society since the writing of this book, I am sure the reader can easily subject himself to contemporary stories mixing dogged determination, special talents, morning rituals and the working-out habits of industry greats.

These kinds of stories might seem fine if readers believe that these men are worthy of emulation, that their stories can inspire and orient. However, there are several reasons why they are problematic. They are distortive since whatever these men achieved in life or for that matter whatever anyone achieves depends on the work of millions of people both dead and alive. To have reached the point of reading this book you must have had caretakers and teachers directly involved in your care; you depend on the invention of writing, on the thousands of engineers and workers both in the past and today who have made the printing press, book, tablet or computer possible. If you are not hungry, or too cold or too hot to concentrate, there have also been thousands involved in that. Whatever political rights you possess, your safety and your health are also guaranteed through the work of hundreds. In order to achieve even the most extremely individual of pursuits such as writing a book or painting a picture, one usually relies on many models, both conscious and unconscious. The dyad of you and the big man makes all of this disappear and does not let you think in the terms that would be most conducive to human emancipation and flourishing; it is indeed a kind of ideational perversion.

Additionally, identification and emulation with the big man is also likely to lead to a dead end as the majority of people cannot structurally become the big man. First, even if you are very successful, you might compare badly with people who were world famous and multimillionaires in their twenties. Following today's winner-takes-all economy, starting an entrepreneurial enterprise also means there is a good chance you will fail, as 85 percent of all small businesses do in their first 10 years. The same goes for almost every other individualist pursuit you may go after. Having constructed a sense of self-worth around financial success and renown of the type that one experiences in the media, one reaches midlife to find that it is hard to reconstruct another successful life narrative.

For many people, residual religious traditions are helpful in constructing an alternate life narrative unrelated to individual success. Trust and belief that God has a plan for you, or in the Buddhist variety, freeing yourself from desire, are general answers for all human beings. They all put people on a universal quest that compensates for the failed individualist one. Indeed, in contrast to the past in which the idea of the special individual came and disrupted the ideas of the church, now the church comes to compensate for the isolation, anxiety and failed identity associated with being an individual.

Because religions are universal solutions used to overcome anxiety, they can quickly turn to proselytizing and a paradoxical erasure of individuality. A former student of mine, a blockchain entrepreneur, came to visit me from San Francisco. Though he seemed happy and driven, I sensed great anxiety underneath. He has started a cryptocurrency fund and was anxiously waiting for people to invest in it. The conversation turned to meditation; he meditated for at least three hours every day. I told him that it wasn't for me. He quickly claimed that my turning down meditation was a form of resistance that shows how much I actually need meditation. Perhaps he was right and I do need meditation! Still his argument leaves no room for individuality. Looking at his anxiety it was clear that he was living according to two very different philosophies. The charismatic individualist founder with an inexorable will, relentless drive and boundless energy directed toward worldly success and the meditative Buddhist who tries and extinguishes the self and its desires.

As much as we push toward a philosophy of individual aggrandizement, we then fall back on practices of submission and the extinguishing of desire. It seems that the persona of the entrepreneur is overly taxing and psychologically unsustainable for many people and is regularly supplemented with a wish to escape its burdens and be swallowed by a community, to feel taken care of, part of something larger. One constantly feels this tension between the burdens of isolated individuals and a wish for sharing and collective ways of life in the elite ideology of Silicon Valley. On the one hand we have the cult and celebration of the lonely multimillionaire entrepreneur; on the other the stress of collective emancipation of mankind through freedom of information, free services and the exponential growth in computing power.

These ideological commitments have not been without dramatic effects on society and economy. The result of both these commitments together has led to the insidiousness of the business model of Google and Facebook and many other firms. Everything is free and collaborative on the surface but in order to accumulate wealth, personal information is covertly gathered and sold to unknown third parties. These third parties often attempt to modify behavior and opinions. This is not just about selling commodities; it can be about radicalizing political opinion or voter suppression. One can argue that this is what advertising and propaganda always did. But by knowing much about you as an individual, it has become much more effective.

In fact, there is a quasi-fascist bifurcation in Silicon Valley regarding human beings. Apart from the entrepreneur superhero "big man," most human beings are seen as childish and foolish to give up their personal information and at the same time disposable – their work will be automated by AI, their bodies a shell for information that will be uploaded to the web. Anyone who works in AI knows that machine learning in almost all fields consists of learning from the work of hundreds of human beings. Translation, medical diagnostics and autonomous driving, for example, rely on the data of hundreds of real translators, drivers and doctors. Still, all this labor is discounted; its almost magical effects are attributed to one entrepreneur, or at best it is ascribed to a handful of engineers.

Dividing human beings into childish machines on the one hand and great men on the other has a long history. By the time of Bonaparte and Beethoven you had a belief in greatness and genius, while on the other hand there was a detailed imagining of the human mind as a kind of association machine. This view was updated in the 1980s when American intellectuals, philosophers and cognitive scientists stressed that humans were little more than biological information processing machines. These biological machines can be nudged and manipulated at will and their life is just a result of their environmental conditioning. On the other hand, in our culture, a handful of people at the top, like Steve Jobs or Elon Musk, deserve autobiographical being; their life found deserving is viewed as a kind of self-authored narrative. A thoughtful and nuanced account of the interaction between time, place, society, culture, genetics and upbringing is characteristically missing in both renditions of masses who are no more than biological information machines, as well as from the lucky few entrepreneurs who are said to make history and are supposedly driven by will and vision alone.

The effects of a culture that is unable to empathize with regular people and that sees humans as disposable machines can be very unexpected. Lacking sympathetic presentations of regular life, one is left with little sympathy for one's own life. This can lead not only to depression but to meaningless acts of violence that aim to show one's relevance. In order to examine this, let us paraphrase Plato somewhat and say that it might be difficult to see the effects of meaninglessness in the small mirror of the soul; its effects would be much easier to see on the big screen.

Batman

On July 20, 2012, James Holmes, hair dyed orange, went to watch the third installment of the Batman series, *Dark Night Rises*, at the Century movie theater in Aurora, Colorado, one of the most progressive and peaceful places in the US. James came from a well-to-do professional family. His father, who had math degrees from Stanford and Berkeley, worked at the time as a highly paid senior scientist doing credit score analytics. His mother was a registered nurse. James Holmes, as a neuroscience student at UCR, fit right in. A fellow graduate student said, "He didn't stand out at all, he was no different from any other neuroscience student at UCR." Another student said, "He was a very smart guy, was a member of multiple honors societies, as was I."

On that day, though, he was going to see Batman. He bought a ticket, entered Theater 9 that was brimming with 400 people and sat in the first row. After about 20 minutes he left the theater through an exit door on the side of the movie screen. The door led to an empty parking lot at the back of the complex. Using a plastic tablecloth holder to leave the door open, he went to his car, changed into a bulletproof vest, a ballistic helmet, bullet-resistant leggings, a throat protector, a groin protector and tactical gloves. Most who saw him thought it was a costume or a publicity stunt for the film. He was playing techno music in his earphones so as not to be able to hear the reactions. He threw two smoke canisters, which caused eye irritation, into the theater and then fired off rounds from three different firearms. He shot first to the back of the room, and then toward people in the aisles. Bullets passed through the wall and hit three people in the adjacent Theater 8, which was screening the same film.

Witnesses said the multiplex's fire alarm system began sounding soon after the attack began, and staff told people in Theater 8 to evacuate. One witness said she was hesitant to leave because someone yelled that someone was shooting in the lobby. Holmes fired 76 shots in the theater: six from the shotgun, 65 from the semiautomatic rifle and five from the .40-caliber handgun. He killed 12 people and wounded 80. Matt McQuinn, for example, aged 27, was shot nine times, including in the chest and neck, while trying to protect his girlfriend.

Like the Batman and Joker, James Holmes was very good with technology, but he was an isolated young man with no meaningful relationships. In his college application he wrote, "I had little experience in computer programming and the work was challenging to say the least. Nonetheless, I taught myself how to program in Flash and then construct a cross-temporal calibration model...Completing the project and presenting my model at the end of the internship was exhilarating."[1] One of his coworkers said that he acted strangely in a laboratory work station by staring at a wall and not verbally responding, only smirking when his coworker asked if he was okay.[2] It is an open question how much he was influenced by the character of the Joker in the film. We can certainly say that both he and the Joker are responding to the same kinds of societal separation.

Separation is also the way in which the role in the film was formed. Following the strictures of Hollywood method acting in which one is supposed to "become the role," Heath Leger, the actor who played the Joker in *The Dark Knight*, drove himself "crazy" in a similar manner to the way that James Holmes became unstable – by social isolation. Leger locked himself alone in a hotel. "I sat around in a hotel room in London for about a month, locked myself away...I ended up landing more in the realm of a psychopath – someone with very little to no conscience towards his acts."[3] Before he committed suicide, Leger wrote BYE BYE ominously scrolled all over the diary; his father and others suspect that immersion in the Joker character contributed to his suicide.

For James Holmes, the film probably resonated with his socially alienated experience; the comic world of the film, a world in which empowerment means treating people as disposable, informed his reality. While the reaction to the shooting was mainly couched in terms of gun-control debate in the US, there was also a realization that the culture of the film itself is problematic. The mainstream newspapers defended the film industry, and reasserted the film as pure spectacle. However, even Warner Bros. admitted a kind of connection between the film and reality and canceled film galas in France, Mexico and Japan and made a "substantial" donation to Colorado's Community First Foundation to benefit victims. We are thus faced with the thorny question of the imitation between fiction and life.

While many are impressed with Heath Leger's Joker performance in *The Dark Knight*, we usually don't imitate him; we are also more likely to identify with the good billionaire, the Dark Knight. This identification and the idea behind it of a rich savior is not the stuff of fantasy and fiction. Donald Trump won the 2016 election precisely through presenting himself as a kind of Batman, someone who will save the US not only from "evil" Mexicans and Muslims but also from the inefficient and corrupt nature of government itself. After all, one of the main themes of the film is that government officials, policemen and even the CIA are ineffectual bumbling idiots. Though the US government won World War Two, put a man on the moon, invented the atom bomb and the internet, it needs the help of the billionaire hero in dealing with the Joker.

It's not, of course, that seeing Batman leads you to vote for a billionaire. It's the culture that believes in the ruling idea of heroic billionaires that gives you both Batman and Trump. This idea has a strange significant hold over the population in the

US. With ineffectual masses and a corrupt government, the only choice is actually between the order of money (Bruce Wayne/Batman) and the unleashing of senseless violence (the Joker). Obviously, James Holmes was an isolated individual with mental health problems. Still, in another society his rebellious antisocial nature would be channeled somewhere else. For example, maybe in the UK he would join a punk or anarchist group, or in Germany he would become a radical environmental activist. In the wholly totalitarian world of US capitalism, the only alternative to tech-billionaire Wayne is the senseless terror of the Joker. The film accurately reflects a culture that views any alternative to the rule of the billionaires as beyond the bounds of sense, indeed as self-disruptive madness itself. This madness is tellingly tied to social justice. At one point the Joker says, "Introduce a little anarchy. Upset the established order, and everything becomes chaos. I'm an agent of chaos. Oh, and you know the thing about chaos? It's fair!" As we see in the sequel, the *Dark Knight Rises*, fairness or redistribution is always equated with violence and chaos. The Batman series seems to want to inculcate the viewer with the idea that progressive

social transformation, "fairness," equals senseless violence and destruction. It presents a reality in which the desire for fairness and a changed order is presented as criminally mad. The film both reflects and distorts reality. Far from being pure fantasy, it quite accurately depicts a government subservient to billionaires and the people of the city themselves as passive victims of inexplicable forces that hold them hostage and victimize them. It only distorts the causes of violence.

One can sum up the "lie" of the film by the very splitting of Batman and Joker. Indeed, at one point the film almost admits to the artificiality of this split when the Joker is interrogated by Batman and says, "I don't want to kill you! What would I do without you? Go back to ripping off mob dealers? No, no, NO! No. You...you...complete me." The truth that is glimpsed here is the very true figure of Joker-swindler-billionaire. The combined figure of Batman-Joker represents the billionaire class that is beyond the law, showing no empathy toward people, fighting against democratic movements across the world, outsourcing jobs to China, spying on them using their phones, holding them hostage with debt, using control of the media to stoke fear of crime and dazzling them with empty technological innovation and entertainment.

Capitalism, economist Joseph Schumpeter said, is a kind of process of creative destruction or, better said, destructive creation. It itself is a kind of combination of discipline with chaos and anarchy. This is the strangeness of capitalism itself. The way it represents itself as cold and ascetic, with a disciplined use of instrumental and technological reason (Batman), coupled with psychopathic disregard for humans and their welfare in the name of individualistic exceptionalism. Both Batman and Joker allow this disorder to be disowned by the billionaire Bruce Wayne, a legitimate figure at daylight. Transforming into Batman hints at the shadow world of billionaires, who represent law-abiding citizens by day but partake in a shadowy world beyond the law by night.

Most importantly in the figure of the Joker, the most troubling aspects of capitalism itself are outsourced, projected and externalized to an otherworldly evil, divorced from their social and economic origins in corporate America. Corporate America disowns the chaos and disruption that it creates, viewing it as an externality, and then dons the black outfit to fight it, as if it was some unearthly hellish evil. The capitalist world from the days of the great colonization of the new world to today's giant tech corporations creates disorder. The disorder wreaked on native civilization, the disorder of dislocation from Africa and slavery, the disorder of the Great Depression and Great Recession, the disorder of workers and professionals who are fired according to economic expediency, the disorder that comes from our proximity and exploitation of animals, and finally the disorder of environmental degradation and the stability of the weather itself. It then, however, disowns and externalizes this disorder as a result of "evil" foreigners. This has already been clear in Germany, where the crash and unemployment of 1928 was blamed on Jews. In the Batman series, disorder comes from Bane, a foreigner from the Middle East. However, after externalizing the source of disorder, it represents corporate leaders as those who will bring back order again.

The original Batman comics were first published in the late thirties in New York after a decade of depression, aimed at readers whose despair was so powerful they were willing to believe in any kind of savior, just as *The Dark Knight* was screened in 2008 to audiences suffering from the Great Recession, with its record high unemployment and the decimation of pension savings and the value of houses. "What does not kill you only makes you stranger," says the Joker, and indeed it might seem very strange that the people who are most hit by the recession will sit in a movie house and see something like a Wall Street billionaire (the kind of person who actually caused the housing crash) portrayed as someone who can save them from the disorder, crime and corruption. The culture of capitalism represented through this film is marked by classical defenses of displacement and splitting. In its scrambled code we get a glimpse of our scrambled consciousness. We see the strange ruling idea that aims to heal and repair the traumas and catastrophes of our time through the individualistic billionaire and his code of honor. Both the distortion of people's traumas and wishes and the idea of savior become much more explicit in the next installment of the series, *The Dark Night Rises*.

Perhaps the most interesting thing about *The Dark Night Rises* is the figure of Bane. Bane presents himself as an amalgam between Al-Qaida militant and a populist leader. Born in the dirty pits of the Middle East, he brings anarchy and chaos to Gotham. He represents the radical Other of the establishment, a kind of Middle-Eastern communist terrorist. Like Nazi propaganda's presentation of the eternal Jew, Bain is made from mutually exclusive and incoherent threats; their only common ground is that they pose a danger to the status quo.

However, his version of evil, even more than the Joker, explicitly ties chaos and violence to the demand for social justice. He robs the stock exchange on Wall Street with the aid of people posing as shoe shiners and food delivery workers. He frees the incarcerated, he encourages redistribution of wealth (that is subtly represented as a kind of anti-Semitic pogrom taking place on New York's Fifth Avenue), and like the French Revolution, he holds popular tribunals for the former elite.

Like the Joker, the film risks identification with this figure. After all, 2.5 million Americans are incarcerated. If we include all their loved ones and relatives, then there is a significant percentage of the audience who would like to see a mass release of prisoners. We can add this figure to those who suffer from increased discrimination and systemic poverty, and the erosion of the middle class and middle-class salaries. In addition, there is a growing resentment for the elite 1 percent that has doubled its wealth since the 1970s. Given these social realities and the fact that blockbuster films are a popular medium, Bane's political measures undoubtedly represent the real albeit implicit or unconscious desire of the majority of the spectators. Not only do spectators wish to be transgressive, powerful and beyond conventional morality like Bane, that is, to put nonviolence and liberalism aside, many of them would like to end mass incarceration and redistribute wealth.

In the film, this popular desire must both connect to real wishes and at the same time be represented as radical individualized evil. Hollywood must appeal to the desires of people, and sometimes these desires are political. It must include in however distorted terms a recognizable world, a world that is relatable to its audience. The Batman series does both. It's a world of gothic urban capitalism, and at the same time it expresses unconscious desire for the destruction of this world, a desire that is then projected and externalized onto the individualist antagonist. The arc of the narrative, however, ultimately restores this same order. In his actions and persona, Batman exemplifies precisely the virtues of those who rule.

Interlude I: How Can Wayne Be an Idea That Represents Reality and Yet Distorts It at the Same Time?

As we saw, the idea of the virtuous billionaire is an important part of reality; however, it distorts reality at the same time. Portraying the successful technologically savvy billionaire in film might be said to simply mimic and fictionalize reality. The entrepreneur embodies the innovation that is necessary to open new markets, new ways of reversing the law of falling profit rates, which then in turn saves the capitalist world system from reaching crisis point.[4] One can say that films are a fictionalization of reality: they put the vigilante Batman suit on someone like Steve Jobs or Elon Musk. Alternatively, we can say that this idea

43

distorts reality itself, as the innovation of the entrepreneur is often, in fact, the result of the work of many people. Presenting an Apple computer as arising out of Jobs's garage is a distortion of what went into it. Most of the technology was developed in publicly funded universities and government institutions, and of course it took hundreds of engineers to assemble and make this technology work as well as workers to assemble it.

One can thus say that the idea of the special individual is a way of organizing reality, for example, the founders usually have the most shares in a company, while also falsifying this reality at the same time. The figure of the innovative entrepreneur works to save the system both on the level of the reality of capitalism and on the level of legitimization. While in the past the main legitimization of inequality was based on investment – the capitalist invests and takes risks and that is the reason why he should accrue his wealth – today it is not so much the risks for his own capital that make wealth legitimate, but the innovation associated with it that is key.

The idea of the virtuous, special billionaire exists as an idea and as a social institution. Social institutions are largely arbitrary, and thus any idea, no matter its character, can become a social institution. This does not detract from their reality. The game of golf, nation-states and Muslim madrasas are very real, though they are constructed. Ideas of football, golf, spring break and Hajj do not distort reality; they create reality, which the term then designates. However, some creations like the figure of the virtuous individualist billionaire distort representation of value. These creations make it seem as though somehow outstanding value inheres in the person and body of the billionaire, while obviously value and wealth creation are the work of many. We cannot discount the innovation, tenacity, drive and entrepreneurship of some individuals. We can also remember that not long ago, other types of individualists were also celebrated; for example, the bohemian artist, the explorer, the scientist and the revolutionary. For good and bad we are strangely bereft of revolutionaries like Picasso, Einstein, Lenin and Mao or even of dedicated reformists like Martin Luther King Jr., Nelson Mandela and Mahatma Gandhi. It seems that these kinds of people are no longer needed now that we have Elon Musk. Ultimately, however, it is less important to argue for or against big men. One needs to show that in its current reincarnation, the institution of big men does damage to a truth of where value actually comes from – the people.

Interlude II: Externalization, Privatization, Embodiment

Creating heroes and villains, big-men individuals, and foreign, dangerous and evil others is part of an all-pervasive process of externalization and privatization. As we saw, the work and virtue of the "good" produced by thousands is regularly privatized – it becomes magically and financially embodied in charismatic individuals. Externalization is all pervasive as well; forming the main strategy to deal with the "bad" of capitalism, one externalizes through "bad" minorities, through people who are outside one's country. Externalization may be done crudely. For example, during the COVID-19 epidemic, President Donald Trump referred to the virus as the Chinese virus, but he also very quickly blamed the situation developing in the US on the media, Democratic governors, the WHO, Barack Obama and Joe Biden. For ruling elites, it's good not only to show that problems and evils that inhere in society are not due to systemic failure, but also to specifically show that they come from very specific people and institutions. NGOs and human rights groups are a favorite point of attack for leaders around the world. This is the privatization of evil. Instead of evils being systemic, they are a result of small institutions and, as we have seen, individual people. Externalization is all pervasive. It happens when corporations do not take into account the costs to the environment and their workers of what they produce, viewing them as externalities. Externalization happened when instead of solving the problems of religious intolerance and economic inequality in seventeenth-century Europe, these pressures were vented by settling the New World. When instead of solving global warming, billionaires offer us the chance to die on Mars. This is another type of externalization of the bad. Finally, the simplest way of externalizing is through the bad man, the psychopath, the villains that we meet in the press and in our films. Evil is thus both individualized and externalized. Instead of changing the pervasive elements of patriarchy in our culture and society, let us have a Harvey Weinstein; instead of altering the capitalist system that is rigged against the majority of humanity, let us have a Bernie Madoff. Instead of understanding how US foreign policy created terrorists, let's kill Osama Bin Laden. I am not claiming here that some people don't do bad things, but that the system we currently live in creates and incentivizes the action of such people. Bernie Madoff is unimaginable, for example, in an Amish settlement or a hippie commune; the system that we belong to creates the possibilities of what we can be. In a system that puts money above all else, we can expect people like Bernie Madoff. In a system that gives unlimited powers to producers over the lives and livelihoods of actors, you can expect a Weinstein. More subtly, in the current system many people are miniature Bernie Madoffs; there are countless mini-Bernie Madoffs on and off Wall Street.

For our purposes, what is important to notice is that individualization and externalization always outdo a real representation of the problem. Individualization and externalization are much more rhetorically and emotionally effective. Think of the emotional difference between letting someone know that the world's temperature is to be 3 degrees higher and telling them that this particular Muslim man has violated several German women. In fact, while for the left the issue is how to represent societal and ecological ills in an effective and truthful manner, the right always has an easy time representing various external enemies.

Calculating Agent

There is a humbler variant of individualism that many different people and institutions conspire to invoke in us – the person as a calculating agent. It is a ruling idea that invites us to view ourselves as self-interested agents who calculate our actions in order to maximize benefit, utility, pleasure and happiness. This image of the human being is inculcated in economics, psychology, neuroscience, business, philosophy and everyday life. This is a normative model, the way we should behave and more or less the way these fields posit us as behaving. This is not a contradiction. The normative model is posited as quite close to actual behavior. Sometimes in order to pique our interest, a popular book like *Predictably Irrational* will show that we don't really optimize our choices, or someone like Daniel Kahneman will receive a Nobel Prize for demonstrating this. A book like *Freakonomics* will show that we are responding to monetary incentives even when we are not conscious of them, as if it is some deep secret that people in our society respond to monetary incentives. In philosophy we will meet the trolley problem in which we pull a lever that derails a train in order to run over one person rather than five. In a variation on this artificial moral problem, we are reluctant to push a fat person off a bridge for the same results. In game theory, we are asked to imagine two prisoners who need to decide whether to rat on the other prisoner or keep quiet. Often it happens that suspecting that the other will tell on them, both tell on each other and are worse off for it. As students of economics, political science and philosophy, we are sure to meet this image repeatedly as if it is the most natural thing in the world. We are implicitly told that we are a utility calculating agent with interesting quirks. But the deviations and variations of the image only serve to strengthen the basic image – man is a calculating optimizer. What is wrong with this basic picture?

Well, one thing is to define interest, benefit or utility in a way that enables one to compare choices along some quantifiable or at least comparable spectrum. Let's take pleasure, for instance. Many mainstream Americans spend a significant amount of their time and money on American football, while many Middle Eastern Muslims spend next to nothing on the NFL but pay a lot to go on a Hajj in Mecca. Now, which is more beneficial, football or Hajj? The answer depends on whom you ask. Perhaps the reader will say, "It's unfair to compare two different cultures!" I can answer, "Why is this unfair? The theory states that I can compare any two utilities." However, let's accommodate this critique and look at the same culture. What has more utility, going for a jog in the afternoon or going for coffee with a friend? There seems to be no common rational ground for choosing one over the other. But surely you might say this is leisure and not that important. In our working lives, everybody wants to be wealthy. This is not strictly true. Nurses and schoolteachers want to be paid fairly, but they did not choose their profession in order to become rich. If we broaden our historical perspectives, we see examples of Christians, Buddhist, skeptics, intellectuals, artists, musicians, hippies and punks who have chosen a life of modest means or even poverty. In fact, relatively few people strictly choose to be rich as their goal.

Even many of the rich choose additional goals to which they are very attached. Elon Musk, for instance, says he is concerned with making humans interplanetary and may even be willing to lose money for that goal. But let's return to the more extreme example of, say, Christian Franciscans or Buddhist monks who have chosen a life of poverty or very modest means, or resistance fighters who have faced death, torture or imprisonment. You might be tempted to say "Yes, but this kind of life brings much utility and benefit to them"; utility is not money, sophisticated utilitarians say, it's utility. In fact, one of the sneaky charms of the concept of utility is that when you use it, some will hear money and others things more ethereal – pleasure or happiness. Let us go with the more philosophical "higher" version of utility. Okay, I will say now, tell me which life has more utility for the person living it: the life of a Buddhist monk, a resistance fighter or a hedge fund manager? This is too large a choice, you will counter, the model was not made for such big decisions. Let's make it small then. Should I spend my discretionary three hours a day meditating or stock trading? How shall we compare the tranquility that comes with meditation to the peace of mind of financial security or indeed the pleasure of a five-star restaurant? The truthful answer is that we cannot. One might answer that we need to quantify and return to money. Fine, let us descend from true and deep life choices to the realms that utilitarians feel comfortable with. Let's say that an expensive dinner costs 300 dollars and a two-day meditation weekend costs 350 dollars. Where does that leave us? Do the costs help you choose? Not really. Beyond basic survival (food and drink), what we do with our income is almost never a choice between comparable utilities but involves a complex mixture of culture, genetics, personality, situational factures, the rhetoric of desire and more. In fact, our view of the human as a rational agent calculating between the measurable benefits of alternatives may fit only the circumscribed world of some choices in the supermarket or stock exchange.

For example, when I go to the supermarket in the US and buy toothpaste, sometimes I am offered a utility function free of charge. They tell me how many cents a gram of Aim toothpaste vs. Colgate toothpaste costs, I look up and see that the active ingredients and their percentage are the same, and then I feel empowered to make the choice. I get the same value for less money. Yet even in this extremely rare clear-cut situation where one can make a rational decision based on measurable utility, many prefer an expensive brand to something generic or that has received less advertising. And even those more rational do not know if it's worthwhile to invest a few more dollars and get those more expensive brands that offer active ingredients that take care of gums as well.

Given all the uncertainties, making larger and more significant financial decisions such as trading in stocks is even less based on strict rationality. However, let us propose that analysts, automatic trading and other tools somehow make the choices that our stock trader makes more rational. Even if we take this ultra-utilitarian stock trader, she or he still goes home and needs to decide whether they want to marry or stay single, how many children they may want, whether they want to live in the city or in a suburb or develop a passion for reading or sports. True, one can say that this trader can go home and read a book on how to make money or she can go play golf in order to make connections, but then how will she know which is better? Perhaps both are less lucrative then looking to marry a rich man? But then what about the benefit that comes from being an empowered, autonomous woman? Even the most relatively trivial consumerist choices like renovating the house vs. going on vacation are difficult to quantify. What brings more satisfaction: having a nicer house or seeing the world? Choosing between quantifiable benefits cannot really inform our decisions. In the actual world we will probably go to a football game or study Koran, rush a fraternity or enlist in the army, work out in a gym or go hunting, according to what people around us are doing and talking about, and not through some calculation of benefit or utility.

So why is the image of the calculating individual so very prevalent, so ubiquitous? First and foremost, it presents persons flatteringly as autonomous beings. I first experienced how prevalent this image is when I was invited to a house of philosophers who were discussing the famous trolley problem. This problem is couched as a kind of narrative. You take a walk along trolley tracks in your town. A trolley is coming fast behind you, you step to the side and as it gets closer you hear shouts of panic from five people that are on board, the trolley's brakes have gone out and it's going faster and faster. You happen to be next to a hand lever that will switch the trolley into a safe sand pit; however, next to the sandpit stands a man totally unaware of the trolley and you have no time to warn him. If you pull a lever you will save five passengers but the man will die. What will you do? In another variation there is no auxiliary track. Just a fat man standing on a bridge; if you push him on the track you will save five people. The philosophers in the living room discussed the intricacies of the problem and different reasons why most people would choose differently in the first and second case. At one point the discussion veered to discussion of other choices, all of them commercial (which summer home to buy, which restaurant to visit, where to buy shoes). It suddenly dawned on me that though seemingly more down to earth, this is the same conversation. This presentation of man as a being who chooses utilities is all pervasive. It is a small and very typical image, a kind of atom of the ruling idea of choice. The philosophers at the table might feel that they are transitioning from serious ethics to small talk, when in fact they are staying exactly in the same place, reinforcing with their words the same image, and we really like this image.

The image of the calculating decision maker flatters us. It highlights every one of us as an agent in control of his or her life, making sovereign rational choices even though this is rarely the case. It creates the illusion of a heightened form of individualism and ignores the fact that much of what we do is generic so to speak, with numerous people of similar backgrounds as our own doing the same. The image of the calculating person making decisions makes people feel smart, empowered and in control. It's not that we cannot all be enabled in this way, but that it takes more effort than just deciding which choices to make. Indeed, being empowered is preconditioned on a complex interplay of a great many things. To feel empowered as an athlete, for example, one needs to go through years of training, be in a certain kind of physical condition, have certain playing skills, but also be embedded in a context of playing on a team, having a coach, etc. A good athlete performs in a certain way. Even the most rational decision-making process will not make you a good athlete, doctor, political activist, engineer, artist, husband or mother. Though this idea of the rational and calculating agent has much appeal, it will ultimately make you as wise and powerful as a pocket calculator.

As is the case with other ruling ideas, there is an attempt to force reality to conform to the idea. We are presented with insignificant choices every day and there is an attempt to give us many "choices" to "empower" us as consumers. Every shopping mall presents itself as a utopia of choice. Amazon sells over 200 million products. If you were to view each product for just one second, it would take you over 360 years to go over the complete catalog. While, of course, nobody goes over the catalog in its entirety, we do spend hours choosing many things that we don't really need, and many of our recreational environments are presented through choice. However, most of these choices are trivial. When we move to more serious matters like our jobs or our real friends and loved ones, we don't have that much choice. Even in economic matters such as serious investment we have much less choice.

Though human life can never be reduced to choices of consumption or investment, the ruling idea of the calculating agent does structure part of our reality as well as push people to see themselves as agents making consumer choices. However, highlighting and strengthening one's image as a choosing agent is detrimental to the creation of meaning that usually comes from other sources rather than through calculating decision making. The idea of the calculating agent downplays a variety of central aspects of human life, including temporality, life-narrative and connection with others, with nature and meaningful work. It often masks such central concerns and central deficits and compensates with trinkets of consumer choice, preventing people from facing up to and changing their lives.

Changing lives can be done as an individual or even more effectively in groups. The idea of the calculating agent is even more problematic politically than it is personally. It is problematic in that it creates the illusion that one's life situation and its difficulties are necessarily a result of one's choices irrespective of context and social structure. If you are a professional, for example, you might feel that you are not successful enough, that you dislike the way you are treated in your job, or that you are under the pressure of debt. If you are working class, your problems can be much greater, such as unemployment, incarceration, and affording suitable housing and health services. Under the image of the calculating individual, these problems are made to disappear as collective problems, problems shared by millions, and they become essentially private. Whatever condition you are in, you have only yourself to blame, and any solution will come only from yourself, from the sheer resilience, virtue, piety or belief that you yourself can master. Perhaps more absurdly, whatever problem society has needs to be addressed on an individual level. In fact, on the fundamental level there are no societal problems, just individual problems and you have calculated badly.

The Bad Men

As my son was doing his American history course, he got me interested in the discussion around the Founding Fathers and their slaves. Later, I went to a panel discussion in a conference session organized around the question "Were the founding fathers racist?" At one point, one of the participants pointed out that though Thomas Jefferson did not release his slaves in his life or death, this is understandable since he inherited slaves as property when he was 14 years old, and it was against the law to release slaves at the time. The speaker was adamant that "Jefferson was not racist." One can easily get caught up in such discussions. My first thought was that if you own slaves, you must be racist to justify this. But then I was suddenly struck by how gullible I have become to accept the terms of the discussion – that being a racist was worse than owning slaves. Is it really worse to be hated and discriminated against than to be owned from birth to death like livestock? Surly it is better to be despised than to be owned like property. It was strange for me to understand the distortion that made a feeling and belief (racism) somehow more prominent than owning human beings, exploiting them, beating and whipping them, separating mothers from children, and all the other practices of slavery. Surly racism is just a single (psychological and individual) part of something greater, which is the history and institution of slavery and all that it entails. Are the feelings of individual people that important? I then listened more carefully to mainstream and conservative discourse around me. Racism and not the legacy of slavery, colonialism and stark economic inequalities is what is front and center. According to many people's understanding, racism is a result of some bad people with bad feelings. It is instructive to listen closely to what conservative pundit Ben Shapiro says in a talk that explains the core principles of conservatism:

> There are consequences to individual actions. You have to first look to individual actions before you simply shout discrimination or exploitation. Yes, discrimination exists, yes exploitation exists, but let's actually identify the people who are discriminating and exploiting and target them for

violation of law instead of just declaring that it's out there in the universe and we're all being crushed by it, because that helps nobody...we just say discrimination exists, America is institutionally racist, and that is a completely worthless statement, it helps no one; name the racist, find the racist, we will all side together.

Shapiro wants to prosecute people not institutions, though I suspect that even Shapiro writing in 2015 would probably agree that slavery was an institution, not a bunch of despicable people enslaving others. The problem of contemporary racism and racial inequality presumably calls for a transformation of society. But here Ben Shapiro has a problem. Due to his strict individualism, nothing collective can be done to remedy or fix social problems, make a fundamental change of culture or society, or create measures that can help provide greater integration or wealth redistribution. A social collective problem must be given an individualist solution. What is the solution? A couple of "bad" people are racist. This is the compromise reached. Shapiro will recognize that a problem exists, but he will turn it into a personal problem of people rather than an institutional one. I suspect from other statements that Shapiro has made that he views Blacks as having a culture that lacks restraint in sexuality and use of violence. In his imagination people get what they deserve.

Listening to one of the speakers describe the slaves of one of the Founding Fathers, I realized that I did the same thing as Shapiro. I imagined the founders as evil. Scenes of sadistically evil men, from Frederic Douglass to Quentin Tarantino, whipping women filled my mind. And then I realized I have been doped by individualistic imagination and thinking again. The truth is probably that slavery felt ordinary to those who were born into owning slaves, very much like our relationship to those who for very low wages clean our houses or offices, or to farm animals. There was no special need for someone like the young Jefferson to be cruel or sadistic or powerfully animated by racist hate. Just as we are not animated with burning hate toward animals or those who mine in Africa. Those who owned slaves were largely not especially cruel; they perceived Africans as naturally inferior. They let overseers do most of the punishment, just like we let all kinds of special professions, jail wardens, animal slaughterers, soldiers and overseers in factories in China do all kinds of cruel work for us.

We tend to view all those who participate in structural evils as heatedly animated by hatred and sadism, but this is largely untrue. First of all, most structural cruelty is out of sight and therefore out of mind; society does a good job of hiding structural cruelty and violence in faraway places like factories in East Asia, mines in Africa, plantations in South America, and internment camps on various borders or islands. Institutions closer to home, like slaughterhouses, prisons and interrogation rooms, are often largely inaccessible. It is true that those involved directly with repressing and doing violence to migrants, prisoners, women, animals, workers, blacks, Muslims, etc., do justify their actions with thoughts and feelings related to the inferiority of those they wrought violence on. Still, as we transition in society away from the working class toward the middle- and professional-class people (who have little personal connection with such work yet still benefit the most from it), we can afford to be magnanimous and lack any hatred or hard feelings. We quickly personalize residual worries and pressures regarding structural evils.

The dynamic is familiar. The subordination of women to men has been one of the most pervasive structural features of civilizations for thousands of years. It expressed itself in countless ways and was deeply imbedded in law, culture (both religious and secular), family, employment and economy. The feminist movement in the West as well as socialism (in China and Russia) has been successful in rectifying some of the most blatant disadvantages suffered by women, but at the same time it is clear that it's an incomplete project, especially regarding working-class women who do the most difficult and demeaning jobs in society for the least pay. Yet recently this structural wide-reaching inequality that encompasses everything from our films to workplace has been individualized and privatized again. Instead of enacting a substantial transformation of society, the #MeToo movement focused on villains like Harvey Weinstein and others who promoted young actresses on condition they slept with them, what became known as couch casting.

However, couch casting should not be seen as some abnormal procedure done by monsters. It was part of inequalities and asymmetry of gender, intersected, it is crucial to stress, with the radical asymmetry between employer and employee. Committed to the fairy tale that hiring an employee is a symmetrical exchange between two essentially equal individuals trading money for time, the real situation of couch casting is highly distorted. A Hollywood producer has dozens of options to cast, and he is always free to reject a candidate and find someone often just as good. While the candidate faces emotional and financial pressures, she is "free" to be unemployed. What is evil is not Weinstein but the situation that makes Weinstein possible: the vulnerability in which people find themselves when they look to avoid poverty. This situation leads to corruption on the one hand and collaboration on the other. Again, this basic social and structural asymmetry is denied in the US. Thus, we are left with predators, the big bad wolf and other figures of evil, an image that serves to displace society-wide radically asymmetric social relations.

We do this with figures like the Nazis. Most Nazis, just like most slave owners, are regular human beings participating in social institutions. The reader will probably object and ask what about whipping and raping, what about sadistic Nazi doctors, etc.? Of course, some people have more sadistic impulses than others, but it is institutions that allow or disallow these behaviors. These sadistic impulses are not articulated; in a way they don't exist in relatively benign situations and institutions. The American soldiers who massacred women and children in Mai Lai led productive, regular lives up until they became soldiers and were sent to Vietnam. In certain situations, evil is not extraordinary but ordinary.

Hannah Ardent was one of the most respected intellectuals in the West for her ideological service to the US during the Cold War, when she equalized Communism and Nazism under the banner of totalitarianism. Yet she became controversial through her reportage of the Eichmann trial in which she dared to claim that Eichmann was a banal bureaucrat mainly focused on self-advancement. This raised a storm since it did a disservice to the ruling idea of the bad person. Our ideology needs the bad person. We love to hate our Weinsteins, our Eichmanns, our Madoffs, our Zuckerbergs. This hate is sometimes shared by the left as well. Communist film maker Sergei Eisenstein liked to present factory owners laughing with fat bellies and cigars while the workers toiled. We want to personalize, but slavery, the Holocaust, colonialism, sexism and capitalist exploitation are not personal; they are systemic and situational. Many of us know of the Milgram's experiment in which ordinary Americans were led to believe they were giving high voltage shocks to other Americans; more than half continued to administer shocks that would have been lethal. A variation on the theme was the Stanford prison experiment in which student guards turned sadistic after spending a couple of days in a mock prison. Almost everybody saw the pictures of ordinary childish American soldiers humiliating prisoners at Abu Ghraib. Still, even the most educated among us find personalization and individualization of evil irresistible.

Making individuals evil is exciting. People love to hate

people like Trump and Zuckerberg, and they both sell media. Our favorite movie villains such as Darth Vader, Hannibal Lecter, Hans Landa, Cruella de Vil, Gordon Gekko, the Joker, Lord Voldemort and the Terminator make profits by bringing excitement and even a kind of joy at their transgressive acts and personalities. Yet their message of some otherworldly evil embodied is not only false but is pernicious to an understanding of where bad things actually come from. We all have bad, aggressive, antisocial impulses, but these are usually held in check by society and by other impulses such as compassion or fear of retribution. Bad things come mainly from situations and institutions that we feel impelled as individuals to reproduce and to which resistance as individuals is extremely difficult. Individuals are strongly incentivized by systematic rewards and grave punishments, by hopes and threats to reproduce relatively closely the society that we were born into with all of its problems and injustices.

A good example is the way we are separated from those who are less fortunate than us. I have moved several times with my family in the US from DC to Boston, from Boston to New Orleans. When we go house-hunting the Realtor immediately differentiates good and bad neighborhoods according to how dangerous they are and how good the schools are. In several places that we have lived people are mugged every day, and sometimes they are hospitalized. Though muggings are a city-wide phenomenon in DC and New Orleans, one attempts to assuage one's fear by being in the "good" neighborhoods. Being a middle-class academic and having no wealth or security to provide our children, our hope for their future security and flourishing is to give them a good education that will with any luck make them gainfully employed. Most under such a situation will try to have their children attend a good school. And yet our efforts to provide them with good schooling de facto contributes to racial and economic segregation in the US.

Changing something as an individual (sending your children to a "bad" school) is very difficult, and doing so almost seems negligent as a parent.

Individuals face such incentive structures in almost everything they do. For example, not only does education predominantly reproduce inequality and segregation, so do most jobs. Individuals are thus often faced with the "choice" between a job that contributes to inequality or being unemployed. As private individuals we are relatively powerless to alter structural inequalities and are constantly encouraged to reproduce or heighten them. For this very reason individualism is so important as an idea that rules over us and subjects us. Together we might alter existing hierarchies and inequalities; alone we are faced with impossible choices for ourselves and the need to project the resultant harm caused by our societies toward "bad" people.

Some Historical Complications with Individualism and Liberalism

Individualism and individual liberty are of course an aspirational ideal, not an actual description of the political regimes that people live under in the really existing liberalism of the UK and United States. Regimes in most liberal places are in fact highly controlling, with low degrees of personal freedom and high pressure to socially confirm and fit in. This is obviously the case in schooling, where pressure to be popular or less hated is intense, as well as in one's work, where the clothes one wears and the things one says are highly controlled and the wrong word can be penalized. In fact, there is no true individualism in the workplace in any way, shape or form.

More deeply, there are fundamental questions regarding the very possibility of individualism. Humans are born neonates, wholly unprepared for life; they are plastic and formless, they must slowly upload the "software" of culture if they are to function at all as human beings. Moreover, most of what we value is valued collectively. Money, language, sports, education and popularity only accrue value in collectives. They have no meaning for a Robinson Crusoe on an island. However, more narrowly, there are specific contradictions in the individualism articulated in liberalism.

In his book *Liberalism: A Counter-History*, Domenico Losurdo asks a fundamental question regarding thinkers and political regimes that claimed to champion universal liberty, property rights and individualism.[5] He shows that thinkers like John Locke, Montesquieu, Adam Smith, John Stuart Mill and Alexis de Tocqueville backed slavery, and expropriation of land not only from natives but also from the poor. They certainly did not have a *universal* concern with freedom of the individual. More interesting is that individual freedom was curtailed even from those at the top of the hierarchy. For example, colonial slave codes existed to discipline blacks, exploit them and deny them freedom, yet enforcing these codes meant curtailment of individual freedoms to white masters as well. White masters were required by law to punish slaves, to prevent their congregation, to ride patrols and to set up courts. Slave owners could not marry black people, women caught with free black lovers in the North had to witness them being turned into slaves and sent to the South as punishment. Masters were required by law to brutally punish regardless of what they thought of the offense of their "property." When fires that erupted in 1741 in New York created fear of slave revolt, two blacks were executed by being burned alive – their master tried in vain to save them. In another case, a black slave confessed to setting fire to a barn. The crowd of white spectators saw to it that he would be burned slowly. His master, sobbing loudly, could do nothing.[6]

Freedom of speech was viciously curtailed to all those involved in abolitionist papers. The editor of an abolitionist newspaper, Elijah Lovejoy, had to suffer three times as an angry white mob broke into his office and smashed his press. Lovejoy installed new machines each time and continued publishing. The fourth time they broke into his office, he tried to defend his press, the attackers set fire to the building, and as he escaped the fire they shot and killed him.[7]

Freedom to assemble did not exist. Not only did it not exist for black people but for anyone who organized on their behalf. What was perceived as the collective security of the white race took precedence over both individual rights of free speech as well as property rights of masters over their slaves. Losurdo designates the regime in the nineteenth century in the United States not as liberalism but master race democracy. Still, this too is not precise as it wholly discounts both the discourse and practice of individualism in the US and the way it projects individualist values around the world. How then are we to see liberalism and the role of individualism within it? A good way to conceptualize it is as a kind of indeterminacy or slippage as ideas and practices vacillate from aspirational individualism to ensuring *collective* rule to rich whites. If the position of the ruling elite is perceived as threatened in any way, then liberal individualism is suspended to the benefit, protection and enhancement of the collective, often at the cost of individuals.

Indeed, conservative thinkers such as Edmund Burke regularly invoked the sacred quality of community: a partnership of those of the past and those of the future viewing society as a kind of extended family of blood relations. The focus on continuity of generations is of course a mild sedative to preclude thinking about what needs to be changed in the here and now.

Often when people research and then recount their own family lineages, one senses a kind of familial sublime that compensates for the frustrations and privations of the here and now. One imagines a kind of essence of familial identity that will survive one's life. If one sees oneself as a bridge between the past and the future, then there is no point in effecting deep change, one's role is just a kind of intermediary, a mediator of the heritage of the past to the future. This of course can have self-affirming connotations to those who see their role as inheriting wealth, enlarging it and then bequeathing it to their children. Often the doctrine of generations extends from the family to the nation; the nation often ethnically or racially is imagined as a kind of extended family. In most countries it stretches into the distant past and is projected toward the future. A Chinese conservative nationalist can say, "What are your concerns with exploitation and environmental degradation in comparison with the 5,000-year-old past of China and with its glorious future?" The nation and family provide a kind of imagined eternal essence that transcends the here and now.

There are many group discourses and practices among elites. However, elite group discourse has limits too, limits that are set by propaganda aimed at society at large, as well as limits that have to do with internal competition. The economic elite often does not want to represent itself as a group since this will contribute to the awareness of what this group does as a group. Such awareness would contribute to the consciousness of most of society that they are indeed exploited and controlled by this group. This, in turn, comes dangerously close to encouraging organization and resistance among those who are afflicted by the status quo. Better that in society's mind they would be presented not as a group with interest, but as successful individuals. Their power to control the rest of society is best represented as an outcome of fair competition in which hard work, and responsible and sometimes brilliant individuals succeed.

Indeed, this is the way in which they are usually represented. Pick up a newspaper or see the news and you will see a series of presentations on "brilliant" and successful individuals. After all, according to these newspapers ruling idea, success and failure are a sign of virtue vs. fault and not some systemic failure to provide equality and opportunity for different groups. The second reason why there is a limit to collective affiliation is that the powerful compete as well as collaborate with each other and at the end of the day measure their success in terms of *personal* wealth not according to how much their group has succeeded.

Additionally, individualism has also been needed as a ruling idea that keeps the threat of socialism at bay. All through the late nineteenth and twentieth centuries, socialism and communism were presented as threats to the individual; their ideals were the ideals of a "society of bees and beavers." It is ironic to note that far from creating individuals, capitalist liberalism creates quite monotonous subjectivities. Under capitalism, everyone wants the same thing (e.g., Profit) and often attempts to follow the market wherever profit is to be made. Thus, masses of people follow ever-new gold rushes and frontiers of capital. Whether it was the physical frontier of the West, the space frontier, the AI frontier, the neuroscience frontier, the hedge fund frontier, big data frontier, internet of things frontier, blockchain frontier, robotics frontier, augmented reality frontier or quantum computing frontier.

Nor is one free under capitalism to interact as an authentic individual with others. Already in 1854, Henry David Thoreau describes well the kind of nonindividual that capitalism creates. It is worthwhile to quote him at some length:

>...trying to get into business and trying to get out of debt, a very ancient slough, called by the Latins *aes alienum*, another's brass, for some of their coins were made of brass; still living, and dying, and buried by this other's brass; always promising to pay, promising to pay, tomorrow, and dying today, insolvent; seeking to curry favor, to get custom, by how many modes, only not state-prison offenses; lying, flattering, voting, contracting yourselves into a nutshell of civility or dilating into an atmosphere of thin and vaporous

generosity, that you may persuade your neighbor to let you make his shoes, or his hat, or his coat, or his carriage, or import his groceries for him; making yourselves sick, that you may lay up something against a sick day, something to be tucked away in an old chest, or in a stocking behind the plastering, or, more safely, in the brick bank; no matter where, no matter how much or how little…I sometimes wonder that we can be so frivolous, I may almost say, as to attend to the gross but somewhat foreign form of servitude called Negro Slavery, there are so many keen and subtle masters that enslave both North and South. It is hard to have a Southern overseer; it is worse to have a Northern one; but worst of all when you are the slave-driver of yourself.[8]

Thoreau was well aware that under such a system, with its pressure to make money, with its servile obsequiousness, constant flattery and business-based pragmatic niceness, true individuality is impossible. Indeed, models of individuals are always far off in time and space, never those actually around you. When Ayn Rand needed to exemplify American individualism in her novel *The Fountainhead*, she created the character of Howard Roark, a modernist architect unwilling to compromise with the establishment. Though ostensibly inspired by Frank Lloyd Wright, the persona is ultimately taken from German Bauhaus, which ironically was a communist inspired movement that sought to do away with class distinctions between craftsman and artist, and to build in a style that was functional, cheap and consistent with mass collective production.

Indeed, modernism itself is unimaginable without the modernist groups that conceived of it and put it together. Suffice to say that individualism is mostly an ideological weapon. If society sincerely wanted individualism, it would free up individuals from hierarchy, as well as provide basic needs. Hierarchy itself precludes authentic expression and self-building as one needs to present a necessarily false self to those above you. As we saw, the market exerts a tremendously de-individualizing force. People make career choices based not on possibilities of personal development and uniqueness but around the very possibility of employment or getting adequately compensated. Films, for example, level out unique individuals by churning out "universal" infantile superhero stories of good vs. bad or formulaic romantic comedies. In short, encouraging true individualism is a serious project that makes demands toward equality and welfare that require broad redistribution, something that can never happen under the current system.

Chapter Three

The New Commandments

Enjoy!

On any regular day, we are called to enjoy. Pleasure is imbedded in both our environment and our conversations. Throughout the day we will negotiate which pleasure we allow ourselves and which not. This goes from relatively trivial decisions, such as should one buy a pastry or some fashionable clothes, should we play a video game, eat chocolate, masturbate or see a movie, to decisions that can affect a whole life profoundly, such as using heroin or having sex with someone who we will be together with long term.

We usually think and talk about pleasure in three main ways. One is through weakness of the will, through pleasures that add legitimacy and through pleasures that are transgressive or criminal. Comedians make fun of themselves for eating ice cream or masturbating. It is indeed funny and even puzzling that we act against our own better judgment, willingly doing things we know are bad for us. Sometimes this is clearly related to our relationship to time; we seem to prefer even the smallest immediate rewards to larger rewards in the future. But it also reveals that we are not in full control of ourselves regarding pleasure. Whether we couch this in biblical terms of desire and morality, psychoanalytical terms of id and superego, or modern neuroscience that contrasts various subcortical pleasure hotspots with the prefrontal cortex, there is more than one entity within us that responds to pleasure. We have long known and felt that we are divided within ourselves regarding pleasure. Pleasure then is represented as a short-term surge and enjoyment with usually bad long-term consequences.

We are increasingly aware of the complex ways in which these short-term surges in pleasure are detrimental to us in the long term. Sugar, intermittent social affirmation on social networks and gaming are good cases in point. Sugar has been linked to diabetes, obesity and heart disease, while intermittent social affirmation has been linked to depression and anxiety. By now we all know that it's not good to indulge in these pleasures, that in a way they activate parts of us that are better left shut down.

Then there is the second talk of pleasure: the legitimate pleasures. At dinner parties people discuss good food they have eaten, films they have enjoyed and concerts attended, or they relate their vacations on beaches and ski resorts. Young adults may discuss drugs enthusiastically, and couples may compliment each other on appearance or sexual performance. In contrast to the comic image of a man uncontrollably eating ice cream, we are proud of these pleasures in that context and see them as evidence of a life well lived. In the first image we are powerlessly latching on to enjoyment. The metaphor of the impulsive child greedily trying to maximize pleasure or the drug addict who is looking to partially do away with self and world since both have become difficult or painful, resonates here. Another way of talking about pleasure makes us into connoisseurs and aristocrats, flouting our freedom to be doing largely useless things. These useless things, this consumption, is the way in which we not only enjoy but more importantly how we show sovereignty in a capitalist world. Thus, pleasures are sometimes for the weak willed, and sometimes buttress legitimacy and power. The third relation with pleasure is to view it as transgressive or illegal. Ice cream may show weakness of the will, an expensive house shows legitimacy, and sex with minors is illegal.

Many pleasures are making their way from illegitimate to legitimate; for instance, homosexual or sadomasochistic sex and recreational marijuana. Other pleasures, especially for men, went the reverse way; for example, some forms of what was once considered by many men to be harmless flirting became harassment, and new prohibitions are enacted on consensual sexuality in the workplace. Clearly, we have a complex relationship toward pleasure: sometimes we proudly share and sometimes we are ashamed. How should we make sense of this? In order to understand pleasure and what we want to do with it we must go back and examine how we got to this point.

To simplify, one can say that until the 1960s, pleasure in the West was largely controlled by Christianity, liberalism and the market. It is often claimed that Christianity, in its doctrinal core, was largely negative toward pleasure. More precisely, like other institutions, the church used pleasure in order to support its legitimacy. It has created a hierarchy of pleasures in which those pleasures that occur within its recognized institutions are supported and those that are outside are not. At one end we get the pleasures of the church itself. The church offers sociability, the pleasure of social recognition and respectability, the pleasure of church ritual, of the sermon, its comfort and inspiration, and sometimes the pleasure of communal eating. At the other end, we have pleasures that are strictly disallowed. Though the relationship of the church to sex is highly complex and has experienced various fluctuations, one can broadly say that the church discouraged or outlawed masturbation, oral sex, homosexuality, pornography, adultery, polyamory, bestiality, intercrural intercourse (copulation between the thighs), having sex with a pregnant woman, and having sex standing up or with the woman on top. At the height of its repression, enjoyment of sex itself was suspect. Thomas Aquinas, for example, warned that a man who had sex with his wife for pleasure was treating her like a prostitute. St Jerome agreed and said that "a man who is too passionately in love with his wife is an adulterer."[1] Any act of sexuality that was deemed either outside the institution of the family or outside the intent to procreate was discouraged. Through the years, the church accommodated itself to various sexual practices; however, at the core of its relationship to sexuality stands procreation, and it remains suspicious of pleasure. The church also saw overeating and drinking or desiring rich foods as a grave sin; gluttony was one of the seven deadly sins. This too was relaxed through the years as people found new motivations for restricting their diets.

Liberalism stresses lack of interference in doing things that do not harm others. People are seen as naturally free, and the burden of proof is on those who would restrict this natural freedom. In practice, it is only recently that freedoms that go against Christian doctrine, such as homosexuality and BDSM, have been allowed. Some sexual practices between consenting adults such as sexual relations between first cousins are still criminalized and given heavy sentencing that can include periods of up to 40 years in prison in some US states, while they are legal in France, Belgium, Netherlands, Russia and Spain. Decriminalization of sexuality has been uneven, with moral panics often causing all kinds of regress from the basic doctrine of liberalism that states that one should have maximal freedom as long as one does not hurt others.

The ability to give consent has been withdrawn not only from those who have not reached the age of consent but also from those who are intoxicated or who have unequal power. Thus, for instance, college students are said to be unable to give meaningful consent to professors, and employees to those above them in the organization. The issue here is complex since those under the power of others often feel that they have little choice but to comply with those above them in the interests of keeping their jobs, getting promoted or getting recommendations. Here, as in the chapter on individualism, we witness the way in which the costs of structural evils such as hierarchy and job insecurity (that create the very possibility of sexual and other kinds of exploitation), evils that benefit a ruling elite, are privatized onto those who attempt such a relationship. In an egalitarian society, sexual exploitation could not exist. Ostensibly, such laws are made to guard employees from unwanted attention by those above them; nevertheless, freedom and pleasure are denied to consenting adults if any of their activities pose any possible type of financial or legal risk to institutions of which they are part. In fact, one can safely say that in adopting these regulations that restrict pleasure, institutes are mainly concerned with legal liability and lawsuits and not with protecting those who are vulnerable.

On the other hand, there has been a shift toward unfettered enjoyment in the realm of recreational drugs with worldwide decriminalization and legalization, and the commodification of marijuana. More ominously, people have been increasingly trusted to successfully withdraw on their own from highly addictive medications such as fentanyl, OxyContin, Demerol, hydrocodone, morphine and Percocet. It is not a coincidence that people are called to freely enjoy drugs but are restricted and controlled in the realm of sexuality in the workplace. In the first case, pleasure facilitates business profits from the sale of marijuana and drugs, in the second, the pleasure of employees to engage in behavior that might pose some risk of litigation to business is curtailed. The freedoms of liberalism are regularly extended to pleasures that benefit owners and managers while new restrictions are placed on the pleasures of employees and workers.

After Christianity and liberalism, we come to the market as a third force that strongly influences our pleasure. At first the market may not seem to have any kind of specific tendency regarding pleasures. Anything today can be bought or sold, even things that negate pleasure. Ascetic diets and Vipassana retreats are sold just like dildos and sweet cakes. However, when we look more closely, the market does deeply affect pleasure. A market-dominated society is likely to repress pleasures that are not commodified while attempting to turn every pleasure into a commodity. Thus, enjoyment of nature turns into a vacation trip, the pleasure of being with friends or loved ones must be articulated through visiting restaurants, shopping or going to shows. Masturbation is rarely done with imagination but using pornography sites that sell viewers' attention to advertisers, and sex itself is increasingly undertaken with lots of marketable gear, as well as being conceptualized as an economic or legal transaction by the use of words like consent. We are unable to conceptualize or enjoy things in ways that do not involve economic exchange. The market not only tries to repress or commodify existing pleasures, but it regularly sets the kinds of pleasure that we seek. This takes several distinct forms. The first can be called infantilization.

Marketers know that the common denominator between adults and children is children. While it is possible for many adults to enjoy a Disney film or a computer game, few children comprehend or enjoy a foreign political documentary. Market considerations require us to try to pitch stories to both old and young, thus infantilizing adults. Contrary to what conservative thinkers believe, infantilization is not really related to being coddled by parents. Parents are actually pressuring children into extraordinary academic achievements and compelling them to take on a large and rapidly expanding portfolio of academic and other activities. Parents are in fact doing their best to provide their children with the very sober attitude that is needed to compete in a difficult job market. What is causing infantilization is the consumer market: video games, television shows, films, videos and posts. These products are designed with a specific pleasure regime in mind. They generate immediate pleasures of agency and aggression through video games and hip-hop, suspense and surprise, and the release of tension through laughter in short videos and television. Often these products are made so that they will hook children quickly but not deliver much long term.

Competition in the market often means that products contend by generating quick and addictive pleasures. Addictive technologies are not new. For example, the process of refining sugar by slave labor imported from Africa to the New World made sugar the most lucrative commodity of the late-eighteenth century. In fact, the sugar industry is a "model" pleasure industry for us to understand the interconnections between addictive enjoyment, exploitation and globalization. It enriched a thin layer of plantation owners, traders and stockholders while at the same time trafficked and enslaved millions, killed countless thousands on their way to the New World, caused tooth decay, and due to the relatively primitive state of dentistry, caused severe health complications for Europe's population. On the level of ideas and ideology, sugar became an integral part of various bourgeois rituals and values, including afternoon tea in England, Kaffee und kuchen (coffee and cake) in Germany, etc. Sugar encourages and makes easy the drinking of coffee. Coffee and coffee houses are part of an important ritual of modern life, unimaginable in the Middle Ages. It reaffirms a hedonic subjectivity, out looking for good coffee or pastry. It is also one of the main ways in which a capitalist society creates itself as an inviting public space. For relatively little money, one can inhabit an enjoyable public space and make it one's own, present oneself in public and socialize, with little awareness of the horrors involved in the production of sugar and coffee.

In ways that I hope to show, today's addictive global digital technologies are doing something similar. Social media, for example, tends toward the repetitive addictive consumption of fragmented material; this type of content consumption benefits a small elite at the expense of the privacy of users, and ultimately the social isolation and anxiety of billions of people.

Anxiety comes, however, not only through the markets of communication and consumption but through the market of work. Job markets often exert opposite pressures on us than consumption markets when we attempt to make sure that both ourselves and our children will be gainfully employed. The job market creates a whole set of expectations that parents try to inculcate in their children that come directly into conflict with the consumer market. These include values of deferred gratification, hard work, drive and study. Often these differing pressures of consumer and job market are felt precisely around pleasure and its postponement. Children often find themselves caught between parents, who represent the future job market, and their media and friends, who represent the consumer market. The contrast between the two is something that goes deep in the formation of their sense of self; however, it is ultimately a conflict within capitalism that plays itself out in our subjectivity.

The regime of pleasure and of repression of pleasures of men and women in Western society includes a mixture of Christianity, liberalism and the market. There are many tensions and conflicts among the three. Both liberalism and the market deeply undermine traditional values in many ways. They undermine the gratifications of community, spirituality, long-term marriage and childrearing as they create hedonistic and competitive individuals. The market also undermines liberalism itself. Liberalism's values of autonomy, dignity and personal responsibility often clash with the logic of the infantilizing and addictive-making aspect of the market itself. Finally, the market attempts to commoditize things that are best left outside of it that resist commodification, such as friendship, incarceration, education, politics, etc. Out of the three, today the market is the most dynamic: liberalism, traditional values and religion are mainly reacting to it. As we shall see in a chapter devoted to this issue, Christianity and more recently Eastern spirituality and meditation compensate for the suffering, anxiety and depression involved in lack of success in the market. We are existentially dependent on the market: religion, meditation and culture are just a flourish.

Yet for all their tension, the average middle-class person living in the US in the 1950s would have all three regulating him or her in various proportions. This person would be Christian, believe in liberalism and rights, and be imbedded in the market. This would largely set the attitudes and practices of pleasure. She or he would thus be somewhat sexually conservative, believe in individuals' rights and be an avid consumer. Yet of all the three, it is mainly Christianity in the past and the market in the present that forcefully set the agenda, largely because liberalism is compatible with very different ways of life and does not postulate a distinct life form. The relative weakness of liberalism reveals itself in the intolerant attitude toward homosexuality, BDSM or even intoxicating substances that are not part of a mainstream way of life. This explains, for instance, the differential treatment that alcohol and marijuana traditionally received by the law. Liberalism typically reveals itself as weak, frequently when ways of life deemed "unnatural" or foreign are rejected. Christianity and the job market, though often in tension, have also consolidated an overlap, especially around the work ethic, responsibility and repression of sexuality and personal expression.

In Western Europe, socialism and social democracy were additional components responsible for our relationship with enjoyment for most of the twentieth century. For a certain period of time, socialism upheld the dignity of working men and of industrial work in general, no matter how repetitive or alienating industrial labor was. This had the effect of essentially repressing our need for enjoyment in the interest of the collective. For some who came of age in the 1960s, this set of values was suddenly experienced as especially repressive, and they have inaugurated a kind of cultural revolution whose results reverberate today.

One of this revolution's enduring legacies as we saw in the

previous chapter was to overthrow a repressive culture largely in the name of basic enjoyments such as music, drugs and sex. The most important intellectual event in the US around that time was the Kinsey report *Sexual Behavior in the Human Male*, published in 1948, and *Sexual Behavior in the Human Female*, published in 1953. Though some of his research was later discredited due to sampling as well as criticism leveled against his participation in sexual activity as part of the research, the report itself had a profound influence. First, he demoralized sexuality. Kinsey invoked science to neutralize moral judgment. He did not think that science should raise issues of what people should do, only what they in fact do. Kinsey focused on the counting of orgasms, discounting distinctions of source, whether it comes from masturbation or sex with one's partner, marital or nonmartial sex, commercial and noncommercial, heterosexual or homosexual, or sex with people or animals. Any orgasm became equal to any other. This way of counting did lead him to a kind of sex positivity. He suggested that masturbation contributes to health and that premarital sex helps with sexual adjustment and satisfaction in marriage. He even claimed that under some conditions extramarital sex enhances marital sex. For Kinsey anything that limits orgasms, including social and legal restrictions on nonmartial sex, religious restraints or restrictions on masturbation or sex work, has no rational or scientific basis. Together with Kinsey, a kind of skepticism regarding knowing what precisely constitutes the appropriate form of sexuality sets in. In contrast to Christian doctrine that knows what productive "good" sex looks like, the new worldview remains both skeptical of restricting sexuality and curious regarding new forms of pleasure. The year 1960 introduced the contraceptive pill, further separating sexuality and reproduction.

The consensus around the liberalization of sexuality and free pleasure lasted until the late 1970s. One can say that the period between 1960 and 1981 was a unique time in human history in which sexual relationships did not seem to have any important consequences in terms of sexually transmitted disease or unwanted pregnancies. Soon, however, a conservative backlash took place around the world. Margaret Thatcher and Ronald Reagan were elected to office, leading to homosexuals who were infected with newly discovered HIV to be perceived by the conservatives as experiencing cosmic retribution for promiscuous homosexuality and drug use.

At the same time, a new kind of feminist argument surfaced that sought to curtail sexual freedom. In the late seventies and early eighties, some feminists started identifying heterosexual relations as coercive and involving the submission of women to men. Regular heterosexual sexuality was said to reinforce the submission of women and dominance of men. Decriminalization of sexuality and its representation are not seen as liberation but as letting private inequalities set what is happening. Prominent among those who have made this argument were Catharine MacKinnon and Andrea Dworkin, who claimed that pornography promotes images of male dominance, that female performers are victims of violence and coercion, and that pornography encourages men to degrade women and be violent toward them. They both held similar views regarding prostitution and BDSM. Together they drafted the Dworkin-MacKinnon Antipornography Civil Rights Ordinance, which defined pornography as a civil rights violation against women. The ordinance passed in Indianapolis; however, it was overturned as unconstitutional by a higher court. Nevertheless, Dworkin and MacKinnon have altered feminism irrevocably. In terms of sexuality and pleasure, the left has always called for liberation while the right has called for restriction. Dworkin and MacKinnon have consolidated a feminist agenda that was supportive toward sexual restriction in many ways.

At the time, the most vocal opposition came from lesbian

sex-positive feminists. They criticized restrictions on women's sexual behavior and the high costs involved for women in being sexually active. They advocated sexual liberation for women as well as for men and in giving all genders more sexual opportunities rather than restricting pornography. They promoted the decriminalization and destigmatization of prostitution as well as organized sex workers in unions. They argued that consensual BDSM sexuality is in fact enjoyed by many women and therefore should not be labeled "anti-feminist", that roles in BDSM are not fixed by gender but by personal preference, and that playful use of power demystifies power rather than enforcing it by making real power in the world look artificial – and thus encourages challenging it.

The argument between the anti-porn and sex-positive feminists was labyrinthine in its complexity. Dworkin and MacKinnon have ultimately lost the war on pornography, sex work and BDSM. Their signaling out of pornography as sexist in a world in which almost all commercial culture is sexist seemed simply sex negative. Liberals of all kinds supported free speech and the pro-porn faction ultimately won out. Problems with pornography today are much more likely to be discussed under the rubric of addiction than of women's objectification and domination. Still, the sex-positive faction has not won the sex war mainly through argument; it has prevailed because it has aligned itself with the market and new technology of the internet. Pornography was a powerful industry bringing in billions of dollars worldwide; it was difficult for lawmakers to go against it. When the internet became public, the choice was made not to censor the new medium in any significant way in the West.

The type of legal feminism propagated by Dworkin and MacKinnon, a feminism that aims to restrict and punish men, did not, however, die out completely. It has sought to further its political agenda, not in pornography and sex work but in sexual harassment in the workplace. Sexual harassment in the workplace was indeed a worthy goal as women who held subordinate positions in institutions had to tolerate demeaning treatment in order to keep their jobs. Yet we must keep in mind that measures against sexual harassment in the workplace were easier to implement since they did not go against business interests like the anti-pornography bill did, but have given even more power to employers over employees.

MacKinnon's brand of legal feminism uses antidiscrimination laws in order to persecute against sexual harassment while broadening the definition of sexual harassment ever more. Irrespective of the argument regarding the relative harm of pornography vs. harassment, it is important to note that the power relations in the economy have set the agenda. Going against the business interests of the porn industry proved too hard, while granting business managers and owners the right to fire employees on any kind of infraction proved relatively easy.

A similar logic prevailed regarding homosexuality and drugs. The 1980s saw conservatives using HIV as a way to roll back advancements made by homosexuals in the 1970s. Implicit in their discourse was the claim that homosexuals had HIV coming to them for their promiscuity and perverse ways. Even today, influential conservative commentators in the US like Ben Shapiro proudly proclaim that being virgins before marriage has entailed zero risks to contract sexually transmitted diseases. Yet it is clear that there will be no turning back on the sexual revolution, now that it is backed by what can be called market hedonism. The logic of market hedonism is strong in the realm of drugs, both recreational and those that are prescribed. Marijuana has crossed from the illegal to legal in many places around the world. The adverse of pleasure – pain – has become unacceptable in a way that it was not before. Prescription opioids have flooded society; are taken to escape anxiety and depression associated with social isolation, meaningless employment or unemployment; and their consumption has lowered life expectancy in the US for the first time in decades. Both conservatives and some progressives are waging a rearguard battle against the relentless advancement of marketable pleasures. Marketable pleasures are in fact at the forefront of today's economic system. People's pleasures are fused with the market at younger and younger ages, while the market itself constantly infantilizes.

Nowhere is infantilization more prevalent than in the turn toward games. Indeed, games seem to turn up more and more in unexpected places. I would like to provide a personal example to illustrate this. I was presenting at a turbulent and difficult panel on the Israeli-Palestinian conflict at a literary conference in Amsterdam in 2017. Two-thirds of participants were Jewish Americans or Israelis, and a third were Palestinians mainly sitting in the back. My presentation included a scene from a film in which a difficult dialog is held between two bereaved mothers. One lost her son to a Palestinian sniper, the other son died in an Israeli jail after a violent interrogation. The Palestinians in the back were asking difficult questions on the symmetry portrayed in the film. I was feeling exhausted, guilty and frustrated. I tried to answer as best I could and sat down. Next on the panel was a well-known professor from an Ivy League university. Though he has written serious tomes on nationalism and deconstruction in the past, at the panel he was explaining to us that his research project was putting together an educational board game on the Arab-Israeli conflict. He then showed us the board; it was extremely similar to Monopoly. There were two kinds of cards in the middle and participants had to answer questions and advance along the rim of the board. At the beginning I was relieved, but then I wondered if board games are really the right format to teach the Arab-Israeli conflict. I had vaguely heard about game studies and gamification but had brushed it off as childish. The next time I met with games in an unexpected setting was in my own class. I was teaching a course on global literature and theory and had asked the students to work in teams and come up with teaching activities. I was surprised that half the class put together Kahoot-based activities. Kahoot is a site that lets the students in the class compete in answering multiple choice questions. The person who answers them the fastest gets the most points. I was surprised that they found this so enjoyable. I started thinking about games, and reading and listening to experts at gamification. What looked to me like an empty but relatively harmless pleasure soon became much more sinister.

Gamification experts start with exciting utopian premises, the cancellation of the difference between work and nonwork, between seriousness and pleasure. Anything can be turned into a pleasurable game they tell us. We soon learn consumers want engagement through games more than anything else. When we read such claims, we begin to ask whether customers want games or are games a way to draw in customers? Some gamification experts are much more explicit.

In a Google Tech talk called "Fun Is the Future: Mastering Gamification," game expert Gabe Zichermann tells us:

increasingly, users are faced with a set of choices that are basically distinguished between – we used to think of them as work and leisure choices – but increasingly they are compulsory and optional choices. Compulsory and optional have replaced fun and work in the language. Once we get into optional time, disposable time, discretionary time, users are naturally going to gravitate to the experience that they find the most rewarding. Notice my choice of words. And by definition, games have a big advantage over just about anything that you might be creating in your own spare time, right? They are designed explicitly to maximize reward. So, if I can freely choose...like do kids not read books today because they don't understand why books are important? No, it's because they have the choice of stuff that's way more interesting than books so they are choosing something more engaging than books. It's a hedonistic response to market choice. It also highlights something really important about the power of games. Games are the only force in the known universe that can get people to take actions which are against their self-interest in a predictable way without the use of force.

Without any kind of noticeable pangs of conscience, Zichermann ends his lecture:

The game always favors its creator. No matter what game you're playing, the house always wins. The deck is absolutely stacked against you. I'm using metaphor, they all point back to a fundamental truism. There is no way to beat the house long term. No, no way. So you have the choice in a more gamified world of either being the house or being played. These are your choices. But there's no ambiguity here. The sooner you build gamified experience, the sooner you get to, you know, taking your cut, because it's ultimately the best business in the world to be in. Two people or multiple people battle it out and you get a cut of everything that happens. You might at Google be familiar with that as a premise.

What begins as a utopian world in which work as something compulsory disappears and becomes play, ends with an almost stark vision, a vision that could have been called Marxist if only it was not described from the position of the powerful against the powerless. Like Marx, it posits a dynamic that leads to a stark differentiation between two kinds of people. Marx's original binary was owners of means of production and wage laborers. Here we have a glimpse of the future already present. A world divided between a tiny elite who own people's attention through gaming platforms and millions of users who are manipulated by it, addicted to it and working against their self-interest.

Digital omnipresent games are a contemporary psycho-technology that circumvents our conscious judgment and decision making; it starts early with children. However, the logic of games goes well beyond anything related just to games. Attention and attachment have become the main resource of the contemporary world, today's new gold. Unparalleled fortunes have been made in record time by harvesting attention. Harvesting attention has reached previously unknown efficiency. Techno-hedonism is a rapidly expanding frontier. It is disrupting all previous pleasures. It promises to swallow most of our discretionary time, that is, most of what we can choose to do. Like a new religion it presents a new escape from the world. Pleasures present a new frontier of coercion by evading conscious choice. Today's predominant model of generating engagement and pleasure does not really need conscious affirmation. As Herbert Marcuse already formulated in the 1960s, today's culture enforces repressive desublimization. It is good to be reminded of what sublimation is. Sublimation is the redirection and transformation of pleasure from simple and intense pleasures to pleasures that are longer and more complex. Thus, erotic urges are said to be sublimated when they are channeled and transformed to, for example, writing a romantic symphony. Repressive desublimization is thus the process in which one is coerced to go through the opposite process, to desublimate.

By the time we are teens we have already been bombarded with simple yet intense enjoyments: pornography, drugs, sweet food, beats that catch you immediately. We may find slower, longer and more complex pleasures much harder to tune into. Even when we view or read something for longer periods of time, such as a lengthy book or a television series, it is in fact composed of hundreds of short suspenseful episodes linked with one another. In those episodes there is rarely a lull in the action. Every episode does more or less what every other episode does. It does not matter at what point in the narrative one is at; the narrative is designed to hook and capture you for as long as possible. Unlike a romantic symphony or nineteenth-century novel, there is never a time of emotional ambiguity or of slow building of empathy toward characters, contemplation or commentary on social forces or psychology. Any point within the narrative is just like any other point, with no real heterogeneity. Even the ending itself is not conclusive (there might be more seasons); it rarely ties everything together. The time and attention of the spectator have already been "harvested"; there is no reason to bother with overall emotional and intellectual gratification.

This process has engendered a certain flatness in culture itself, culture that until the middle of the twentieth century was still able to reflect and create depth of feeling like world sorrow and unfulfilled yearnings and desires for what does not exist. Today we live for the first time in societies in which the victory of desires over repression lives hand and hand with the triumph of society over individuals. Yet at the same time in which pleasure is seemingly offered in abundance, deep frustrations exist. Pleasures are often used to ward off a sense of meaninglessness, a defense against a sense of displacement, contingency and death. They do this by seeming purposeful, necessary and rational; they appear to provide self-evident reasons for our actions. Often pleasures such as visiting a restaurant, shopping or a taking a vacation trip are conceived of as reward or compensation for unsatisfying work. Often, too much is expected of pleasure in a world in which other sources of affirmation and meaning have disappeared; pleasure is burdened with more than it can handle. This is especially prevalent in the realm of sexuality, where many feel that their sex lives do not measure up to the image of what they think sexuality should be like, and the meaning and fulfillment that sex should provide. Sex becomes a site of apprehensions, frustrations and misunderstandings for many people. This is likely to be because sex is strongly influenced by the marketable images yet is still fundamentally (outside of prostitution) a nonmarket activity, an exchange that does not entail a monetary transfer. It is for this reason that market norms (pornography) and nonmarket norms (real sex) combine unevenly and create frustration and confusion.

It is very likely that sex, sleep and other activities that are still outside of the market will become marketized and techno-commodified. Just like socializing with friends used to be wholly outside the market and is now done using social media imbricated within market and monetary circuits, so will other human behaviors go. Hedonistic technological marketization is the way that society will go at least in the short-term future. Corresponding to this hedonic marketization is a belief in enjoyment. Both lead us to see the world as an environment that affords a series of enjoyments. Our relationship toward these enjoyments and pleasures really occludes us from seeing the world as it is. Pleasure today is an affective tie that precludes us from feeling the pain of the world as it is. As long as there is no serious critique of the pleasures of the market, there will be no natural limit to the colonization of our life and attention.

Be Famous

The idea of the famous person is a central ruling idea in our culture. In fact, most of our everyday culture is organized around people who are famous. As I mentioned before, much of our popular media is organized around a dozen famous and powerful businessmen, presidents, actors and sport celebrities. The media coverage that this handful of individuals gets is simply overwhelming. In the media, humanity does not really exist, only the celebrities do. Nor is the coverage only low brow. Ostensibly serious, in-depth journalism in the *New York Times* or *Wall Street Journal* will detail lifestyle choices of Jeff Bezos or Elon Musk. Most of the time, we accept that this is the way it should be. In fact, we find celebrities exhilarating and motivating. Through them we experience vicariously what it is like to be extremely rich, beautiful or physically skillful. We get motivated by seeing their performances, by hearing them talk. We attempt to repress our negative emotions toward them; we try to bear no grudge against people who are said to create so much value and whose decisions affect millions. Many of us sometimes explicitly, sometimes more covertly, simply want to be them.

Nevertheless, let's zoom out from a kid who wants to become a sports star, a young man who wants to be a billionaire, or a young woman who consciously or unconsciously wants to be adored and loved like a famous actress. Let's zoom out of Earth and view Earth coolly from an alien's perspective. Is it not strange that billions of people aspire to something that precisely only few can achieve? Is it good to live your life star or billionaire gazing? Is it not related to many of the feelings of depression and anxiety that most of us increasingly have? What could be the alternative, both personally and socially? In order to answer this question, we must look at the culture of fame and fortune today and ask where it came from and what its function is in today's world. Only then can we evaluate the good and bad things that it does and perhaps seek alternatives. So where does the culture of fame come from?

At first, we may simply see fame as an eternal motivation of human nature. Did not the ancient Greeks try to achieve immortality through courage and death in battle? To die young famously or anonymously as old men, that was the ancient question. In the Iliad, Achilles says, "My mother Thetis tells me that there are two ways in which I may meet my end. If I stay here and fight, I will not return alive but my name will live forever (kleos), whereas if I go home my name will die, but it will be long ere death shall take me." A closer look shows that we are very different from Ancient Greeks. In contrast to the ancient world, today's fame does not come from a glorious death as a young man in battle, nor does it lead to a kind of glory and honor that is immortalized. In general, we don't want to be famous for immortality. As Woody Allen once wrote, "I don't want to achieve immortality through my work; I want to achieve immortality through not dying. I don't want to live on in the hearts of my countrymen; I want to live on in my apartment."

Today, wanting to be famous has little to do with battle – none of the very famous people today are warriors – nor do we believe in fame bringing immortality. Ask most people who Gloria Swanson, Robert Taylor, Dorothy Lamour, Carole Lombard or Errol Flynn are, and you will get blank stares, though in their day they were arguably more famous in the US than today's most famous Hollywood actors. Greek immortality is out, so when does one begin the story of today's kind of fame?

Being famous today has its roots in the entrepreneurial spirit of the Renaissance, and it is there we must turn to. As we saw, the modern way to be an individual was the same route to becoming famous. Both were articulated in the arts. In the Middle Ages, artists were anonymous, but by the Renaissance artists of truly global renown came into being, like Michelangelo, Raphael, Donatello, Titian, Botticelli, Da Vinci and, as we saw, Dürer. It is important to remember, however, that in the Renaissance, the fame and prestige that this kind of person accrued was miniscule compared to the prestige and power that royalty and popes had. "Celebrity" artists and various entrepreneurs were insignificant upstarts in the ecology of power and fame of that time. After all, where would you have had the chance to know them? A book market was starting, but there was no mass media to speak of. Nor did these entrepreneurs/artists hold power; they were usually beholden to patrons, who were part of the nobility or the church. The idea of wanting to be a famous entrepreneur or some kind of artist would have been strange to the overwhelming majority of the population who just reproduced what their parents did, which was mostly being peasants. Sometimes young men joined the church or the army in search of mobility, but rarely did they attempt anything else. So how did this idea of fame through art become so popular?

This idea has had to break through an impossibly oppressive system designed to keep everyone in their place, a system and its ideas around noble birth and God's will that have lasted for a thousand years. These ruling ideas of a previous epoch have died an extremely slow death. Such ideas transform themselves and often make limited comebacks. A quick look around the globe from the world adoration for the British royal family to the rulers of Saudi Arabia shows that royalty still plays a role in legitimizing authority. Royalty has an even more pronounced hold on people's imagination in popular culture. Disney films follow the exploits of princesses; television series are devoted to kings and queens. A bit less explicitly, almost all works of fantasy are couched in some variation of the Middle Ages, almost always presenting protagonists as royalty. If the protagonists themselves are not royalty, they intimately become involved with them. *The Lion, the Witch and the Wardrobe, The Hobbit* and *Game of Thrones* all revolve around royalty. Our imagination seems to be stuck in the veneration of kings and queens of the Middle Ages. Even when we imagine the future, it's often some variation of this past.

Even more effectively than how royalty is used is the way in which God is used to buttress authority and legitimacy in Turkey, Russia, Iran, Israel and the US. Yet at the same time it is also clear that today's sources of legitimacy and authority cannot rely solely on royalty and God. The legitimacy of Saudi Arabian princes and Muslims can be undercut by a lack of shared economic growth, degradation of the environment, and lack of personal or health security. Nor are the tremendous forces and dangers created by technological innovation and initiative since the eighteenth century related in any meaningful way to royalty or religion. Industrial production, AI, atomic energy, space technology, design DNA, information revolution, pharmacology, brain interventions and bio-materials are powerful entities that are increasingly mobilized by huge multinational companies. These companies have little need for royalty or God; their stress on science and technology is ultimately incompatible with a traditionalist worldview. Those in power will ultimately need to legitimize their rule by the way they deal with social, ecological and technological opportunities and dangers. This is not something futuristic; already today the legitimacy of China's ruling party is intimately connected with air pollution and the environment. What is true for the effects of the industrial revolution today in China will soon be true for the unemployment effects of AI and thought privacy issues of brain interventions in the future everywhere else.

Thus, there seems to be a limit to how much the ruling ideas of the Middle Ages, such as the veneration of royalty and religious figures, can sustain themselves indefinitely or make a comeback. Yet we need to go back well before the onslaught of the Industrial Revolution to see how these ideas were undermined precisely by the idea of the famous individual, an individual whose renown is based on achievements in the economy or the arts. Merchants, artists, administrators, lawyers and artisans adopted the idea that wealth and recognition should come from talent and hard work, not from being born into a noble family, and that the individual, not God, is responsible for his or her fate.

Attempting to be famous by talent combined with work

is essentially a new kind of practice and value that replaces courage (nobility) and piety (clergy). In a medieval society with its fixed social hierarchy, talent did not open any new avenues. The feelings associated with talent, such as ambition and pride, were explicitly frowned upon in traditional culture. Work, predominantly in agriculture, was often considered a kind of curse (e.g., "In the sweat of thy face shalt thou eat bread" Genesis 3:19). Working ensured survival; it was not something that created novelty, value and possibly renown. Fame as a result of talent and work were once revolutionary ideas. They were an ideational battering ram that toppled the castles of the feudal order. A new kind of people took over the world. Their name in Europe was the bourgeoisie. Using trade, slave labor and later on industrial production, they amassed enormous fortunes.

Early on, through their revolutions, they seized state power in the US and France. Later on, using trade and industrial production, they seized power all over the world.

The bourgeoisie created a new culture: the great novels, theories, symphonies, paintings and operas of the eighteenth and nineteenth centuries. They gave birth to the new sciences of evolutionary biology, modern archeology, modern history, economics, sociology, anthropology and psychology. Often these achievements are associated with illustrious names like Mozart, Napoleon, Darwin, Mendeleev, Pasteur, Marx and Wagner. Indeed, one of the main organizing ideas of theirs was the deserved success and fame of the great individual. Deserved success and fame is a ruling idea.

By the middle of the nineteenth century this idea began to be used not only against the nobility and the church "above" but also toward the demands for economic equality from workers "below." Talent, drive and accompanying success transitioned from an idea used to promote equality, recognition and legitimization to people who are not nobles or priests, to an idea that is used to justify why the rich are rich and the poor are poor. It transitioned from an idea designed to be a weapon of the rising powers of the middle classes in the face of their superiors, to an idea used as a weapon to keep down the lower classes. At this point, the ruling idea is called upon to do two very different things. Here we can already see something interesting about the ruling ideas, the way they can shift their function depending on context. An idea of recognition and fame based on hard work and talent that seems identical to itself becomes essentially different according to function. It is "colored" differently when it is used to fight the clergy and nobility than when it is called upon to legitimize economic inequality.

Once new economic elites seized power, they reimagined society. Instead of imagining the existing social order as essentially the will of God, the elites imagined the existing social order and its glaring inequalities as a result of merit. From that point onward, inequality was often legitimated through talent, hard work and uniqueness of the individual. Renown and recognition were simply seen as the result of the right combination of the above in great measure. Almost any representation of industry "greats" from Henry Ford to Elon Musk by mainstream media includes precisely this mixture of presenting their talent and hard work coupled with their unique individuality. Reporting on industry greats has been a long-standing tradition since the end of the nineteenth century, the gilded age of the robber barons. However, since the nineteenth century there have been other developments that exacerbated the cult of fame.

In the early twentieth century, the young film industry discovered that actors when presented in the popular press could market a film in ways not available to other aspects of the movie, such as story line, writer or director. Actors' lives then became directed by agents in order to maximize attention and adoration. In the 1990s, the internet introduced an economy driven by attention. By the 2010s, the whole economy moved to a model in which products are paired with content that viewers and readers connect to and find relatable. This content most effectively takes the form of stories and gossip about people they know. As a consequence, these people whom everyone knows become an essential prerequisite of the economy.

Nevertheless, the economy could not benefit from stardom if people did not connect and bond with celebrities emotionally. This bond takes various forms, from mild to extremely strong. On the mild side, when seeing the face of a likable movie star on a tabloid in the supermarket, one gets a slightly warm feeling of seeing someone both attractive and familiar. Like affable talk show hosts, they serve as emotional decoration in our lives, casual acquaintances who make no demand on us and whom we cannot get anything out of. For fans and children, the relationship is often more complex. Celebrities are idealized. People sometimes proudly relate that they have met such and such famous person in the street or saw them at the restaurant. In a strange way, people feel as though some value has been conferred on them by such a sighting. Paraphernalia of musicians sell for astounding sums and function like relics of holy men; these objects confer value to those who have them. Celebrities are the holy men of a consumer economy based on marketing, saints in a society based on attention. In the attentional economy of today, the quest for God, Enlightenment or political transformation has been replaced by the quest for celebrity. Wanting to be famous is wanting to be loved for just existing, like a baby whose parents give attention, love and care, without the arduous and often unsuccessful attempt to win love and esteem in the real world.

It is both simplistic and misleading to simply criticize the power of celebrity. Celebrity does many good things besides selling products. Famous people often provide a worthy model for young people. They orient, inspire and motivate, often spawning a whole culture. Take The Beatles, who undoubtedly inspired a great flowering of rock bands in the UK, or James Brown, who created funk and laid the roots for hip-hop, or the success of tennis player Bjorn Borg in the 1970s and early 1980s, which led to a whole series of first-rate Swedish players who had a leading role in international tennis in the 1990s. An older example of renown and fame that has contributed to a whole culture is the fame of the French intellectuals. Starting with Voltaire and Rousseau, the tradition spewed a galaxy of thinkers who have fundamentally altered the world, from Rousseau, whose works serve as a main inspiration for the French Revolution and the political structure of the republic, and Sartre and Frantz Fanon's deep intellectual encouragement for anti-colonial struggles around the world, to Foucault's influence on gay liberation and gender politics. If one believes that these men and women are worthy of emulation, then their stories can be exciting and inspiring to orient people.

Some may counterargue that fame is not worthy of serious consideration and is mainly a kind of emotional decoration for often dreary lives, that it puts a bit of color and excitement in people's worlds, that it is a kind of harmless, pleasurable experience in vicarious living. One experiences a bit of what it's like to have success and adoration, or alternatively one experiences schadenfreude or sadness and grief when celebrities get into trouble or when they die. This interpretation that sees celebrity as a kind of emotional ornamentation can seem persuasive; nevertheless, it is misleading.

In our cultural practices we ascribe special value to those who have fame; by following the vicissitudes of their lives and not of others, the media makes claim that they have special worth. However, it is precisely the way we ascribe value to celebrity that is distortive and problematic. It is distortive since whatever individuals achieve in life *always* depends on the work of millions both dead and alive. To become a celebrity or even just a regular person means having depended on the work of thousands. To have reached the point of simply reading this book you must have had parents or caretakers who looked after your physical survival. Someone has also patiently taught you to read. More broadly, you depend on the invention of writing, on the thousands of engineers and workers both in the past and today who have made functional this book or tablet or whatever you are reading this on. Being able to concentrate on this text means that you are not too hungry, too sick, too cold or too hot, and that you probably also found a quiet place for yourself. Thousands were involved in guaranteeing these enabling conditions. Whatever political rights you possess, your safety and health are also looked after by the work of hundreds. In order to achieve even the most extremely individual of pursuits such as writing a book, painting a picture or creating a video, one usually relies on many models both conscious and unconscious. However, when one watches or reads about a famous person, all those other people seem to disappear. This idea and image of the famous man obscures thinking and feeling in terms that would be most conducive to human emancipation and flourishing; it is a kind of sophisticated psychological exploitation. It exploits our built-in predisposition to form attachments to faces, voices and personalized performances that are repeatedly shown to us. This predisposition was necessary in order to survive as babies and children; it is also part of our ability to form long-term relationships in adulthood.[2] Nevertheless, in our own society it has been hijacked in order to attach us to attractive strangers who are used to sell us consumer products. It has also had a largely unintended consequence of young people growing up today aspiring to be celebrities.

In an important way, people's deep desires today are an unintended consequence of the need to sell them things. People are made to desire merchandise through celebrities, but they also desire to be precisely the thing (celebrities) that helps sell merchandise. Nevertheless, for most people, wanting to become a celebrity will lead to a dead end. Millions of people cannot attend meaningfully to the exploits of more than a couple of dozen people. One cannot have even four million famous people. Celebrity culture has negative effects even on those who do not wish to be famous. Though most people don't explicitly compare themselves to the globally famous, the globally famous form a kind of background of our lives. First, even if you are relatively famous – let's say a couple of thousand have seen your blog, you wrote a book or maybe you are in a position of power in a big organization – you still compare badly with world-famous people who are constantly in the media.

Having constructed a sense of self-worth around renown, many who reach midlife find it hard to reconstruct another successful life narrative when they fail to achieve it. This is likely to lead to crisis and perhaps a life experienced as a failure. People then often turn to religious traditions or pop spirituality that offers to help provide another life narrative unrelated to individual fame. Trust and belief that God has a plan for you or being mindful and releasing yourself from desire are indeed unrelated to fame. All they do is put people on a parallel track to another quest once the track of fame and success has not materialized. Indeed, in contrast to the past in which the idea of the special and famous individual came and disrupted the church, now the church comes to compensate for the isolation, anxiety and failed identity that resulted from the idea of the famous individual. To the extent that we believe in individual will power, drive and resourcefulness (that is not believing in God), many fall back on practices of being mindful, that is, viewing our own thoughts and desires as something ephemeral. Thus, we are called upon in meditation to view our thoughts, desires and feelings as somehow external to our being. These thoughts and feelings, though they may be distorted, are often indicative of our life situation. Concentrating on your breath while making your thoughts become just a "cinema" of consciousness essentially means making ethereal the situation that these thoughts represent.

It is true that we have some freedom regarding how to interpret any situation that we find ourselves in, and more radically we can disengage the self from it. For some, their loss of the dream of celebrity is overseen by a plan from God; others compensate with toys or vacations or continue to believe that at some point in life they will become rich and famous. However, this desire itself is problematic. Trying to become rich and famous for long periods of time is itself often unsustainable for many people and is regularly supplemented with a wish to escape its cold egoism and be part of something larger.

A good, but slightly different example for this is the tension between the burdens of the isolated individual and an ethos of sharing in the mainstream beliefs in Silicon Valley. On the one hand is the cult and celebration of the lone multimillionaire entrepreneur and the fortune that he possesses, and on the other is a stress on collective emancipation of mankind through freedom of information, free services and the exponential growth in computing power. The result of both these commitments together has led to the business model of Google and Facebook and increasingly other firms. Everything is free and collaborative on the surface, but in order to accumulate wealth, personal information is covertly gathered and sold to unknown third parties. These third parties do not just want to sell commodities, but, as we have seen with the Facebook–Cambridge Analytica scandal, also want to modify political behavior and opinions.

The cult of the famous creates another alarming split in Silicon Valley regarding human beings. On the one hand, there is the leader, the entrepreneur superhero, and on the other, the thoughtless, childish humans, those "idiots" who are willing to hand out all their personal information, and whose work will be automated by AI. Anyone who works in AI knows that machine learning in almost all fields consists of learning from the work of hundreds of human beings. Machine translation, medical diagnostics and autonomous driving, for example, rely on the data of hundreds of real translators, doctors and drivers. Still, all this labor is discounted, its marvelous effects in efficiency and accuracy ascribed to one entrepreneur and "his" invention.

Dividing human beings into childish automatons on the one hand and great men on the other has a long history. Already at the beginning of the nineteenth century, the time of Bonaparte and Beethoven, it was widely believed that some people were towering geniuses while at the same time scientists and philosophers imagined the regular human mind as kind of an association machine. This image has been updated but has stayed fundamentally the same. Today we have great entrepreneurs and celebrities, with their lives seen as self-authored. They rise to become autobiographical beings. On the other hand, we have the rather slow biological information processing machines, with trivial desires of recognition and connection that we can manipulate and commodify. A nuanced account of the interaction between time, place, personality and upbringing is characteristically missing in the renditions of both the famous and regular people.

The effects of a culture that denigrates ordinary life, is unable to empathize with regular people and sees humans as disposable evolutionary machines can be very unexpected. Lacking sympathetic representations of regular, non-famous life, one is left with little sympathy or even the ability to reflect and realistically evaluate one's own life. This can lead not only to depression, but to a twisted comic-like view of reality and acts of violence in a desperate bid for fame and meaning. Celebrity culture depletes regular life from meaning and contributes to isolation, anxiety, depression and sometimes violence. We might begin to understand the damage of celebrity culture by imagining life without celebrities.

We can begin with our own world without famous people. No Hollywood stars at the counter in the supermarket, no president's personal life on the front page of the newspaper, and no articles relating the exploits of business greats. That thought can make some people anxious. There are so many famous people whom one loves and many whom we love to hate. It seems like a drab world in which the stars fall from our "sky." You might grow depressed with what seems like a grayish, uninteresting and mundane world. But then perhaps the abolition of celebrity as our illusionary joy is really an attempt to change the conditions that require this parasocial relationship in the first place. To abandon an illusionary relationship to stars means to form a real constellation around ourselves. Famous people are not some extra to our own world; they are essential to keep it running like it does. Abolishing them means fundamentally changing ourselves, making a world in which we are all stars of our own solar systems.

At a certain point in life we internalize a kind of ideal. When my 12-year-old son tells me he will be famous and very rich by the time he is 16, how should I respond? There are many things that call for affirming him. First, why be a spoilsport or, as he sometimes calls me, a hater? Second, since making him fit society is hard enough, why go against society? One can use his desires in order to get him to further values that I partially believe in, for example, education or doing creative work. Parents are under pressure to make their children fit, succeed and thrive in society. If your son says he wants to be famous, then it seems the best option is to let him be. The problem is what happens when he does not become famous? When there is a discrepancy between the ideal and its fulfillment? When the ideal will be used to beat himself on the head with – to see himself as a loser? These ideals work as a slow poison. Would it not be better if most people aspire to meaningful work, friendships and loving relationships? Perhaps a society in which many have these three aspirations is possible, while a society made up of a couple of billion people all famous is logically impossible.

Chapter Four

Values and Virtues

Values in the Workplace

Most workplaces and companies around the world have core values that are instilled during orientation days and reiterated during company vacations. The company Bright Horizons Family Solutions, for example, which provides day care at more than 900 day care centers, has the HEART Principle as its core values: Honesty, Excellence, Accountability, Respect, Teamwork. These sound like excellent values to have when you are employing people whose job it is to take care of your children. We might think the values are a good thing; they almost seem to guarantee goodness. Philip Morris International, the global cigarette maker, also has great values. On their website they write:

> Trust, collaboration, and integrity are the core values that embody our commitment to society, our shareholders, our business partners, and our colleagues. They guide us as individuals and collectively as a company. They are with us every day and everywhere. We honor this commitment regardless of the challenges and pressures we face in conducting our business. Acting with integrity, honesty, and in full compliance with the law and our own policies is indispensable in securing a prosperous future for PMI.

Would we say that these are excellent values for a company that creates cancer-inducing, addictive substances? Would it not be better if Philip Morris had fewer values? Perhaps with less trust and collaboration it would be less effective in causing cancer? What kind of values can redeem a product that is both addictive and potentially causes death?

Enron, a company that was engaged in massive fraud while simultaneously being named as "America's Most Innovative Company" by *Fortune* magazine for six consecutive years, had the values "excellence," "respect," "integrity" and "communication" carved on the marble floor of the atrium of its global headquarters in Houston, and devoted its orientation to instilling its workers with them. Instagram, a company that creates addicting and ultimately impoverishing and isolating social media practices, talks about "community first" and "inspiring creativity."

Talk of values trickles all the way down to almost all businesses and organizations and is currently used all around the world to motivate and control workers.

In 2016, I found myself out of an academic job in the US, unemployed and worried. I created an opportunity to teach at Jinan University in the mega city of Guangzhou in China. I took my family and a few belongings, and we relocated to the Jinan campus. University campuses in China are like cities in themselves; they have centers in which you can buy glasses, clothes and sports equipment, eat dim sum soup, etc.

They also have barbers and hairdressers, as Chinese students like to wear their hair fashionably. In the mornings I used to wake up early and go for a walk past this center, and every morning the workers at the hairdresser's salon would be lined up military style in front of their "leader". Here is a picture I took:

One time at lunch I saw

the young woman who appears second on the right, working on an English textbook. She smiled at me (one often gets smiles in China for being an "exotic" white foreigner). I asked her why they were standing at attention in the morning. She told me that it's pre-work assembly and it happens all over China. As we stayed longer, we indeed saw it everywhere. But on that day it was novel for me. I asked her what was being said. She explained thus:

> The leader (employer) elaborates every day on a different virtue from the Confucian five constants: *Benevolence* (rén 仁), *righteousness* (yì 义), *propriety* (lǐ 礼), *wisdom* (zhì 智) and *fidelity* (xìn 信). Today she elaborated on lǐ – propriety. She said that there is much to learn from ancient rituals that were designed to maintain respect. In ancient China these rituals were designed to uphold proper relations between monarch and subject, father and son, husband and wife, elder and youngster, and teacher and student. Our leader would like us to use the feelings associated with this virtue when we deal with customers. Behind the niceness, they must also feel respect and propriety. This is important because using WeChat, customers from the campus who used to be a "captive" audience can now order a meeting at the hairdresser's anywhere in the area. In this uncertain time, we need propriety more than ever both at work and at home so we can live in harmony and develop. This was what the leader said at the assembly.

Though ostensibly a communist country that broke with tradition, China is quick to use traditional values in the interests of affirming and stabilizing the inevitable hierarchies that come with state and global capitalism. The rhetoric of the manager might sound a bit foreign to us, especially the rather direct way that it affirms respect and deference to authority. The system in the US, for example, is based perhaps less on respect and deference and more on fear of being fired. Yet Amazon in its leadership principles has the following: "Leaders are right a lot. They have strong judgment and good instincts. They seek diverse perspectives and work to disconfirm their beliefs." These words show an interesting paradox between authority and Popper's falsifiability principle that claims that it is the duty of scientists to try to disprove their theories, a principle that has found its way into management discourse. Still, deference to authority does matter.

What the hairdresser used as propriety, Amazon calls customer obsession: "Leaders start with the customer and work backwards. They work vigorously to earn and keep customer trust. Although leaders pay attention to competitors, they obsess over customers." Nor are classical virtues absent. Like frugality: "Accomplish more with less. Constraints breed resourcefulness, self-sufficiency, and invention. There are no extra points for growing headcount, budget size, or fixed expense."

If the company needs to be competitive and is poised for expanding in international markets, values are naturally less deferential and more aggressive. Huawei, for example, calls itself "wolf-culture":

The first character of wolves is bloodthirsty. Employees of Huawei are extremely sensitive to the market information and can respond promptly to any changes. The second character of wolves is resistant to coldness. The fearlessness of difficulties and eagerness of making progress are insisted by every member of Huawei, no matter how complicated the hardship is. The third character of wolves is taking actions in teams. The atmosphere of team cooperation is particularly strong in Huawei and people are encouraged to develop and share personal opinions with each other.[1]

Later on in the same document they enumerate their values:

> The organizational culture of cooperation, honesty, sacrifice, study, creation, benefit and fairness are applied to problem solving and goal achievement of each employee in Huawei.

There is good reason to believe that such rhetoric works. The extent to which workers come to believe the values of the company is called "employee alignment" in management speak. When one looks at statistics of how many workers, even those working 12-hour shifts in factories in China, are aligned with management, we usually find that it stands at 60-70 percent. How can one explain this? How can people believe in vacuous-sounding discourse that contradicts most of their actual experience at work? Before we answer this question, let's look at the role of virtues in another kind of institution – education.

Values in Education

Here is a picture I took of an elementary school my son went to in Guangzhou, China, with a banner encouraging the students to be studious and meticulous in their work.

In the Anglophone world, school posters are used to instill values; here are some from Michigan state and Australia:

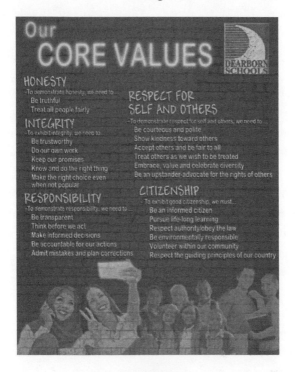

(Dearborn Public Schools, Dearborn, Michigan, USA), (Alphington Grammar School, Victoria, Australia). Universities also have similar mottos, core values and mission statements. Here is another passage from an educational organization that tries to instill values in its members:

> For one person, work is a "curse," "God's punishment," a burden that one should remove as rapidly as possible. For another, it is a necessary part of existence that gives human life its meaning. For one, bravery and loyalty are nothing but great stupidity. He would rather be "a coward for a few minutes" than to "be dead for the rest of one's life." For another, bravery and loyalty are the characteristics used to value and esteem people. He holds to his word, in good times or ill. He cannot live without honor and would rather die than be a coward.

For a contemporary reader, this passage might sound a bit over the top, too exulted, so to speak. Most of us today seem to think that it's better to be a coward than to die. Yet some variation in the values and virtues in the passage should be familiar to any reader; for example, the university where I work has as its motto "Only the Audacious," and Facebook has "Move Fast and Break Things." It would perhaps be a surprise to learn that the passage comes from the chapter called inequality in the booklet material for the Hitler Youth taken from Fritz Bennecke (ed.), *Vom deutschen Volk und seinem Lebensraum. Handbuch für die Schulung in der HJ* (Munich: Franz Eher, 1937). We often appreciate people who embody virtues and values, and yet as the example above shows, sometimes these virtues are used in service of things we abhor. Thus, we have to broaden our gaze and consider the overall social and historical context. Even values and practices of mindfulness, equanimity and tranquility are not free from the examination of the larger political context.

In his book *Zen at War*, Brian D. Victoria documents the way in which Buddhism has been used to support Japanese militarism and imperialism from the Meiji Restoration through World War II.[2] Values of śūnyatā (emptiness) and selflessness, mutual dependency, and inner peace, which Western audiences perceive as deeply and inexorably ethical when extoled by someone like the Dalai Lama, can be just as instrumental in furthering some of the worst atrocities. Without careful acknowledgment of the consequences of actions, that is, without an analysis of how a chain of actions are related to common goods in the world, like well-being, health, equality, etc., it is impossible to judge virtues, values and practices. It is perhaps for this very reason that corporate culture likes "values" as well as contemporary variations of Buddhism such as mindfulness meditation as they simultaneously compensate and mask the harm created by much contemporary work.

We are thus left wondering what it means when some of the same values appear in China, the US, Nazi Germany and imperialist Japan. To answer this question, we must go back and examine the history of those who suspected that there was something wrong with values. Some of this early critique was expressed as a critique of virtues. Virtues are closely related to values. They can be looked at as the implementation of values in action and character. Let's look at the history of the critique of virtues.

The Ancient Critique of Virtues
Socrates was the first to discover the ambivalent character of virtues themselves, their power to motivate and orient behavior as well as their clever use by those in power. His insights mark the birth of critical systematic thinking on virtues. The starting point was the normative culture of ancient Greece that was organized around the virtues of courage, temperance, cunning, justice and wisdom. These values were exemplified by Homeric

heroes as well as statesmen.

Socrates's main philosophical endeavor was critical. His main practice was to approach people on the streets of Athens in what today would be considered performance conceptual art and argue with them. He would go up to young men who were part of the Athenian elite and challenge them to define a certain virtue. These young men aspired to embody civic and political virtues like courage, justice or piety and thus Socrates began by challenging them to define those virtues. More specifically, Socrates often led the conversation in a certain direction with his questions. He often compared the virtues to skillful work associated with medicine, barrel or shoe making, what was known in Greek as techne or craftmanship. Socrates thought that the classic virtues should reliably create value, just like shoe making generated dependable value. He was trying to contextualize virtue in what he considered beneficial work.

Since Socrates' arguments finished with aporia, that is, a lack of ability to reach a definite conclusion, one ends unsure of what virtue itself is. Socrates thus undermined his interlocuters' belief that they know what the virtues are. He challenged the normative character traits that were said to form the foundation of successful and just civic action and political prestige. It was for this undermining of a naive belief in the virtues and what is seen as their religious foundations, for his corrupting of the youth, that he was put to death.

With Socrates, the suspicion starts that those who invoke virtues are not doing it for any clear, discernable and most importantly reliable benefit for society. In fact, it seems more and more that values and virtues themselves are a way of evoking positive self-representation of the speaker while simultaneously occluding broader social reality and social benefit. Socrates sensed that the young men of rich and politically influential families who proposed to follow virtue and the sophists who purported to teach it were full of hot air and empty talk, and that their virtue rationally should correspond (but did not) to more humble pursuits such as barrel and shoe makers.

The Middle Ages presented a re-traditionalization of society. While Socrates tried to wrest the virtues away from their connection to religion and politics toward work and crafts, the church and nobility of the Middle Ages did the exact opposite. Artisans, their work, craft and value were wholly devalued again and virtues were welded once more to the church and aristocracy, inseparable from the Christian belief system. Virtues became central to Christian ideology and they could not really be questioned. They were seen as God-given and transcendent; criticizing them was not like in Socrates's time, when it was seen mainly as an offense only against the social order; now it was an offense against the metaphysical order; you were going to Hell in the next life and punished by the church in this one.

Bourgeois Virtues

The rise of the bourgeoisie marked a new set of virtues distinct from those that came before. This happened both in theory and in practice. In the eighteenth century the bourgeoisie, or as they are known in anglophone countries, the middle class, was still fighting for its ascendency against aristocracy and the church; it was a revolutionary class. At this time intellectuals, writers, philosophers, poets and painters were articulating new kinds of virtues. One of these new virtues was work. In contrast to the nobility with its hereditary/divine rights, the middle class sought to legitimate its increasing power through work.[3] And indeed many of the virtues of the middle class are related to work. Self-interest, rational calculation of means and ends, sobriety, persistence, grit, these are new virtues – all related to work. These are novel virtues specifically in comparison to the previous virtues articulated by the nobility, which was animated by virtues such as valor, religious piety, generosity and vengeance. Nobles were taught to make alliances by gifts and favors, to throw lavish feasts, to be cunning and ruthless, to conquer and slaughter one's enemies, to be alternately merciful or violent and by this very fickleness demonstrate one's absolute sovereignty, one's power beyond reason, deliberation or utility. The nobility aspired to warlike virtues, the bourgeoisie constant ones that accumulate over years.

Members of the bourgeoisie instrumentally use their reason and skills day in and day out to become ever more efficient in accumulation. Their calling is serious work that alternates with rest in the comfortable surroundings of their homes, a compromise between endless toil and small domestic pleasures. Much of European literature from Moliere's *Le Bourgeois Gentilhomme* (1670) to Chekov's *The Cherry Orchard* (1903) dealt with contrasting these different sets of values, nobility on the one hand and the bourgeoisie on the other. The divergence of values can be discerned in high literature as well as in popular fiction. The contrast between the virtues of the nobility and those of the bourgeoisie who ultimately vanquish the nobility is well illustrated by Bram Stoker's popular novel *Dracula* (1897). Dracula is a Transylvanian nobleman who lives in the Carpathian Mountains; he is handsome and charismatic and proud of his boyar past, of belonging to the highest rank of feudal East European aristocracy. The novel tells us that he is a statesman and a solider. He takes up arms as befitting his status, of voivode, or war-lord, and defends Christian Europe against the Turks when they threaten to conquer Europe after the fall of Constantinople. Surviving through the centuries in his deteriorating castle with three beautiful brides, he attempts a comeback to the rational West.

The new middle class and its values are aptly represented by both Jonathan Harker and Abraham Van Helsing. Jonathan is a newly recruited solicitor from Exeter, England, working under Mr Hawkins as an estate agent for Dracula; he is a professional and almost gender-neutral man who will be symbolically cuckolded by Dracula, who will drink his fiancée's blood. At the beginning of the epistolary novel, Jonathan relates his travels to Eastern Europe to help the count. East Europe presents a land before the bourgeoisie and before capitalism. Nature is enchanted with both black magic and Christianity, with nobles and peasants. Jonathan fittingly indeed finds himself above the peasants and below the noble count. Though he is repeatedly warned by the peasants of the evil nature of the count and his castle, he presses forth since he is engaged in "important business." Jonathan represents the bland side of work, work as duty and middle-class responsibility and respectability. Though bland and uncharismatic, it is Jonathan together with Van Helsing who will win using their bourgeois virtues against the charismatic count. In the 1890s when *Dracula* was published, Europe was still largely ruled by monarchic dynasties, from the royal family in England in the West to the Habsburgs in central Europe to the Romanov tsars in Russia. Nevertheless, it was clear that they were a kind of living dead, an anachronism that refuses to die. We might fall prey to their charm, they might still be parasitical and drink our blood, but their day is definitely over; we the bourgeoisie with our science, our work and persistence will ultimately drive a stake through their heart and chop their head off.

Of course, well before Dracula's head was chopped off, the French Revolution chopped off the heads of the king and many of the French nobility. Nevertheless, for our purposes it is more interesting to note how the ancient virtues were demolished by argument. In his *Groundwork for the Critique of Morals*, Kant gives a strong argument against the ancient virtues as the basis of morality:

Moderation in affects and passions, self-control, and calm reflection are not only good for all sorts of purposes but even seem to constitute a part of the inner worth of a person;

111

but they lack much that would be required to declare them good without limitation (however unconditionally they were praised by the ancients); for, without the basic principles of a good will they can become extremely evil, and the coolness of a scoundrel makes him not only far more dangerous but also immediately more abominable in our eyes than we would have taken him to be without it. (4:394)

Kant effectively critiques the most important Greek virtue of sophrosyne (Greek: σωφροσύνη) that is often translated as temperance, moderation, prudence, purity and self-control. His argument is that by themselves virtues don't guarantee one being a good person. Kant replaces the virtues with what he calls the categorical imperative: "Act as if the maxims of your action were to become through your will a universal law of nature." One should follow rules that are largely divorced from circumstance and that any rational being would follow. The critique of Kant's morality is labyrinthine, and one cannot fully delve into it here. Still, some common criticisms claim that his formulation suffers from formalism as well as idealism; it provides no specific information on what people should do in our world as it is. Secondly, it cannot explain why certain actions are right or wrong without appealing to some kind of goods and bads that are interpreted as such by the doer. It is my argument that without social and historical context as well as a political interpretation of this context, the categorical imperative as well as virtue ethics are empty. A Nazi, a communist revolutionary, a Christian saint, a Buddhist, a capitalist and a third world terrorist can all claim to follow both virtue ethics as well as the categorical imperative. The results of having virtues depend in a particular way on the historical, ideological, cultural and societal context. However, before we examine how to think about this context and its relationship to virtue, let us ask why values and virtues are so useful. What enables them to be used as ruling ideas?

Virtue is useful for making sense of everyday social experience, especially our relationship with family and friends, as well as being aimed at what can be called aspirational and memetic desires. Our everyday interactions growing up are filled with parents telling us to be honest and industrious, same age companions either being loyal or treacherous, and spouses spurring us to be conscientious and hardworking. Our everyday perception of people is mediated through the concepts of virtues and their opposite, vices. This person is dishonest, that person reckless. We often experience gratuitous cruelty from our classmates, and our institutions are filled with obsequious employees who flatter superiors.

As we grow up, we also look for aspirational role models who can orient us. The way that we describe why we think these people are worth emulating is conceptualized and verbalized using virtues. Traditionally this has been highly gendered as well. Boys wanted to be courageous, valiant, ambitious, sexually experienced, demanding, heroic, self-confident, strong, reticent, analytical, logical, tough, athletic, aggressive and sacrificial. Girls were supposed to be accommodating, emotional, talkative, gentle, kind, tactful, nurturing, submissive and easily influenced.

Mimicry seems to be still one of the basic ways in which we learn to do and be who we are. Since we are born as helpless creatures that undergo upwardly of 20 years of apprenticeship in being human under various caretakers and educators, it's understandable that role models, and the language of virtue that comes necessarily with describing the traits of character of role models, would be something that we are highly sensitive to. The language of virtue is the way we talk about what we would want to be like from the time of childhood. However, and this is the crucial point, this language is used to subjugate us later on. When people talk to us about virtue and being conscientious and industrious, there is something comforting about it since this kind of discourse has been used by parents who had deep love for us and cared for us. When we hear it again, it sounds like the same thing. Employers, priests, government officials and self-help gurus use it all the time. But this time it is not from people who genuinely care about you. In his powerful remarks written in 1938 in the article *Their Morals and Ours*, Trotsky had this to say on the morality propagated by business managers, preachers, gurus and HR people:

> The bourgeoisie, which far surpasses the proletariat in the completeness and irreconcilability of its class consciousness, is vitally interested in imposing its moral philosophy upon the exploited masses. It is exactly for this purpose that the concrete norms of the bourgeois catechism are concealed under moral abstractions patronized by religion, philosophy, or that hybrid which is called "common sense." The appeal to abstract norms is not a disinterested philosophic mistake but a necessary element in the mechanics of class deception. The exposure of this deceit which retains the tradition of thousands of years is the first duty of a proletarian revolutionist.

Trotsky tells us that what the bourgeoisie says is fundamentally different from what he does. The concrete norms that govern behavior, norms of exploitation of people, public goods and infrastructure, of strict monopolies, all of these actual behaviors are hidden under religion and philosophy or what has become common sense. The virtues are an integral part of this. In the ancient world they were precisely the intersection of religion (hero and gods worship), philosophy (especially Aristotle who elaborated on them) and common sense of parents and educators. Today they are at the intersection of corporate culture, parents and self-help gurus. The "concrete norms" of maximizing profit come at the cost of creating radical inequality, resurrecting the radical right, degrading air and water, and making people anxious and depressed. Thus, when tech giants extol virtues like connecting people (social media), making them knowledgeable (search engines) or experienced (virtual reality), what they are doing is engaging in subtle forms of class deception. While few people deeply believe that these virtues are what these companies are about, the extoled virtues do serve as a kind of soft deflection from directly confronting the evils involved in these enterprises. The thought that one is serving forces of exploitation, degradation of human beings and nature by monetizing friendship and knowledge, by further isolating people always lurks in the background. That is the reason why both tech billionaires and ordinary software engineers usually severely limit their children's use of technology. Bill Gates did not let his children have a phone until the age of 14, Steve Jobs said he severely limited technology for his children, and Tim Cook did not allow his nephew to join online networks. Yet when they come to work, they all repeat the peaceable mantra, "We are just making people social or knowledgeable" and in effect, we are in the business of creating good citizens.

Universities, especially elite ones, work in a similar manner. Under the high rhetoric, almost everyone feels that universities reproduce and exacerbate inequality. Tulane, the university that I currently teach at, is located in New Orleans, a city with a 60 percent black population. Nevertheless, only 8.6 percent of students are black. This racial disparity overlaps with a class disparity; there are literally zero children of working-class black or white backgrounds in my university. This is not a mistake to be corrected by creating another diversity office; this is one of the major functions of the university. Professional parents hyper-parent their children to the best universities and colleges that they can in order to reproduce them as professionals because they are afraid of them becoming part of the working class.

Since the professional class in the US is predominantly white, when it reproduces itself, it necessarily excludes blacks, who are overwhelmingly working class. Thus, when you go through the university campus you will see black women preparing food and black women cleaning toilets as well as Latin American men working in the construction of new buildings in which predominantly white children of the professional class will be reproducing themselves.

Nonetheless, as one goes around campus, nobody thinks or behaves as though reproducing inequality is one of their goals. Construction workers, cleaners and secretaries do what they must for their unlivable wages; professors follow their career goals, institutional intrigue and advancement politics; students study for their future career as well as pleasurable experience. Action, thought and incentives are essentially private.

Virtues come into the picture in the motto of the university, in its strategic plan and core values, in the newsletters that we receive that show us how inclusive the university is and how relevant its medical research is to the public good, etc. On a more personal level, virtue comes in when individuals feel challenged or discouraged in their lives. They figure in our world as something that helps to sustain and motivate. In my department, a black secretary will go to church, where a pastor will tell her to be loving to everybody as well as to be chaste, that is, not to have sex before marriage; students may listen to a motivational speech on YouTube that tells them to be tenacious in following their goals, to have faith, persistence, discipline, responsibility and confidence, to continue fighting when they get hit. A female professor might read a book on lean-in feminism on how to be courageous and succeed in a masculine workplace. Nothing is wrong with this. People need motivational talk. They sometimes need to be told to toughen up, take responsibility and insist. The problem is not the means but the ends that are chosen. The world does not really need more hi-tech billionaires, sports or Hollywood stars. Pursuing with courage, boldness, perseverance and other virtues *system-conforming* goals in a system that creates radical inequality, mental illness, global warming, racism, war and poverty is simply a bad thing. To see this, one just needs to imagine that the same motivational talk advocating values of responsibility, insistence and grit would have worked just as well in a meeting of slave holders or Nazis.

Management uses virtues to combat what is known as worker disengagement. Research indicates that about 68 percent of the workforce is disengaged. The reasons for this are many, and they include lack of recognition or feedback from management, lack of opportunities for advancement, low pay, and absence of training opportunities. Layoffs signal that one is both exploitable and disposable. Virtues and company values are there to create corporate culture, a kind of positive motivating feel for the workplace, preventing it from feeling deeply depressing or demoralizing. Often virtues are used to whitewash. The term *Leadership* that is used extensively is a central virtue. It denotes a sense of action and agency while keeping the term vague enough so that anyone, no matter how low in the organizational hierarchy, can be a leader. For those in power, *Leadership* suggests legitimacy and a feeling that they deserve their privilege. It is conveniently spiritual, connoting an "Eastern" wise man, while at the same time, a man who is ultimately concerned with the bottom line. Other examples of today's hypocritical discourse include *Nimble, Lean* and *Flexible,* which denote a company that regularly fires people. *Resilience* means that workers have to put up with whatever working conditions their employers provide them with.

Lastly, not only are virtues prevalent inside communications and meetings of an organization to keep people engaged, but they are also used extensively in both external and internal outreach and marketing. Pick up a brochure for any university and you will see industrious and ingenious medical researchers working for the benefit of *humanity*, not themselves. The outward face of many organizations is always couched in terms of values of universal benefit. This has long been the case. Since the Middle Ages, religious institutions in particular have often pursued land, power and money while presenting themselves as based on love and compassion. The bourgeois revolutionaries of liberalism in the US touted the virtues of universal freedom and equality in a slave ownership society.

It is because virtues have been so badly abused by religious authorities and the bourgeoisie that the best thinkers, artists and political activists of the past 250 years have come to view virtues as something inauthentic and disgusting, to be critiqued or brushed aside. Those who have been resolutely anti-bourgeois include thinkers and writers such as Jean-Jacques Rousseau, Honoré de Balzac, Stendhal, Karl Marx, Charles Dickens, Matthew Arnold, Gustave Flaubert, Emile Zola, Thomas Mann, Oscar Wilde, John Ruskin, Ferdinand Toennies, William Morris, Thorstein Veblen, Dorothy Day and thousands of others. In fact, one can almost say that a list of anti-bourgeois writers, artists and thinkers is almost coterminous with the best that has been created, period. Very rarely did an authentic creative person look at the bourgeoisie and like what he saw. People have shown their contempt of bourgeois virtues in many ways, from leading lives of bohemians, beatniks or hippies, to organizing revolutions, to drawing a mustache on the Mona Lisa. In response, the bourgeoisie, the church, royalty, business leaders and the mainstream press liked to claim that the anti-bourgeois were amoral and immoral. They have routinely described these anti-capitalists as sharing the values and orientation of the Nazis, calling them hotheads, fools, deviants, bums, and vicious and violent persons. Nevertheless, their critique of bourgeois life and virtues essentially stands. If the world will survive ecological catastrophe and other ravages of capitalism, it will come to appreciate the anti-bourgeois, and their view will become more mainstream.

Virtues are important, but as Socrates suspected, they cannot stand alone and we must question their utility and social effects. The people who exercise them must be accountable in terms of their larger effects on society and the world. We must always ask, "Virtue to do what?" and figure out patiently who is doing what to whom and what real effects it has. We must think systematically and not fetishize individuals who seem to embody virtues within a system that creates so much violence and destruction; otherwise the virtues simply contribute further and more energetically to the world becoming a much worse place.

Chapter Five

Knowledge

Knowledge and being knowledgeable is one of the most important ruling ideas. From the very beginning it has been central to the rise and power of the capitalist class. No group of people before it handled knowledge in such a systematic way, nor used this knowledge to both create its power as well as to legitimize itself. It has created truly objective knowledge, useful knowledge as well as distorted knowledge to enrich and empower itself. It has been central to its self-representation. In the last chapter we illustrated the value of work through the character of Jonathan Harker in the story of Dracula. Knowledge is aptly embodied by Doctor Abraham Van Helsing, who is described thus:

> He is a seemingly arbitrary man, this is because he knows what he is talking about better than anyone else. He is a philosopher and a metaphysician, and one of the most advanced scientists of his day, and he has, I believe, an absolutely open mind. This, with an iron nerve, a temper of the ice-brook, and indomitable resolution, self-command, and toleration exalted from virtues to blessings, and the kindliest and truest heart that beats, these form his equipment for the noble work that he is doing for mankind, work both in theory and practice, for his views are as wide as his all-embracing sympathy. (page 56)

This paragraph is almost a laundry list of values of the elites: self-control, empiricism, resolution, toleration. However, ultimately Van Helsing's authority and legitimacy stem from his intelligence and knowledge; he is philosopher, metaphysician, scientist and doctor. Knowledge proves to be the ultimate legitimization of the rule of elites, though with its own complex tensions and contradictions.

Marx defines the ruling elites as those who own the means of production (e.g., factories or stocks in companies). According to this formulation, Van Helsing does not fit the core of the concept. He is a knowledge expert whom the real ruling elites surround themselves with, to vanquish the residual aristocracy (Dracula) as well as to keep power and wealth for themselves.

Indeed, since the nineteenth century, the powerful owner class has made highly effective use of knowledge experts. They both legitimize themselves and make themselves dominant by these experts' knowledge, just as they made themselves rich by slaves and wage laborers. These experts and their knowledge occupy a strange and ambivalent position. In contrast to slaves and wage laborers, their lives are not the lives of constant exploitation; sometimes they might even lead a comfortable life full of interesting research; nevertheless they work on the behest of owners to whom they are truly subordinate. They might feel grateful to or resentful of these owners. Dealing with knowledge, while distancing themselves from overseeing production and trade, they sometimes come to appreciate it for its own sake, while for the owner, knowledge is mostly a means to power and money. They might look down at owners using their own scale of values. Owners can seem crude, exploitative and uneducated. It could also happen that people whose job it is to produce with relative autonomy accurate depictions of reality, irrespective of tradition and authority, might come to understand the owners themselves as the cause for all kinds of socially induced misery in the world. This is often the source of the conflict between intellectuals and the bourgeoisie. In the nineteenth century, writers such as Twain, Dickens and Marx wrote and organized against slavery, child work and workers' exploitation. In the early twentieth century, political revolutionaries like Lenin and

Trotsky or modernists were physically fighting the bourgeoisie. After World War Two, twentieth-century intellectuals like Fanon, Sartre and Chomsky critiqued imperialism while third-world intellectuals took arms against it.

Much of intellectual history in the past three centuries can be viewed as a list of various rebellions against the bourgeoisie. Intellectuals joined and created many movements hostile to the bourgeoisie, such as third-world nationalism and communism. Thus, the virtue of knowledge in a bourgeois society always risks revolution. It is for this reason that knowledge is both promoted and constrained at the same time. Technical knowledge is highly promoted, while true historical and social knowledge is often highly restricted since it challenges the status quo.

Nonetheless, knowers and intellectuals usually stay within their orbit and serve their masters well. For example, since 1930 there have been three times as many scientists working for corporations in the US than in universities. In some deep sense, knowledge in our societies vacillates between providing an accurate depiction of reality to creating knowledge that is biased toward furthering elite interests. How are we to assess this knowledge? Does it possess the virtue of truth? The question of whether the knowledge accrued by this class from the seventeenth century to our own is wholly objective or whether it holds bourgeois biases is a complex one.

One can start simply by a kind of almost naive division of knowledge. Many scientific discoveries are objective; what is discovered is essentially independent from humans in general, not to mention of their political formations. It would be ludicrous to say that chlorophyll and black holes are bourgeois inventions that serve bourgeois interests. The very strangeness and novelty of the entities that science discovers largely speaks to their objectivity. A big daddy God in the sky and a bad Muslim enemy are familiar and easy to understand for any child, and thus can easily serve as ruling ideas. Not so quasars and mitochondrion, strange beings that do not address us intuitively. Their very peculiarity and almost indifference to our life-world and our social conflicts powerfully attests that they are not some invention.

On the other side of our trust in the impartiality of knowledge, we have things like nineteenth-century anthropology with its role of both gathering information to better colonize and control native populations but also to demonstrate their inferiority. We also have knowledge and theories whose specific interpretation often legitimizes power; for example, the social Darwinist interpretation of evolutionary theory, Adam Smith's account of the invisible hand or Thomas Malthus's scientific argument that poverty is inevitable since population growth is exponential while resources grow linearly at best. These are types of knowledge that are deeply useful for legitimizing hierarchy in society. Political science and public policy are both good examples for fields that were born in the Cold War to legitimate the American political system in contrast to the Soviet one. More recently, we have Middle East studies and other area studies that provide understanding of areas usually with US or Western interests in mind. Can one say that information gathering and systematization has become less "interested" today. If anything, knowledge accumulated for private use and ownership by corporations is now unprecedented. The richest corporations in the world like Facebook and Google have become powerful by amassing extraordinary amounts of knowledge about regular people in order to monetize attention with advertisements. This knowledge gathering is definitely not in your best interests. Nor is it objective in any strict sense, since without their platforms you would not be generating this information in the first place.

Finally, one also thinks of what forms of knowledge are actively repressed by the knowledge monopoly of the bourgeoisie. Good examples for such knowledge include the history and culture of non-Western civilization and indigenous populations, culture, history, and resistance of working-class and poor populations within the West, and the vast area of women's contribution to humanity. In fact, add all these up and we can safely say that the knowledge and perspective of 99 percent of humanity has been actively repressed. Since the 1980s, we have witnessed a gradual introduction of these perspectives into some departments of universities. The introduction of comparatively tiny programs of Africana studies and gender studies, and programs that teach a miniscule proportion of students (most students take practical courses such as business and STEM fields) has been met with overwhelming resistance from the right. Nevertheless, even these repressed efforts have enabled us to imagine how knowledge of human beings, their society and history, fundamentally changes once we really include the perspective of most of humanity within it.

A less explicitly political challenge to bourgeois knowledge has to do not with a highly-skewed perspective propagated by rich men of Western European origins, but by scientists' own hyper-conformity to accepted ways, fashions and paradigms of understanding the world. At the very start of the 1960s, two intellectuals, Thomas Kuhn and Michele Foucault, were concerned with the relationship of scientific statements to reality vs. their conformity to accepted ways of understanding the world. In his *Structure of Scientific Revolutions* (1962), Kuhn demonstrated the way in which the scientific community as a group, with its particular in-group pressures, sets whether a paradigm is upheld or discarded. Scientific truth is strongly influenced by group agreement. It was clear from his exposition that scientific careers exerted a tremendous pressure on what scientific theories were held to be true at a certain time. Scientists are socialized for the most extended periods of time, and advancing in a career as a scientist means meaningfully participating in a certain kind of paradigm that includes both ways of doing things (experiments, observations, etc.) and ways of talking about them that are acceptable to the scientific community.

Around the same time that Kuhn developed his notion of paradigm, Foucault introduced the notion of epistemic change, later on called episteme, in his book *The Birth of the Clinic: An Archaeology of Medical Perception* (1963). The birth of modern medicine and the medical specialist in the eighteenth century was not the birth of some supposed neutral objective observer of particular diseases. Rather as Foucault articulated three years later in *The Order of Things: An Archeology of the Human Sciences* (1966), it was a general movement from the taxonomic era, an era in which knowledge was organized in kinds, to an organic historical era, in which things are organized as process. The clinic was not simply established on observation but on a type of general discourse. The authority of the clinician is founded not on strict observation of symptoms but on the way that knowledge is organized and fits into a valued prevalent discourse. Foucault reached a similar conclusion to Kuhn.

There is a feeling of truth that a proposition possesses that is not related to its correspondence to reality but to its fit to the ruling episteme/paradigm. Truth under the Aristotelian paradigm is not the same as after the paradigm shift to Newton, in the same way an eighteenth-century doctor could observe the same disease as a nineteenth-century one reaching different conclusions, yet both would express the truth for their time. Some will say that this is merely an effect of the growth of knowledge; the truth is simply expanding. Partially this is correct, of course. We know much more of the world today; our knowledge of physics, biology, geology, and even history and human sciences has expanded. Nevertheless, theories and their related procedures are like a flashlight that we use to illuminate a certain region of our world. When we change flashlights, we don't just expand our vision, we look at different things. I experienced this firsthand. In the 1990s, I was doing graduate work in cognitive science. Since the 1970s, cognitive science had been the ruling paradigm; it viewed the mind as an information processer. It had a philosophical basis in functionalism, the view that the mind is the "software" of the brain and can be studied independently of it. It had a psychological basis in studies of attention and memory, a linguistic basis in Noam Chomsky's generative grammar, a systems theory basis of cybernetics, and the AI research of Herbert Simon, Roger Shank and Marvin Minsky. It had typical experimental procedures having subjects do short tasks of reading or recognition and then measuring their reaction times. Nevertheless, 10 years later, by the early 2000s, this whole way of seeing things and doing experiments was simply dropped. It was replaced with a brain-based paradigm using fMRI that sought to localize brain function. This was a new paradigm with new premises and new questions shining a different light on the world and putting the whole cognitive paradigm into sudden dark irrelevancy.

Kuhn and Foucault's take on science flourished in the 1980s and was embedded in a broad post-modern constructivist critique of science. This critique came from a kind of left-libertarian perspective, whose general motive was to generally undermine authority and reveal the constructed and interested nature of all types of knowledge.

In the following decades, left-wing postmodernism died out, imploding under 9/11, American wars in Iraq and Afghanistan, Hurricane Katrina, the 2008 recession, and global heating. The socially constructed nature of discourse that was a fitting theme in the years in which Western powers were experiencing economic growth and stability seemed less relevant when the traumatic events of the 2000s were taking place. Finally, in an age in which half of the ruling elite was denying global heating, it seemed positively dangerous to critique scientific discourse.

Nonetheless, postmodernism lived on. In the 2010s, it moved from the left to the right in order to undermine universalism and science. This surprise move was not as novel a development as many believe and had classic precedents. One can say that the conservative right has always employed a kind of postmodernism, an opposition to universal truth from its inception as a reaction to the French Revolution. Opposing the French revolutionaries, Edmund Burke, the father of conservative thought, argued that their use of reason and universalism was abhorrent and violent. He called on people to respect and adhere to the characteristics of tradition and history of a particular people. Revolutionaries were foisting their beliefs in universal truths on traditionally minded people who did not want them. Joseph De Maistre, the eighteenth-century conservative philosopher, argued from a religious perspective that human ability to know is highly limited and that the revolutionaries were arrogant and violent, and that one should be humble and return to being subjected to the king and church.

Today the right is very skeptical about universal knowledge, often making particular claims that Western traditions are threatened by Muslims, Asians, Blacks, South Americans, Marxists, anarchists, feminists, homosexuals, social justice warriors or students. Western identity that is defended against the effects of true historical knowledge and universal morality is paradoxically a tradition that prides itself on its universality and claims to truth. Since the advent of Christianity as well as the Enlightenment, Western culture claims universality while at the same time practicing a kind of ethnic or racial supremacy of Western Europe and its offshoots. Western identity in itself is largely an incoherent category. It holds a major internal contradiction between Christian and Enlightenment commitments. It attempts to represses the contribution of non-Western Europeans to its own traditions, for example, the fact that rational inquiry originated in ancient Egypt and that Jesus was a Middle Eastern with anti-imperialist proclivities, and that both the Muslim world and the West share Abraham and

Aristotle at the core of their cultures. Also, Marxism is a Western philosophy, an important extension of the Enlightenment, and has analyzed institutions that existed almost entirely in Western Europe (like industrial capitalism). Most importantly, Western identity is inconsistent with the core of Western Enlightenment itself. In contrast to tribal or local culture, it does not really uphold a strong sense of identity. The Enlightenment expressing itself in both science and capitalism quickly de-particularizes and de-traditionalizes; it often trivializes local knowledge: what is knowledge of the British ritual of afternoon tea in comparison to Newton's laws of gravity, or the German Lederhosen dance next to Kant's *Critique of Pure Reason*? More practically, what is the power of a local eatery, coffee or tailor in comparison with Macdonald's, Starbucks or H&M? In general, while it was often claimed that socialism enforces a gray monotony, it is actually capitalism that does that. YouTuber Natalie Wayne asks and answers, "What the hell even is this country? Just the same terrible shit copy-pasted all over the goddamn place: Longhorn Steakhouse, Golden Corral, Staples, the Red Lobster, Petsmart, Chipotle, Fridays, Dave & Buster's."

Inconsistently, Western conservatives appeal to both Enlightenment and capitalism while wanting to retain a particularistic superiority at the same time. In order to more closely examine the tension within the elite and its use of knowledge, we have to turn to examine the Enlightenment itself.

Enlightenment

A good place to begin is with Emmanuel Kant's essay "Answering a Question: What Is Enlightenment?" The essay expresses clearly the virtues related to knowledge of the rising middle class:

Enlightenment is the departure of the human being from its self-incurred minority/immaturity (*unmündigkeit*).

Minority is the inability to make use of one's understanding without the direction of another. This minority/immaturity is self-incurred when the cause of it lies not in the lack of understanding but of resolution and of courage to make use of it without the direction of another. Sapere Aude! Have the courage to make use of your *own* understanding!

Laziness and cowardice are the causes why so great a part of human beings, long after nature emancipated them from other people's direction nevertheless gladly remain under age all their lives, and why it becomes so easy for others to set themselves up as their guardians.

Knowledge and the virtues of courage figure prominently in the understanding of the Enlightenment. It is relatively easy to notice that the problem of humanity is stated as self-incurred. It is not that most of humanity is subjected, exploited and brainwashed with ruling ideas, it is simply that it is not courageous enough to make autonomous use of its own understanding. It would be a good political exercise to think what various oppressed and subjected people – the woman servants in Kant's house, the workers in the factories, the Africans in the German colony of the Brandenburger Gold Coast, etc. – would make of the text.

Indeed, though Enlightenment ideals have been criticized by Marxists, anti-colonialists and feminists, and by the discourse theory of Kuhn, Foucault and Derrida, they are still alive and recognizably dominant in our culture. It is true that society vacillates between these values and more particularistic and populist ethnic and nationalist values, yet it is worth noticing that the most powerful institutions such as hi-tech giants as well as schools and universities are committed to the Enlightenment.

If one looks, for instance, to the mottos of universities around the world from the US to China, one gets things like "Truth and Virtue," "Wisdom and Knowledge," "Knowledge itself is liberty," "Let knowledge grow from more to more; and so be human life enriched," "Knowledge is the light of the Mind," "For God and for Truth," "Let your light Shine," "Learning and Labor," "Light, Liberty," "Making life better," "Let there be light," "Light of Enlightenment," "Light and Hope," etc. As one can see, light is a classic metaphor for the way the En*light*enment thinks of knowledge.

On September 10, 2014, an installation by Chris Burden was lit up at Brandeis University near Boston. It was called the light of reason. Here is a picture of the opening:

Three rows of regal Victorian lamps light up the entrance to the Rose Art Museum. A crowd is sitting in the front of the picture. A string quartet in the back provides music, and on the left about two dozen students are using the visibility of this event in order to protest campus sexual harassment. The Waltham mayor, Jeannette McCarthy, said in an earlier press release, "The kind of light installation for which Mr Burden is famous is in keeping with the legacy of Justice Brandeis, who always wanted to bring in the 'sunshine.'" Burden was not always installing Victorian "lights of reason" at elite universities. Responding to the Vietnam war, his best-known work from 1971 is called Shoot, in which he has a friend shoot him in the arm with a .22 rifle. In Fire Roll (1973), he set his pants on fire and then rolled on the ground to extinguish them; in Velvet Water (1974), he tried to breathe water. One of his best-known pieces is Trans-

Fixed, in which he lies face up on a Volkswagen Beetle and has himself crucified. In the late seventies, together with the general depoliticization of art, Burden turned to large installations.

In a way, the picture above sums up the social situation today as a kind of sellout of the avant-garde to the establishment, while feminists and LGBTQ+ are on the side of the picture pushing for reform largely within the Enlightenment that is viewed not as exploitative but as non-inclusive or sexually coercive. It is also good to notice who is not in the picture at all: the working and nonworking poor both Waltham the city that Brandeis as well as the rest of the world, the light of the Enlightenment does not shine on them.

In general, dominant forms of knowledge and its celebration pass over the poor and working class. And yet the rhetoric of pursuing knowledge is quite persuasive; we are moved by those who think for themselves, who "boldly go where no man has gone before." The rhetoric of science today, its ideology, so to speak, has not changed much. It presents itself as a mixture of sublimity and discovery. Here is a typical passage from Carl Sagan's famous book *Cosmos*:

The Cosmos is all that is or ever was or ever will be. Our feeblest contemplations of the Cosmos stir us – there is a tingling in the spine, a catch in the voice, a faint sensation, as if a distant memory, of falling from a height. We know we are approaching the greatest of mysteries. The size and age of the Cosmos are beyond ordinary human understanding. Lost somewhere between immensity and eternity is our tiny planetary home. In a cosmic perspective, most human concerns seem insignificant, even petty. And yet our species is young and curious and brave and shows much promise. In the last few millennia we have made the most astonishing and unexpected discoveries about the Cosmos and our place within it, explorations that are exhilarating to consider.

They remind us that humans have evolved to wonder, that understanding is a joy, that knowledge is prerequisite to survival. I believe our future depends on how well we know this Cosmos in which we float like a mote of dust in the morning sky.[1]

Passages like this abound in the popular presentation of science. The emotions of wonder and sublime that they evoke have sent thousands of children to become scientists, often ultimately working on minute, un-sublime problems for the rest of their adult lives. They form a kind of ersatz religion. It is easy to make fun of this rhetoric and view it as a certain privileged segment of the population (the middle class of Western European origin), explaining why what it does is so important and needs this expenditure of wealth and inequality. Yet it would also be foolish to view the results of science as always tainted by race and gender as is sometimes done across the humanities and social sciences today.

As recently as 1998, Saul Perlmutter, the leader of the international supernova cosmology project at Berkeley, made the public announcement in which he showed evidence that the expansion of the universe is accelerating. By showing the frequency of light coming in from supernova and examining the redshift, the fact that the wavelength becomes longer as one moves away from things, he demonstrated that the expansion of the universe is accelerating. This essentially lets us know how the universe will end. The trillions of its stars will move further away from one another, their fuel will run out, they will become white dwarfs and then will finally die out. For billions of years there will be only black holes in the universe and then just particles in dark cold space. The universe will end in ice not fire. The evidence for this result today is overwhelming. It is hard to ascribe an important role of class, gender or race in this discovery. Of course, Perlmutter comes from a certain class, race and gender (middle class, white, male) that has facilitated his ability to conduct research. Yet it is hard to imagine that the results would have been different in another more just world in which other classes, races and genders have the accessibility to conduct high-end research. It seems that we can neatly divide between the rational procedure of evidence and results of science, and the conflicted, political, social world that underpins it. However, things may not be so simple.

The Scientist as Virtuous Hero

To see why this is so, we have to turn to the public face of scientists, to how science is presented to the public. In 2018, comedian and post-addiction guru Russel Brand interviewed "rock star" physicist and science popularizer Brian Cox on Brand's podcast *Under the Skin*. Cox started by saying that science is the study of nature and a humble pursuit: "It's about just essentially looking at small things and asking very simple questions, almost childlike questions, why is the sky blue, why is that leaf green?" This is, of course, a far cry from experimental paradigms such as the particle collider at CERN that Cox himself is involved in as well as projects employing thousands of people and millions of dollars, and asking questions regarding things that nobody has even seen, and very few people care about, like the nature of the Higgs boson particle.

Be that as it may, one can plausibly argue that simple wonder is perhaps the start of a chain that leads to these highly esoteric questions and procedures. It seems that like the case of Perlmutter's findings we can still separate politics and science. However, the line between the descriptively scientific and the normative is not clear. For example, Cox moves on to say that we are the most "valuable structure that we know of in the universe" since as Richard Feynman said, we are "atom's contemplating atoms." Cox acknowledges that this is not self-evident:

When I say that sometimes people get very...you know people are liable to say, Oh humans are damaging the planet and we're better off without them, this is nonsense right. The point is, the most remarkable thing about our physical universe is that there are places where atoms can contemplate atoms. At one place that we know of, there might be others, we might be quite rare, we don't know, we've looked a bit and we've seen no sign of anyone else, it's called the great silence, astronomers call it. The great silence because we listen with radio telescopes and we look out into space, we see no sign of any other civilizations and so it could be quite a lonely existence that we have here but therefore very valuable indeed.

Here we see how scientific fact (the rare existence of intelligence) becomes a value statement, even a political argument. Science here is quickly made to buttress anthropocentrism, which in today's climate politics is in fact a political position. We might not be the center of the universe, but we are indeed the most valuable thing that exists in it. Is this a retreat from the decentering, sobering effect of Copernicus and Darwin? Does science by itself tell us that we are indeed the most worthwhile thing in the universe? Some scientists have argued that the only real criterion for life is survival and therefore bacteria and cockroaches are more worthwhile in evolutionary terms than us. Some rightly point out that different life forms do wonderous things, like live underwater, convert sunshine into energy or fly through the air, which we humans cannot.

Citing the father of the atomic bomb, Robert Oppenheimer, Cox goes on to say that science can teach us how to run society. The very humble nature of science – that we don't know things for certain, that as scientists we find delight in being proven wrong, that our opinion counts for nothing – those things can be translated to the way societies are run. This probably implies that we should be careful when making changes in society.

Cox also suggests using the concept of complementarity when thinking of society: an idea originally formulated by Niels Bohr originating in early-twentieth century quantum mechanics, the fact that one must hold two apparently mutually contradictory ideas in order to get a full picture of subatomic reality. Cox suggests using complementarity to think about society. While libertarians prioritize individual freedom above all, and others like communists prioritize the well-being of society, we need to realize that there is no individual freedom without society and no society without individual freedom and that the two are interlinked in highly complex ways. One needs to be comfortable in holding these two ideas together (individualism and society) at the same time. Again, science is made to support a certain ideology.

Defending liberal democracy, Cox goes on to say that every time someone finds himself being an outlier in terms of opinion, one should be waving the flag, cheering "I don't live in North Korea." He lauds not the results of Brexit (he is a fan of the European Union), but thinks that Brexit demonstrated that people can overturn the status quo in a democracy. As is evident very quickly, the scientist is made to argue politics.

Later in the interview, Russell Brand challenges him regarding the legitimizing function of science, the fact that it can be used like Christianity was used for legitimizing power. Cox reiterates that "science is a body of knowledge, it does not tell you what to make of that knowledge, it can tell you there are two trillion galaxies observable in the universe full-stop. Does not tell you what that means. What are you to make of that." Nevertheless, a couple of minutes later he laments that civilization needs meaning. In response to the need for meaning he cites Elon Musk and Jeff Bezos, who claim that humanity needs frontiers: both frontiers of knowledge and physical frontiers. He laments that we don't have frontiers on Earth anymore, that there is no Wild West. Therefore, the next stage is to go up to the stars, where we will find meaning again. Cox shows no awareness that the Wild West was a frontier for European colonists only, nor of the brutality of settling this frontier. When Brand challenges him by saying that the frontiers he would like to see are frontiers of love, equality and care, Cox answers that new political order can only develop in the frontier, that society is too entrenched and ossified to be changed today on Earth. He cites the movement from Europe to America that created the American Constitution, which he sees as one of the most important documents of how you might run a society. If in 100 years, the Mars colony is looking to become independent, it can create new ways of being and interacting. The physical act of coming to new places will allow humanity to do things that are not possible here because of the historic weight that we have on ourselves.

Cox thus uses his scientific authority as well as his coy charm to buttress specifically anthropocentrism, Western European style parliamentary democracies, the American Constitution and colonization projects, as well as to valorize billionaire entrepreneurs. How far away from pure observation we come at the end of the talk.

When listening to Cox and other scientists in the public realm, we are always struck by many questions. Is science truly only descriptive and lacks normativity? Is normativity something that is "sneaked in" later on? What about the connection made by Brian Cox as well as earlier by Karl Popper between falsification and democracy, a connection used to legitimize Western democracies while delegitimizing communism and Marxism as non-falsifiable? On the other ideological side, what are we to do with Albert Einstein's endorsement of socialism?

Science and research as well as scientists themselves do not happen in a vacuum. It is interesting to look at the way that virtues and values of science alternate from the utmost humility in which a scientist is a kind of strange hybrid between a child and a meticulous adult, asking simple questions and trying to propose evidence-based answers, to the virtue of scientist as the courageous conqueror of new powers and new worlds. Interestingly, popular culture has been very sensitive to the latter presentation of the ambitious scientist. He is often made to overlap with the head of large corporations, probably because people like Gates, Bezos and Musk involve themselves in science endeavors and, in the case of Gates, also scientific education. In popular culture they are presented as kinds of negative seers. The villain Wallace from the film *Blade Runner 2049* does not say things that are much different from the truly likable Brian Cox. Essentially soliloquizing in front of a naked, vulnerable replicant that has just been "born," he says (according the script):

We make Angels. In service of
Civilization. Yes, there were bad angels
once... I make good angels now.
That is how I took us to nine new worlds.
Nine. [disdainful] A child can count to nine on
fingers. We should own the stars.

Every leap of civilization was built off
the back of a disposable workforce. We
lost our stomach for slaves. Unless...
engineered. But I can only make so many.
That barren pasture, empty and salted.
Right here [points to the new born woman's womb]. The
  dead space between the stars. This the seat that we must
  change for Heaven.

[With a swift motion he CUTS the Model across the ABDOMEN with a surgical knife, she stands for an uneasy second before she collapses bleeding...he continues his monologue]

I cannot breed them. So help me I have tried.
We need more Replicants than can ever be assembled.
Millions so we can be trillions. More.
We could storm Eden and
retake her...

Such talk is not so fictionalized as we may think. Presenting his
plans to set the infrastructure to the colonization of space, Jeff
Bezos says in his presentation, "We can have a trillion humans in
the solar system. A thousand Mozarts and a thousand Einsteins.
This would be an incredible civilization!"

Indeed, Bezos, like Wallace, reaches the stars on the back
of a disposable workforce. His workers urinate into bottles
to avoid missing deadlines all while making in a year what
Bezos makes every 11.5 seconds. An Amazon driver reported
that when he crushed his hand accidently with his van door,
he was publicly shamed and asked to finish his deliveries
before seeking medical care. Of course, the products that
Bezos buys cheaply or delivers are made in China with even
more disposable people. The Wah Tung factory, for example,
produces Disney's dolls sold on Amazon and has a quota of
2,500 toys per day. Women workers work overtime to make 245
dollars a month. Since they are internal migrants with no rights
to childcare, they part with their children and send them to the
countryside. Workers live eight people per room, with no hot
water, and do 11- to 13-hour shifts; if targets are not met, lunch
breaks are canceled. Workers are ordered to handle dangerous
chemicals like benzene, which causes leukemia, with relatively
little protection, and to sandblast jeans to make them look worn,
causing a lung disease called silicosis. Forced public shamings
are held in the courtyard in cases of rule breaking or even if
something broke down due to management's fault.

As one can see, often dismal social realities exist behind
the rhetoric of discovery and frontiers. The idea of furthering

knowledge is not innocent; it is often used to displace and "postpone" social conflicts and injustices unto a new place where supposedly there will be an abundance that will make redistribution through politics superfluous. New knowledge is both exciting and important. Science has fundamentally changed what we think of ourselves and our history. Yet we should be wary and be on guard for the use of knowledge to legitimate existing political structures.

Chapter Six

Technology and Disruption

We are used to the idea of technological progress. It is an idea bombarding us constantly and one of the few things that society seems to deliver reliably. No matter at what time you are reading this book, in your own lifetime you have experienced technological progress. For my generation, it has been the internet and the iPhone; for my parents, it has been compact disks and personal computers; for my grandparents, it was nuclear power and spaceflight. While technological progress is real, there is an idealized, largely false way we usually think about it.

Pick up a book on the future of any developing technology such as artificial intelligence, genetic engineering, virtual reality, internet of things or colonization of planets, and you will quickly see that the more things change, the more they stay the same. The future is just like the present only better, more efficient and faster; it is filled with wonderous technology that enhances life dramatically. Synthetic biology will provide an abundance of sustainable biofuels, Personally tailored genomic medicine will cure cancer, perhaps even reverse aging. Space technology will colonize other planets, terraforming them to make them more like Earth. Yet in imagining the future, work, family, education, entertainment and culture all stay more or less the same. One book describes a small business on Mars, another an artificial pet dinosaur for the family. In such accounts, human beings and society stay reassuringly the same; it is just technology that changes. Writers make these technological changes vivid and compelling; however, these scenarios go against all that we know about the real historical and societal effects of technological change.

Every major technological change in the past was accompanied by a deep social and cultural disruption. The invention and implementation of agriculture, for example, has altered every facet of human civilization. I would like to go into detail on the changes that agricultural technology created to illustrate how totally transformative technological change is. Before agriculture, people lived in small bands of 10 to 30 people as hunter-gatherers. Hunter-gatherers lived in what is arguably a completely different world than the world created by agriculture. It is a world with different ways of sustaining oneself and of reproduction, a world with distinctive kinds of family, religion, identity and worldview. Let's start with survival. Hunting and gathering were mobile activities that everyone partakes in; they have little division of labor. It is true that mostly men did the hunting while women nursed children, but both activities took a small fraction of the day. The rest of the time was spent scouting, relocating, gathering fruits and vegetables, setting up camp and making tools, all work that *everybody*, man and woman, took part in. There was no surplus of food and no permanent settlement. For a mobile band, every additional possession was literally a burden. The ability to accumulate possessions and power did not exist; since there was no one richer or poorer, and no specialized institutions of violence like the army and police, the ability to sanction and control others was very limited. Hunter-gatherers thus lived in a very egalitarian society.

The technological revolution of agriculture has dramatically transformed human existence. It has created a division of labor and specialization that enabled the creation of types of human life unknown before: kings, warriors, priests, tax collectors, potters, bakers, carpenters, shoemakers, weavers, astrologers, fishermen, foresters, gardeners, moneylenders, dyers, innkeepers, interpreters, jesters, smiths, peasants and slaves. In agrarian societies, power stemmed from appropriating surplus grain and produce from peasants, not from hunting skills or personal charisma. An urban class of governing elite was formed as well as religious and military institutions to legitimize and enforce the appropriation of surplus.

Religion changes fundamentally as humanity transitions to agriculture. Since this book is about ruling ideas, I would like to focus on this change. Especially since what we call religion today has in the past integrated cosmology, history and ideology and was the main source of how people thought of the world and their place within it.

Hunter-gatherers believed in animism; it is the belief that spirits inhabit natural objects in the world. Thus, a mountain or a lake can possess spirit. For hunter-gatherers, the spiritual is not separated from the natural. Every natural thing is imbued with both practical and purely relational significance. One can view this from the perspective of an extended concept of personhood: in the hunter-gatherer world, a rock or a tree can be a person with whom we have a kind of relationship. These inanimate persons call on us and capture our attention. Shamans function as intermediaries from the more-than-human agencies like animals, plants and landforms and help communicate with the human world.

With the advent of agriculture, religion gradually separates from nature and becomes a tool of the ruling elite in its appropriation of resources. In Ancient Mesopotamian agrarian societies, a person's main duty was to serve the gods by gifting them food, drink and shelter. The most familiar agrarian religion for the reader is probably that of the Old Testament. And we might want to consider the many different ways that it is different from animism. The first thing we can notice is that its God demands exclusivity, backed up by fear of violence. This exclusivity translates to a total fidelity to a *specific* priestly class that mediates between him and the people. A professional priestly class is a classic characteristic of agrarian religions.

Agrarian religions expand great effort and detail to show why this class is important and to legitimize its privileges.

The considerably long passages from the Bible are filled with requirements for the temple, including tributes, sacrifices, offerings, etc. This is the revenue stream offered to priests. However, agrarian religion does not only legitimize and empower priests, it legitimizes kings and royal lineages.

The Bible's most memorable narratives, the stories of Moses and David, are stories that show how God has chosen an unlikely, sometimes even reluctant leader, and how fate, success and ascension to leadership are ultimately due to God's will. In the Moses story, this is quite explicit as Moses relies on constant interventions by God. In David's story, the narrator makes sure that we understand that, though the odds of David becoming king are extremely slim, this is the providence and will of God. Viewed from a theocentric perspective, the story makes simple sense. What happens is God's will. However, our view of the story changes dramatically once we accept that scribes wrote it to justify the Kingdom of the House of David. In actual history (like all history), it is not God's will that puts someone like David in power, but essentially, like all rulers, the more mundane and sometimes ugly machinations of power. Viewed from this perspective, the narratives of the Old Testament are legitimization narratives for those who rule. For all practical purposes, a peasant living under the hereditary line of King David is brought to accept their rule and exploitation since this is the will of the threatening all-powerful creator of the universe. In contrast to modern democratic legitimization that is ostensibly at least built on the will of the people, biblical legitimization is built on the rather obscure will of God, an obscure will that can conveniently be represented by the priestly and kingly caste.

This kind of legitimization afforded by agrarian religion is hardly unique to ancient Israel. Agriculture, as I claimed, brought surplus that was appropriated by rulers, and scribes and priests came up with deeply emotionally persuasive narratives to justify this. In older agrarian religions, this is relatively up front and explicit. In contrast to hunter-gatherer animism that attempts to interact and control nature, agrarian religions are mainly used to control and stratify people. Their main social function is to legitimize hierarchies. In the East, the Hindu law book of Manusmriti divides society into Brahmins (priests and teachers), Kshatriyas (warriors and rulers), Vaishyas (farmers, traders and merchants), Shudras (laborers) and Dalits (street sweepers, latrine cleaners). For a thousand years, caste regulated every aspect of Hindu existence. Castes have lived segregated from one another and could only marry within the caste. Brahmins, for example, cannot even accept drink or food from laborers. Such hierarchies and segregation in agrarian religions are often based on religious purity; those higher up are socialized to feel disgust at the lower orders of society. In the West, both religion and philosophy were made to justify hierarchies. This reflects precisely the disdain that priests, slave masters and wealthy families in all agrarian societies have felt regarding peasants as well as craftsmen – that is all those who use their hands to work. In the following quote, Xenophon makes Socrates say the very opposite of what he said in Plato's early dialogues:

> For not only are the arts which we call mechanical generally held in bad repute, but States (cities) also have a very low opinion of them – and with justice. For they are injurious to the bodily health of the workmen and overseers, in that they compel them to be seated and indoors, and in some cases also all the day before a fire. And when the body grows effeminate, the mind also becomes weaker and weaker. And the mechanical arts, as they are called, will not let men unite with them to care for friends and State, so that men

engaged in them must ever appear to be both bad friends and poor defenders (bad patriots) of their country. And there are States, but more particularly such as are most famous in war, in which not a single citizen is allowed to engage in mechanical arts.[1]

I doubt that the real historical Socrates expressed these views. The reasons given are highly suspect; they are nothing like the deep and often surprising reasoning that Socrates became famous for.[2] Such banal "reasons" to look down at craftsmen would have been in the mouths of every aristocratic person in Athens. Craftsmen are effeminate, not warrior like, they stay inside, what they do is not healthy (in contrast to war that is healthy?). At the end of the day, under these "reasons" stands the basic attitude of something like "We don't like the craftsmen because they are not like us, they don't participate in 'our' (meaning aristocratic) way of life." This is typical of rationalization of hierarchy. Its reasons are always empty and hollow. They never lead to anything surprising or novel; they just reinstate the value of the status quo. In the East, Confucius also gave "rational" reasons why hierarchy should be respected. He argued that social harmony is the result of constantly looking after one's relationship with one's superiors, women should submit to men, subjects to their rulers.

It is true that in very specific circumstances agrarian religion allows a critique and even revolt against authority. One can even go so far as to say that the originators of new religions have always been seen as a threat to the existing social order. For example, Judaism, at least mythically, originates with a slave revolt, that a direct covenant between the people and God allowed the prophets to criticize political authority, and that Jesus rebels against the spiritual authority of Jewish leaders who are complicit with imperial Roman rule. Nevertheless, it is my argument that agrarian religions are based on the legitimization of a priestly class that monopolizes the sacred, and lies, exploits and is often cruel to the population. Besides the fact that expropriation is often so severe that the population is kept at subsistence levels, literal sacrifice of lives was required of them. Human sacrifice is not something incidental to the system but is an important symbol that anything no matter how precious can be taken by the priestly class. Far from being rare, human sacrifice was prevalent in most agrarian civilizations. In 1487, for example, at the reconsecration of the Pyramid of Tenochtitlan, in what is now Mexico City, a conservative estimate of 20,000 people were sacrificed in one ceremony. Children would be tortured throughout the year as the Aztecs believed that the god Tlaloc needed the tears of children to wet the earth for him, otherwise he would withhold the rain. At one site the remains of 42 children revealed bone cavities and infections due to torture designed to make them cry continually. Several of the children had their fingernails pulled out. In Peru, Incan priests would take well-fed and well-dressed children from the ages of 6 to 15, lead them to a feast with the emperor and then lead them to the mountaintops for sacrifice. Similarly, in Genesis, God asks Abraham for a human sacrifice only to revoke the request at the last minute, marking the end of a custom that was very popular in the ancient Near East. The Bible also tells of the King of Moab, who gave his son as a burned offering in order to incite the gods to help him in his war against Israel.

New Institutions under Agrarianism

A new kind of religion monopolized by a priestly class was not the only new hierarchical institution created by the agricultural revolution. The need to keep track of agricultural surplus through taxation essentially created writing. Writing necessitated a kind of specialized institution, schools devoted to the teaching of reading and writing. A school is a new kind of institution radically different from the informal process of imitating tribe elders that took place in hunter-gatherer bands. Literacy was a transformative invention. Theorist Walter Ong argued that writing restructures thought, creates linear rather than cyclical time, moves meaning from sound to space, makes messages reproducible and transmissible, separates meaning from sensory context, and turns people inward as they read and write alone. And yet for all its different effects, one of the most prominent is to create a gulf between those who can read and write and those who cannot. For the literate, it was easy to think that they were rightfully the superiors of the nonliterate. An Ancient Egyptian text called *The Satire of Trades*, written in approximately 2000 BC, consists of a father's exhortation to his son to go to writing school and train as a scribe:

I have seen how the belabored man is belabored – thou shouldst set thy heart in pursuit of writing. And I have observed how one may be rescued from his duties – behold, there is nothing which surpasses writing...I shall make thee love writing more than thy (own) mother...I have seen the metalworker at his work at the mouth of his furnace. His fingers were somewhat like crocodiles; he stank more than fish-roe...The Barber is (still) shaving at the end of Dusk... The small building contractor carries mud...He is dirtier than vines or pigs from treading under his mud. His clothes are stiff with clay...The Weaver in the Workshops, he is worse than a woman, with his thighs against his belly. He cannot breathe the (open) air. If he cuts short the day of weaving, he is beaten with fifty thongs... The arrow-maker, he is very miserable as he goes out into the desert [to get flint points]. Greater is that which he gives to his donkey than its work thereafter [is worth]...The laundry man launders on the [river] bank, a neighbor of the crocodile...

Behold, there is no profession free of a boss – except for

the scribe: he is the boss...

Behold, there is no scribe who lacks food from the property of the House of the King – life, prosperity, health!... His father and his mother praise god, he being set upon the way of the living. Behold these things – I [have set them] before thee and thy children's children.[3]

This is not very different from today's knowledge elite pushing their children toward academic achievements. Indeed, it has been shown that model minorities use the threat of downward mobility (e.g., if you don't study hard you will work at McDonald's) in order to pressure their children toward academic success. The beginnings of these hierarchies between intellectual work that demands high literacy and menial work can be traced back to agrarian societies.

Those wielding the power of reading and writing must have inspired awe. This awe was probably translated to a willingness to do what these elites required. For example, there seems to be more evidence that those who partook of the grueling work of constructing the pyramids in Egypt did so as a religious duty, duties that were codified in texts.

In agrarian societies, we see a related change in socialization. In hunter-gatherer bands, the stress is on teaching children to be independent and self-reliant (since as hunter-gatherers they will need initiative in order to secure food). In agrarian societies, one teaches them obedience that helps them conform to the known ways of planting, cultivating and harvesting, and to their social status within a hierarchical society. A new type of docile human was being created. The agricultural revolution splits society into recognizable classes: a tiny urban governing class and a mass of serfs or slaves who create the surplus for this governing class. Auxiliaries to this governing class are what one would call urban professionals (scribes, architects, bureaucrats, judges, generals, etc.) who benefited from serving the political elite. When we add a standing army and police, we get the state.

The tiny elite with its small cadre of professional auxiliaries on the one hand and the rural masses on the other had distinctly different cultures. Rural village culture was insular, it did not know much beyond village life; its culture was various simplified and degraded versions of the state religion mixed with superstition. Urban culture developed philosophy, literature, art and science, but also a strong contempt for manual work and peasants, who were viewed as subhuman.

A good illustration is estate records all over the world that regularly list peasants with livestock. The agricultural revolution orchestrated the first large-scale dehumanization of human beings. The governing class expropriated peasants to the limit of their physical ability to survive. Peasants lived in abject poverty, mainly on porridge and a few home-grown vegetables, sleeping on floors covered with straw. Child labor was regularly used in the mines. For example, in the salt mines of Hallstatt, Austria, children as young as six years old were found with arthritis of the elbow, knee and spine. Some had fractured skulls or were missing bits of bones that were snapped from the joint under severe strain. Vertebrae of all individuals in the mine were worn or compressed. In other agrarian societies, people often sold their children, and their master, the lord of the manor, had the *jus primae noctis*, the right of the first night with all the brides.

Perhaps most characteristically, the agricultural revolution created the institution of slavery, which existed in all agrarian societies around the world. There are no known hunter-gatherer societies with slavery. On a very basic level, only in agrarian societies that produce surplus could slavery exist. Masters buy slaves with their own surplus and often slaves work at creating surplus. They do not make sense in a society where surplus and private property do not exist. Many ancient agrarian societies were fully fledged slave societies where up to one-third of the population were slaves. Perhaps the first known society to rely on slaves to that extent was Athens, which both won its slaves through wars with Persia and other people and bought them. From the fifth century to the third century BC, indeed, one-third of the population of Athens were slaves. Some were domestic slaves while many others worked in the Laurium silver mines.

This forced labor enabled all the achievements in the arts and sciences that are seen as the birth of Western Civilization. A third of the population of Rome from the second century BC to the fourth century AD was composed of slaves who did everything from farming to domestic chores. A bit less reliant on slavery was the Ottoman Empire, which until the mid-nineteenth century relied on one-fifth of its population to do its most difficult work.

The transition from hunter-gatherers to agrarian societies created specifically exploitative and violent institutions and social roles. The charismatic leaders in hunter-gather societies who had no formal authority and were constantly negotiated with, developed into a warrior caste that won its prestige and power on the basis of conquest. This class was often served by the class of priests that gathered information on every household, monopolized the sacred, and transformed relatively harmless animism into religions based on jealous and angry gods. The gods demanded absolute loyalty and devotion and constant sacrifice. In the past, these sacrifices meant humans, food, drink and anything precious. After the great religious transformations of the axial age, it increasingly meant surveillance and social control of individuals and families, obedience to religious authorities, and prayer and study.

To summarize, the agricultural revolution was deeply disruptive and transformative, creating the high achievements of philosophy, art, theater and math while tethering the majority to an abject oppressive life as peasants, serfs or slaves. The disruption of the agricultural revolution, far from being an unmixed blessing, resulted in institutions and social arrangements that we still find deeply troubling today, including patriarchy, wealth inequality, and the coercion, control and violence of the state.

Industrial Disruption

Modernity and the industrial revolution were no less disruptive. Modernity arguably begins with a kind of cultural revolution, the Protestant Reformation, that was enabled by the printing press. This cultural revolution marked a considerable change in society and culture. Reading and interpreting scripture for oneself became an important value, inaugurating the birth of the religiously inspired individualism. Work that was traditionally viewed as punishment for sin or as degrading became imbued with religious significance. Under these new values, people worked harder, were more rational and thriftier, and reinvested their savings in new enterprises. With the technical invention of the compass and the limited-liability corporation we see the rise to dominance of a new class of merchants and bankers.

About 200 years later, we witness the most intense disruption that human society and the natural world has even known – the Industrial Revolution. This disruption was so extreme that we still don't know if we will survive it. One can start with immediate disruptions that this revolution has caused and then move to the long term. The invention of bulky machines powered by steam engines created the need for factories, which needed a supply of labor that could only be found in the cities. Through the great enclosure, a process in which the nobility pushed peasants off their land to allow more sheep to graze in order to supply more wool to factories, the peasants found their way to the cities, lost their connection to extended families, to friendships and to the natural world. Masses of people streamed into unsanitary and crowded urban spaces. Many were injured during their work, fell ill or were fired when they reached a certain age. Urban workers also suffered from crime, alcoholism, depression and anxiety. Work became highly regimented and repetitive. Children worked from 4 in morning to 11 at night. They were fined for small infringements like whistling or talking at work; other violations such as organizing were answered by flogging. Indeed, for those affected directly by industrialization, the transition has been nothing less than traumatic.

Industrialization has indeed been disruptive in many ways. Society became mostly urban rather than rural; living in gigantic cities, the family lost its significance as a productive economic unit, that is, as a group that works together. On a positive note, life expectancy ultimately trebled, and literacy became nearly universal. Mobility and communication have increased massively, first between rural areas to metropolitan areas of the same country and then a one-way immigration to world metropolitan centers (like New York, Vienna) and finally to the situation today when many professionals move worldwide to wherever there is opportunity. Industrialization promoted the creation of new, this-worldly ideologies and belief systems including liberalism, nationalism and socialism as well as mass political parties that represent them. It has deepened the connection between science and technology as well as expanded man's objective knowledge of the natural world as well as human pre-history. Due to a tremendous growth in the past 200 years of per capita income, the standard of living for most people in industrial societies has risen. Almost all people in those societies live with electricity, heating, air conditioning and plumbing.

Nevertheless, all the horrendous negatives and abundant positives pale in significance to the most critical disruption of all. For the first time, man not only disrupted human society but disrupted the whole of the Earth itself. The Industrial Revolution enabled exponential growth of human population as well as the extreme growth in the release of carbon.

It is true that growth and spread of human population caused the extinction of species and decimation of forests long before the Industrial Revolution. Humans have long been a kind of invasive global apex predator, a species that quickly killed off much of the Australian megafauna 45,000 years ago. Nevertheless, it is only with the Industrial Revolution that the most significant disruption of all is taking place, the massive release of CO2 into the atmosphere, that is threatening the Earth's delicate 10-mile-thick biosphere with various catastrophes. Some argue that there will be enough time for human beings to accommodate, that humans since the Ice Age have been adept at both moving around and acclimatizing to different weathers. Such scenarios forget the utterly different state of humanity in the twenty-first century. After humanity had already settled all the planet, there were only five million people. This is radically different than almost 8,000 million that exist today; that is 1,600 times more people. A great majority of these people live in coastal cities where sea-level rise is likely to be devastating. These include the partial submersion of the cities of Bangkok, most of Shanghai, the whole of Mumbai, Alexandria, Basra, Venice, Jakarta, Lagos, Houston, Penang, New Orleans and Rotterdam by 2050, the age when today's children will be full adults. Two billion people are likely to be affected. Rising temperature will create extreme weather, including floods, hurricanes and droughts in many parts of Africa and the Middle East. At the very least, millions will be displaced. This will be the result of technological disruption whose direct roots are in the Industrial Revolution. On the pages of the *New York Times* or *Wall Street Journal*, disruption is made to look "cool," a maneuver of one company against another. In fact, even disruptions such as the way Uber disrupted taxis or how Netflix disrupted television, a disruption that has benefited consumers, has at the same time created suffering for thousands. Yet such disruptions pale in comparison to the ones that will result from global heating.

To summarize, you cannot have your cake and eat it. One cannot have technological development without deep societal disruption. Technological development leads directly to the reconfiguration of society. It is misleading, even pernicious, to present society continuing as it is while technology is rapidly changing. It is the job of a democratic society and true public servants to provide a plan and a rational blueprint that envisions technological development together with societal change.

Chapter Seven

Neo-Nietzscheans

A characteristic aspect of contemporary ruling ideas is their strong affinity to Friedrich Nietzsche's philosophy. At first this might seem unlikely, because of the relative distance in time, place and milieu from our contemporary world. Initially, Nietzsche's way of thinking might seem alien to today's culture, as he lived in very different circumstances. Nietzsche was born in 1844 in Röcken, a tiny village in the Prussian province of Saxony. His father was a pastor and his mother a teacher. He attended private schools, and excelled in Christian theology and German. In 1864, he commenced studies in theology and classical philology at the University of Bonn in the hope of becoming a minister. He soon lost his faith and concentrated on classical studies. In 1867, he volunteered for the Prussian artillery division but had an accident and left a year later. In 1869, while only 24, without doctorate or habilitation, he received an offer to become professor of classical studies at the University of Basel in Switzerland. In 1872, Nietzsche published his first book, *The Birth of Tragedy*, which was not well received by his department and philological colleagues. Due to poor health, short-sightedness and migraine headaches, he soon resigned from the university. Nietzsche continued to write books, about one every year, until his death in 1900. Though he influenced philosophy, culture and politics, his initial notoriety came from his critique of Christianity.

It might seem strange for readers to think of Nietzsche's philosophy as ruling ideas, when our image of Nietzsche is precisely of an iconoclast philosopher who attacked the ruling idea of God. Indeed, this attack was not obvious at that time, and it did incur costs. In 1883, Nietzsche tried to obtain a lecturing post at the University of Leipzig after writing his *Thus Spoke Zarathustra*, the book in which he pronounces that God is dead. It was soon made clear to him that he was unemployable by any German university. Nevertheless, as much as his ideas seem to undermine authority, they have been adopted enthusiastically by both those who are often deeply authoritarian, the Nazi party and American conservatives. Granted, Nietzsche is a multifaceted complex philosopher with contributions to epistemology, aesthetics and cultural critique, a thinker whose ideas cannot strictly be reduced to what aristocrats, fascists or libertarians take from him. Indeed, Nietzsche asked some fundamental questions regarding truth and the will to know, as well as questions regarding the relationship between power and knowledge. He convincingly undermined the claims to disinterestedness and objectivity made by philosophers and other intellectuals; he was also an acute commentator on the art and society of his time. Nevertheless, it is worthwhile to look into the reasons that Nietzsche's ideas have found such resonance with reactionary elites everywhere.

Nietzsche's basic philosophy critiques the Western cultural tradition from its foundational figures of Socrates and Christ to the Enlightenment. He broadly saw this tradition as life negating, moralizing, rationalizing, emasculating and risk averse. According to Nietzsche, these different traditions are imbued with slave morality, the morality and worldview that people hold as a result of their resentment of the strong and successful. As an alternate positive ideal, Nietzsche harked back to two distinct times. One was the bravery of the Ancient Greeks before they were tamed by philosophy, the other the cunning individualists of the Renaissance. He contrasted the risk and adventure of the great individual to the search for the common good and equality of the many.

Nietzsche's *intellectual legacy* is complex; he has influenced some of the most creative thinkers in the twentieth century, most notably Martin Heidegger, Georges Bataille, Jacques Derrida, Gilles Deleuze and Michel Foucault. Yet it is undeniable that his *political use* in the twentieth century was as a kind of weapon against socialism. Aristocrats, conservatives and libertarians needed his ideas as the Soviets and the Communist Party took power in Russia, only 17 years after Nietzsche's death. His ideas were first used as a political weapon against socialism by fascists and Nazis. Clearly Nietzsche diverged from fascism in many ways, especially in his disdain of the masses; still, fascist imperialists were very much influenced by Nietzsche's elitism as well as his call to go beyond good and evil and the quest for power. Nazis, for example, could find many places in Nietzsche's writings where he calls for imperial war as a kind of rejuvenation of man and culture through a letting loose of violent instincts. He often represents his Übermensch as someone who frees himself from the compassion of Christians or the quest for equality of democrats and socialists. On a more philosophical level, fascists could find much use in Nietzsche in order to disparage reason, glorify intuition and myths, and reject democratic progress.

Nietzsche's affirmation of inequality, revitalization of culture and critique of Christianity are integrated. Nevertheless, for exposition purposes, it might be good to separate them out. Let's start with inequality, and the most radical inequality, that of slavery. At many places in his writings, Nietzsche explicitly affirms slavery. In *Beyond Good and Evil* he writes:

> Every enhancement of the type "man" has so far been the work of an aristocratic society and so it will always be – and that is how it will be, again and again, since this sort of society believes in the long ladder of rank order and value distinctions between men, and in some sense needs slavery.[1]

Nietzsche had made countless similar statements consistently in his writings. For instance, in his preface to a book, *The Greek State* (1871), he writes:

> In order that there may be a broad, deep, and fruitful soil for the development of art, the enormous majority must, in the service of a minority be slavishly subjected to life's struggle, to a greater degree than their own wants necessitate. At their cost, through the surplus of their labor, that privileged class is to be relieved from the struggle for existence, in order to create and to satisfy a new world of want.
>
> Accordingly we must accept this cruel sounding truth that *slavery is of the essence of Culture*...The misery of toiling men must still increase in order to make the production of the world of art possible to a small number of Olympian men.[2]

In many ways Nietzsche is historically correct. High culture, the culture of written literature, philosophy, science, mathematics, etc., has only come into being as a result of the surplus expropriated from the masses, often from slaves. He is also right to point out that it is hypocritical to push this underlining truth away from view. Nevertheless, his thought actively precludes the possibility of working toward making a society in which people can be both free and cultural. For Nietzsche, Europe should revert back to slave owning.

This attitude of his to slavery is something that he held steadily throughout his life from a very young age. In 1864, at the height of the American Civil War, whose news certainly reached Europe, the 19-year-old Nietzsche wrote a thesis. He quotes a Greek aristocratic, Theognis, approvingly and calls the following segment of the poem very accurate:

Never do the enslaved go upright
But the crooked necked are ever gnarled
Just as a squill does not bear roses or hyacinths

A slave woman does not bear a free child.

Sometimes Nietzsche even despaired at the success of the democratizing tendencies starting with Christianity and continuing with the Enlightenment and the French Revolution. In *The Genealogy of Morals* he writes:

> Let us stick to the facts: the people have triumphed – or "the slaves" or "the mob" or "the herd" or whatever you like to call them – if this has happened through the Jews, very well! In that case no people ever had a more world-historic mission. "The masters" have been disposed of; the morality of the common man has won. One may conceive of this victory as at the same time a blood-poisoning (it has mixed the races together) – I shan't contradict; but this intoxication has undoubtedly been *successful*. The "redemption" of the human race (from "the master," that is) is going forward; everything is visibly becoming Judaized, Christianized, mob-ized (what do the words matter!). The progress of this poison through the entire body of mankind seems irresistible...[3]

Many Nietzsche readers repress such quotes in which Nietzsche pays the Jews the "compliment" that they are world-historical people since they succeed to poison, through race mixing and propaganda, the "entire body of mankind." Such readers then cite Nietzsche's basic disgust with many German anti-Semites for their envy of well-educated and wealthy Jews, and provide quotes in which Nietzsche is "philosemitic" (for example in his admiration for the vengeful God of the Old Testament). Of course, one can ironically comment that if Nietzsche were to know of the many Jewish intellectuals who have since the 1960s sided with the cause of inequality, including almost all the major thinkers of libertarianism and neoconservatism, maybe he would have paid them a real compliment as valiant promoters of inequality like himself. Jewish people do not have a single political or ethical orientation. The fact that a message of love and consolation to the poor and meek came from a Gallian Jew, Jesus, and spread through another Jew, Saul, does not say much about the people as a whole. No people are either bent on furthering equality or on inequality; every nation is split in this respect. The Jews are just a scapegoat, an externalization, and stand in for certain equalizing trends of history that Nietzsche hates. What is important to realize is that the quote above is not some aberrant statement, and that we should read his words not through some emotional hatred for Jews, but as the essential way that he reads world history, through his *fundamental* commitment to inequality. For Nietzsche, Christianity created an ideology, a slave morality as he calls it, of giving value to the poor and weak. The Enlightenment and the French Revolution translated it to demands of the masses for liberty, equality and fraternity. Out of the failure of the French Revolution to provide real equality and freedom, the masses turned to socialism.

Though one can principally disagree with this narrative, for example, one can claim that the Enlightenment drew its main impetus from the critique of the church, it is not a wholly implausible reading of history. The argument indeed could be made that the Enlightenment movement did ultimately draw from Christian values of Western Europe.[4] Regardless of this argument itself, what was scandalous and interesting about Nietzsche is not that he argued for the causal sequence of Christianity>Enlightenment>Socialism but that he negated it, that he thought that the sequence was not an improvement but a degeneration and decadence, that it undermined aristocratic culture and aristocratic virility. An increasingly plausible interpretation of Nietzsche is to view him as someone who projected his insecurity about his masculinity onto cultural history. His ultimate argument can be characterized as saying that Christians, Enlightenment philosophers, anarchists and socialists are unmanly men who whine about the evils and inequalities of the world and wait for Heaven or future revolution to solve their problems, instead of affirming these evils and inequalities – like real men should. The first thing that is interesting about Nietzsche is that he is one of the first intellectuals who told this narrative of the emasculating effect of the Christianity-Enlightenment-Socialism historical sequence.[5] However, even more remarkable is the way in which he injected the brilliant metaphysical motif of affirming reality into this rather crude narrative, by universalizing and arguing that these effeminate men, the Christians, socialists and anarchists, who cannot affirm the world as it is (with all its cruelty) find weak compensations in the beyond:

> The Christian and the Anarchist – both are decadents. But even when the Christian condemns, slanders, and sullies the world, he is actuated by precisely the same instinct as that which leads the socialistic workman to curse, calumniate and cast dirt at society.[6]

Socialism is simply a resentful negation of the world. Socialists aspire for a world that will snuff out everything that enables individual greatness:

> The Socialists demand a comfortable life for the greatest possible number. If the lasting house of this life of comfort, the perfect State, had really been attained, then this life of comfort would have destroyed the ground out of which grow the great intellect and the mighty individual generally, I mean powerful energy. Were this State reached, mankind would have grown too weary to be still capable of producing genius.[7]

Nietzsche's theory was that building a better society goes against life itself.

> It is disgraceful on the part of socialist-theorists to argue that circumstances and social combinations could be devised which would put an end to all vice, illness, crime, prostitution, and poverty...But that is tantamount to condemning *Life*...[8]

In fact, though Nietzsche as an archeologist of culture invested much effort in looking at the original transformation of Western culture from its original warrior-like heroism to internalizing Jesus and Socrates, it is socialism that is the most dangerous current avatar to this trend that threatens not only great individuals but also great races:

> Who can guarantee that modern democracy, still more modern anarchy, and indeed that tendency to the "Commune," the most primitive form of society, which is now common to all the Socialists in Europe, does not in its real essence signify a monstrous reversion – and that the conquering and *master race* – the Aryan race, is not also becoming inferior physiologically?[9]

For Nietzsche, democratization comes with mixing of races and degeneration. Thus, it is extremely important for him to stop any initiative that encourages political awareness and organization among workers. He writes:

> Who do I hate most among the rabble of today? The socialist rabble, the Chandala-apostles who undermine the worker's instincts and pleasures, their feelings of modesty about their little existences – who make them jealous, who teach them revenge...Injustice is never a matter of unequal rights, it is a matter of claiming "*equal*" rights...What is *bad*? But I have

already said it: everything that comes from weakness, from jealousy, from revenge. The anarchist and the Christian are descended from the same lineage...[10]

Claiming equal rights as he says is always bad and a form of injustice; unequal is precisely just and fair. Such is the philosophy of Nietzsche, an extended affirmation of inequality and subjection between the great individual and the masses, between master and slave, between the master race and subjected races. All this is articulated as a philosophy of liberation from cowardly and resentful moral commitments, moral commitment that we, Nietzsche's readers, made to feel like little aristocrats, have internalized because of Christianity, rational philosophy, truth and socialism. But how is this liberation to occur in practice?

Nietzsche's liberation from constraining and emasculating moral commitments comes through war. It is through war that we can rejuvenate real noble values. Here he explains why war is so important:

War Indispensable. It is nothing but fanaticism and beautiful soulism to expect very much (or even, much only) from humanity when it has forgotten how to wage war. For the present we know of no other means whereby the rough energy of the camp, the deep impersonal hatred, the cold-bloodedness of murder with a good conscience, the general ardour of the system in the destruction of the enemy, the proud indifference to great losses, to one's own existence and that of one's friends, the hollow, earthquake-like convulsion of the soul, can be as forcibly and certainly communicated to enervated nations as is done by every great war...Many other such substitutes for war will be discovered, but perhaps precisely thereby it will become more and more obvious that such a highly cultivated and therefore necessarily enfeebled humanity as that of modern Europe not only needs wars, but the greatest and most terrible wars – consequently occasional relapses into barbarism – lest, by the means of culture, it should lose its culture and its very existence.[11]

Nietzsche's prognosis as well as the proposed cure has been received enthusiastically by elites everywhere. First by European imperialists and nationalists of World War One, then closely followed by the Nazis. The Nazi thinkers modified Nietzsche's ideas by taking on the racial doctrines of Houston Stewart Chamberlain, a close variation on Nietzsche's race theory, as their main inspiration. Other changes were also needed. Ruling ideas are always instrumental since their purpose is power over others, not truth; they adopt themselves constantly to circumstances. The Russian Revolution of 1917 demonstrated the importance of the workers and the masses to *any* viable political platform. Nazis accommodated by introducing mass politics to the right. Nazi and fascist ideology stressed the component of the master race in order for it to be adopted by the *German* masses. The German masses could suddenly also think of themselves as kind of masters over all those who did not belong to the race. This strategy was not wholly new; other rival empires, the British, the American and the Japanese, each in its own way had used race as a central category to enlist the masses to the cause of elites. A British foot solider in India could feel in many ways that he belongs to a master race. A poor white in the American South might be poor, but he is not black. A Japanese official in South Korea or the Philippines could presume submissiveness from the entire population due to his or her race. Such uses of race by imperial elites were not new. What was new in Nazism was the way it adopted the organization and whole political culture of socialist movements for its vision of Aryan race supremacy. This included mass political parties with newspapers, clubs and youth organizations, mass events, etc. This was a novel political movement of the twentieth century, Nietzschean content with socialist form.

World War Two, just like World War One, was a war between empires. Four of these empires (German, British, American, Japanese) used race supremacy in various forms. White supremacy was codified both in law and practice throughout the British colonies (e.g., India, Africa, Southeast Asia, Middle East) and in the US. Nevertheless, the US and Britain made exceptionally good use of the propaganda in which they presented themselves as anti-racist democrats fighting against the racist and anti-Semitic Nazis. Ironically, this use of anti-racist propaganda effected like a boomerang on allied societies themselves. It facilitated the success of the civil rights movement in the US and more importantly the decolonization of Africa and India. The period after World War Two was a time of anti-colonial struggles gaining momentum all around the world. It also had an effect on the ruling ideas. Direct racism was no longer respectable; for example, books and research on race science became unacceptable in universities. White supremacy was on the defense. The carnage of World War One and World War Two diminished the enthusiasm for war, Nietzsche's favorite cure for decadence that was supposed to rejuvenate one's masculinity and courage. In response to these circumstances, Nietzsche's ideas, ideas that were so helpful for elites, had to be transformed, and this would happen not in Europe that had lost its world dominance completely after World War Two but in the US, the most powerful superpower.

In simple terms, the change meant slightly altering or masking three elements in Nietzsche's formulation with close substitutes. First one replaces talk of the master race with talk of Western civilization. Western civilization is a paradoxical amalgam of what conservatives call Judeo-Christian values, the Enlightenment, anti-Marxism and anti-Islamism. The very incoherence of a concept that includes both Judeo-Christianity and anti-religious Enlightenment but excludes those who share monotheism and Aristotle (Muslims) and the continuation of the Enlightenment (Marxists), reveals that the underlining concept of Western civilization is still at least partially racial – what in actuality is included is white people originating in Western Europe. The racial core of the concept is hidden under cultural terms. This change was largely cosmetic in nature.

Another substitute is to change Nietzsche's cure for the degeneration of Western civilization. Nietzsche's cure was imperial and colonial wars, wars that will subjugate whole peoples and rekindle valor, cruelty and competition. Instead of war, we are now called to wage brutal competition in the market economy, where some of the same values will be exercised.

Third, it meant changing Nietzsche's honest statement that masters and slaves are locked in a zero-sum game, in which benefit to one is the cost of another, to a trickle-down model in which benefits trickle down from the rich masters to the poor.

The US had, of course, its own traditions of legitimizing inequality; a good example is the Constitution of the United States. Charles A. Bead and others have argued persuasively that the constitution was motivated primarily by the personal financial interests of the Founding Fathers, though the text itself appears largely egalitarian.[12] Legitimizations of inequality are largely masked in the US by the formal commitment to equality stemming from Enlightenment values. At the turn of the twentieth century, Nietzsche's blunter yet more philosophically sophisticated variety of legitimizing inequality was quickly adopted by various thinkers and opinion makers. Ayn Rand, for example, took Nietzsche's emphasis on individual greatness and egotism, as well as risk taking, and translated them directly from the aristocratic medium of war and politics in which they were written by Nietzsche, to the American entrepreneurial medium of economics, in which they serve as the legitimization of extreme wealth inequalities.

We saw that post-World War Two, elites needed additional strategies of legitimation as racism took a blow after the Holocaust. But it was not only racism that took a blow in the twentieth century; capitalism did as well. In the Anglo-American world, from the time of Adam Smith, capitalism was always defended by representing it with examples of pastoral small-town life. In this small town, there are farmers and artisans who produce for local consumption and shop owners who sell their wares to people they know. Within bounds, everyone looks after their own interests and yet the town ultimately serves its people well. This kind of legitimization of capitalism was becoming less effective after the Industrial Revolution in the US and even more unconvincing after the Great Depression. Life under capitalism could not be presented as a small-town utopia. First of all, increasingly people lived in large cities. In 1830, only 8.8 percent lived in cities; by 1940, the time that Rand was writing her novels, it was 56.4 percent. The Great Depression with its negative effects of unemployment lasted into the 1940s and forced a new narrative. In the richest country the Earth has ever known, 25 percent were unemployed, many women stopped having children and people stood in the long lines of soup kitchens. In such a time, presenting capitalism in a pastoral light was unconvincing. A new kind of legitimization was needed for a time in which laissez-faire capitalism no longer worked. Rand used Nietzsche for this exact purpose. She celebrated the toughness, inequality and harshness of the world, the iron will of the exceptional men. She shares with Nietzsche the belief that some were born to rule and others to follow. Those who follow, the unoriginal masses, use an ideology of altruism in order to weaken the great men. They preach selflessness (an unreachable goal that goes against man's instinct) in order to instill a sense of guilt, sin and unworthiness. They thus contaminate the consciousness of those who are strong with their own misery.

Instead, they should be thankful to the "exceptional" men for whatever trickles down to them, for they are the ones who benefit the most from the genius of the elite of entrepreneurs and business leaders. In *Atlas Shrugged*, she lets John Galt, one of her characters, argue her views:

> In proportion to the mental energy he spent, the man who creates a new invention receives but a small percentage of his value in terms of material payment, no matter what fortune he makes, no matter what millions he earns. But the man who works as a janitor in the factory producing that invention, receives an enormous payment in proportion to the mental effort that his job requires of him. And the same is true of all men between, on all levels of ambition and ability. The man at the top of the intellectual pyramid contributes the most to all those below him, but gets nothing except his material payment, receiving no intellectual bonus from others to add to the value of his time. The man at the bottom who, left to himself, would starve in his hopeless ineptitude, contributes nothing to those above him, but receives the bonus of all of their brains. Such is the nature of the "competition" between the strong and the weak of the intellect. Such is the pattern of "exploitation" for which you have damned the strong.[13]

Rand's essential message of the Great Man is constantly updated and propagated, sometimes quite bluntly. In his *Forbes* opinion piece "Give Back? Yes, It's Time For The 99 percent To Give Back To The 1 percent," Harry Binswanger, a part-time professor at CUNY and the New School, and heir to the Binswanger Glass Company, founded 1872, writes the following:

> It's time to gore another collectivist sacred cow. This time it's the popular idea that the successful are obliged to "give back to the community." That oft-heard claim assumes

that the wealth of high-earners is taken away from "the community." And beneath that lies the perverted Marxist notion that wealth is accumulated by "exploiting" people, not by creating value – as if Henry Ford was not necessary for Fords to roll off the (non-existent) assembly lines and Steve Jobs was not necessary for iPhones and iPads to spring into existence.

Harry Binswanger has concrete suggestions on how we can all show our respect and appreciation for those who created all this value and wealth, which he thinks his readers will appreciate:

> Here's a modest proposal. Anyone who earns a million dollars or more should be exempt from all income taxes. Yes, it's too little. And the real issue is not financial, but moral. So to augment the tax-exemption, in an annual public ceremony, the year's top earner should be awarded the Congressional Medal of Honor.
>
> Imagine the effect on our culture, particularly on the young, if the kind of fame and adulation bathing Lady Gaga attached to the more notable achievements of say, Warren Buffett. Or if the moral praise showered on Mother Teresa went to someone like Lloyd Blankfein, who, in guiding Goldman Sachs toward billions in profits, has done infinitely more for mankind.

It is important to delineate what is Nietzschean here and what is not. Nietzsche was not enamored specifically with money making and trade. Nietzsche, as we saw, presented society as a zero-sum conflict between the strong and the weak. According to Nietzsche, the strong prey on the weak and the weak respond with resentment and articulations of slave morality. Libertarian Nietzscheans, in contrast, introduce the doctrine of free trade. Whatever exchange rational humans go into voluntarily is always "win-win." Free trade in not only rational and beneficial to both parties, it has many additional virtues as well. Here is a personal narration from the best seller *Antifragile* by Nassim Taleb that is worth quoting at some length:

> After more than twenty years as a transactional trader and businessman in what I called the "strange profession," I tried what one calls an academic career. And I have something to report – actually that was the driver behind this idea of antifragility in life and the dichotomy between the natural and the alienation of the unnatural. Commerce is fun, thrilling, lively, and natural; academia as currently professionalized is none of these. And for those who think that academia is "quieter" and an emotionally relaxing transition after the volatile and risk-taking business life, a surprise: when in action, new problems and scares emerge every day to displace and eliminate the previous day's headaches, resentments, and conflicts. A nail displaces another nail, with astonishing variety. But academics (particularly in social science) seem to distrust each other; they live in petty obsessions, envy, and icy-cold hatreds, with small snubs developing into grudges, fossilized over time in the loneliness of the transaction with a computer screen and the immutability of their environment. Not to mention a level of envy I have almost never seen in business [...] My experience is that money and transactions purify relations; ideas and abstract matters like "recognition..." and "credit" warp them, creating an atmosphere of perpetual rivalry. I grew to find people greedy for credentials nauseating, repulsive, and untrustworthy.
>
> Commerce, business, Levantine souks (though not large-scale markets and corporations) are activities and places that bring out the best in people, making most of them forgiving, honest, loving, trusting, and open-minded. As

a member of the Christian minority in the Near East, I can vouch that commerce, particularly small commerce, is the door to tolerance – the only door, in my opinion, to any form of tolerance. It beats rationalizations and lectures. Like antifragile tinkering, mistakes are small and rapidly forgotten.

I want to be happy to be human and be in an environment in which other people are in love with their fate – and never, until my brush with academia, did I think that that environment was a certain form of commerce (combined with solitary scholarship). The biologist-writer and libertarian economist Matt Ridley made me feel that it was truly the Phoenician trader in me (or, more exactly, the Canaanite) that was the intellectual.

The reader might be easily led to sympathize with the writer, especially if the reader spent time in academia. However, academia really only serves as a backdrop to highlight the virtues of trading. More precisely, Taleb combines Nietzscheanism with the older pastoral narrative of trading. Trading strangely is not described in the way that it is done now, with algorithms that undertake millisecond transactions of buying and selling. Taleb goes back to the Levantine souks and lauds them to no end. The anti-modernism, the revitalization of a mythic past of his description, is a classic Nietzschean mystification. Having grown up in Israel-Palestine, I have some experience of the Levantine souks that Taleb is talking about. First, like all places of shopping, they hide both long sequences of production and shipping and all the human and environmental costs that these entail. A market also does not show you how many of the products that you buy end up in landfills or polluting the seas. Nevertheless, souks are often colorful places where it's nice to work. Yet it would be a great exaggeration to view the people working in the souk as "forgiving, honest, loving, trusting, and open-minded." The people in the souk are like people everywhere. Sometimes you may enjoy their friendly banter, sometimes they rip you off, but mostly they will pressure you to buy things you don't really need. There is nothing utopian in a souk. From the point of view of sellers, we see that their job includes hours of deadening work when nothing happens. Go into any kind of market that is not very active (which is most of the time!), even into a modern mall, and you will see dead-eyed people, waiting listlessly, smoking...a waste of human time and human lives. One invariably wishes that all the buying and selling be automated in order to free people for other things. In general, the figure of the trader can be valorized only with great difficulty. There is nothing brave, creative, warm, funny, loving or any other human trait that we appreciate that is intrinsically tied to trading. It is for this very reason that even today in a world devoted to trading, our films, books and songs give us very few representations of traders that we appreciate. In reality, selling and trading is a fairly petty human activity that does not exercise what makes us most human. Yes, there is the staging and rhetoric of merchandise, figuring out how much people will be willing to pay, but all in all the homo-trader cuts a rather dismal figure.

For Taleb, academia with its petty rivalries and frustrations forms a useful background for highlighting the supposed charisma of the market. Taleb's rhetorical move from the boring, trifling and minor to more charismatic is classically Nietzschean, though perhaps not as dramatic as the original formulation, where one is supposed to transport oneself from trivial, middle-class existence to become a warrior Übermensch.

Though we might think that using Nietzsche to legitimize and celebrate traders and capitalism seems forced, we need to be reminded of a series of terms that come to highlight capitalism's more Nietzschean qualities, terms like creative destruction and disruption. Such terms make capitalism exciting. They celebrate a kind of immoral heroism. In this they are indebted to Nietzsche, who taught us how to celebrate destruction and the sacrifice of the many for the few. Nietzsche begins section 24 of his *Genealogy of Morals* thus:

> But have you ever asked yourselves sufficiently how much the erection of every ideal on earth has cost? How much reality has had to be misunderstood and slandered, how many lies have had to be sanctified, how many consciences disturbed, how much "God" sacrificed every time? If a temple is to be erected a temple must be destroyed: that is the law – let anyone who can show me a case in which it is not fulfilled!

Here Nietzsche offers a novel legitimization and even sanctification of violence, destruction and lies in the name of creativity and the new. As we briefly discussed, fascists have been the ones who adopted it in the first half of the twentieth century. However, after a brief respite from the horrific destruction of World War Two, the concept of creative destruction or more recently disruption has become highly effective and wildly popular in glamorizing the negative effects of capitalism. It would do to look at the origin of the concept.

Creative destruction started as a concept that economist Joseph Schumpeter developed in his 1942 book *Capitalism, Socialism and Democracy*. Schumpeter sees the history of capitalism as disrupted by various abrupt technical revolutions. The paragraph that introduces the term "creative destruction" is worth quoting:

> ...the history of the productive apparatus of a typical farm, from the beginnings of the rationalization of crop rotation, plowing and fattening to the mechanized thing of today – linking up with elevators and railroads – is a history of

revolutions. So is the history of the productive apparatus of the iron and steel industry from the charcoal furnace to our own type of furnace, or the history of the apparatus of power production from the overshot water wheel to the modern power plant, or the history of transportation from the mailcoach to the airplane. The opening up of new markets, foreign or domestic, and the organizational development from the craft shop and factory to such concerns as US Steel illustrate the same process of industrial mutation – if I may use that biological term – that incessantly revolutionizes the economic structure from within, incessantly destroying the old one, incessantly creating a new one. This process of Creative Destruction is the essential fact about capitalism. It is what capitalism consists in and what every capitalist concern has got to live in.[14]

Schumpeter draws radical conclusions from this. First is that firms are not in the business of just making a profit but actually in the business of attempting "to keep on their feet, on ground that is slipping away from under them." In contrast to economic theory of the time, Schumpeter claims that it is not lower prices that drive competition but competition from *new* products that is mostly on the mind of firms. Schumpeter's insight was highly original in the 1940s but has become common sense since; in fact, it has become the predominant way that capitalism is thought about and represented in the media. When one reads the economic section of major newspapers, creative destruction is presented as an exciting competition between CEOs on technological innovation and winning market shares. At the same time, many aspects of the impact of innovative competition or creative destruction are left unarticulated. These include the environmental, psychological and health costs of this competition caused by unemployment, pollution in general and emission of CO_2 in particular. These problems are hard to deny, and yet they are usually occluded when we cover business and economics. This is even truer in the way in which the history of the market economy is represented. From Aristotle to Adam Smith to contemporary economics courses, the story is told that a baker before the invention of money wanted a butcher's meat but the butcher did not want bread. They could not trade because there was no medium of money. In another example, we are told of an American Indian who had an extra pony but had to wait a long time until he found another Indian who was willing to exchange this pony for a blanket. The fact that no barter economy has ever been witnessed by an anthropologist, nor money invented to facilitate it, does not bother those who would like to present the market economy as the height of efficiency and rationalism. In fact, barter where it very shortly existed, exists only after people are familiar with money. Most early societies used gift exchange economies and not barter. Even the myth about barter economies is passed by quickly, no more than a couple of minutes are devoted to it. The core of contemporary economic teachings is marginal utility theory, a theory that puts an individual or firm decision in the center, not an analysis of the way a society maintains and reproduces itself. Society and its history are brushed out from explanation. There is little of even the rise of capitalism itself in the sixteenth century, not to mention colonialism, African slave trade and children's work – these are supposedly not economic phenomena, though the motivations for each of them were strictly economic. It is quite astonishing the way that we have accepted discussion or mention of the deaths related to purges in Soviet Russia but to mention the deaths related to capitalism is taboo. The book titled *Le livre noir du capitalism* (*The Black Book of Capitalism*, 1998) provides a list of twentieth-century death tolls attributed to the capitalist system. The list includes two world wars, anti-communist campaigns and repressions, colonial wars, and famines that total more than 100 million deaths. Strangely, this appendix concentrates only on the twentieth century, the most "communist" century. If we properly go back to the beginning of capitalism, we need to begin with the gold-crazed Spanish conquest of the Aztec Empire (1519-1632), which took more than 24 million lives, the conquest of Yucata with 1.4 million and the conquest of the Inca Empire with 8.4 million dead. It is true that many have died from disease, but this disease was brought to America by the drive to expand the economy of Europe. The African slave trade is not only responsible for deaths on ships and the miserable lives of slaves themselves but to the almost one million men who died in the civil war, a successful attempt to destroy what is the capitalist institute of chattel slavery. The American Indian Wars lasted from 1540 to 1920, killing millions. If we go back to the "peaceful" nineteenth century, we have the French colonization of Africa with half a million dead; the 10 million who died extracting rubber during the reign of Leopold II of Belgium; and the Conquest of the Desert, a genocide of the Mapuche people by the Argentinian army, which took place between 1870 and 1884, murdering 40,000. The list of genocides and ethnic cleansing in the name of profit goes on, of course.

Capitalism in the nineteenth century had sugar, cotton and later on rubber as its central industries. The raw material for these industries was based on exercising atrocious violence in the plantations – so much for tolerant Middle Eastern souks. In fact, it is a classic falsification to view the system solely from the point of view of the marketplace, that is, concentrating on the point of trade alone, effacing the whole process of production as well as use and disposal. We see the same difference today between visiting a sumptuous mall to visiting a factory in Bangladesh or Bordo Poniente, a giant waste dump situated near Mexico City. Nevertheless, when confronted with exploitation of both human beings and the environment, capitalist legitimizers call Nietzsche to the rescue. Suddenly the rationality of the system is not its most important characteristic but its dynamic ruthless competition that has given value.

We can understand how this appeal to Nietzschean virtues is made if we think that those who legitimize the capitalist system need to sometimes say contrary things. This is similar to Freud's joke about the borrowed kettle. Freud tells the story of a man charged by his neighbor with returning a kettle that he borrowed in a damaged condition. The man replies that he gave it back undamaged, that the kettle had a hole in it before he borrowed it, and that he never borrowed the kettle at all. Similarly, when someone argues that capitalism has major problems, the answer is that first, it's a wonderful system with no problems, see how trading is a rational exchange for mutual benefit, how colorful and tolerant Middle Eastern markets are. Second, it's true that there is suffering and injustice but it's the best system we have. Third, great suffering and injustice are the price for greatness. Taleb gives the first excuse that markets are colorful and rational, the second excuse, to paraphrase Churchill, is that capitalism is the worst form of government except for all those other forms that have been tried, and the third is where Nietzsche is useful. Whenever suffering of the great masses needs to be defended, Nietzsche progeny comes to the rescue and explains that it is necessary for the cause of human greatness. In Nietzsche's writings, he argued for the suffering of the masses needed for individual aesthetic genius; today's reactionaries, not so enamored with art and artists, often talk about conquering space or going to Mars. What greatness actually is does not really matter; in reality it is just a placeholder for justifying being the masters.

Chapter Eight

Ruling Ideas: The Past, Present and Future

The famous Dickins story *A Christmas Carol,* written at the height of industrial Britain in 1843, tells the story of Ebenezer Scrooge, a money lender and miser. Scrooge is visited at night by the three ghosts of Christmas, past, present and future, that demonstrate to him the devastating results of his greed for himself and those around him. His love of money made him end a relationship with his neglected fiancée, Belle, in the past. It made him ignore Bob Cratchit, his overworked and underpaid clerk, who cannot earn enough to treat his son, Tiny Tim, in the present. The ghost shows him his own funeral attended by local businessmen only if lunch is provided, a poor couple who rejoice his death since they were in debt to Scrooge, and Tiny Tim's funeral. This is the future. After being presented by the visions of these three ghosts, morning comes and Scrooge is a changed man, charitable and compassionate. We like the story because we are fond of the idea that seeing the past, present and future holds the power to radically transform us. Yet usually our past, present and future are not presented in a way that has the potential to transform us. In our culture and media, they are presented in a way that makes us stay the same. Ruling ideas color the way we see past, present and future. Before we can transform ourselves, we need to shed the representations of time that are instilled in us.

The Imagined Political Past

Ruling ideas of all shades use specific points of the past in order to anchor and embody themselves. They come with stories of a time in which things were either much better or much worse. They necessarily distort the past, especially when we deal with the collective past. For example, depending on where you live and your political beliefs, different points of time in the past are taken to be especially benign. We can order this chronologically from the distant past to relatively recently, as well as ideologically from conservative to leftist. Classic European conservatives pine for periods before the French, American and Industrial Revolutions. Indeed, the birth of conservativism itself may be said to be an ideology that came to reverse the French Revolution and reinstall king and church. Conservatives are fond of the time before the Industrial Revolution and urbanization. They may stress the cultural achievements of classical Greece and Rome – their art, philosophy and architecture. They are proud of Homer, Plato and especially Aristotle. They may feel strong attachment to the faith and spirituality of the New Testament; the joys of rural simple life, folk wisdom and the Christian faith of farmers of the Middle Ages; and the glory and splendor of its nobility. They appreciate the great masters of the art and literature of the Renaissance: Leonardo da Vinci, Michelangelo, Nicolaus Copernicus, Petrarch, Raphael and Shakespeare.

Conservatives in the Middle East may look back to the time before European colonization, to the Islamic Golden Age that spanned at least six centuries from the eighth to the fourteenth, in which the Islamic Empire thrived economically, as well as being prominent in the arts and sciences. During that time, scientists developed algebra, trigonometry, medical research and surgeries, optics, and a precise estimation of the Earth's circumference. Scholars wrote and edited encyclopedias, and partook in state-funded massive translation projects from Greek, Sanskrit, Syriac and Pahlavi that have helped integrate and globalize knowledge from India and Greece, knowledge that launched the Renaissance in Europe. The Muslim world could boast of the finest poets such as Rumi and Hafez; the most refined furniture, painting and decorative rugs; and awe-inspiring architecture from the Mosque-Cathedral of Cordoba in Spain to the Taj Mahal in India. Muslims dominated the trade with China and technology such as ship building and maps. Most importantly, Muslims today tend to view such times as times in which the Ummah (the Muslim community) was united, piteous and virtuous, a time in which most people followed the word of God. It is this past that Muslim conservatives look back to. In China's long history there are various times that can be chosen, yet the Chinese also hark back to the time between the ninth and the thirteenth centuries. This is a time in which China was the wealthiest and most prosperous empire in the world, an empire that invented gunpowder, the compass and the printing press. During the Song Dynasty (960-1279), for example, China saw a quick expansion of both population and economic growth. It had a meritocratic scholar-bureaucratic elite instead of an aristocracy or military ruling society like in the West. China had the largest cities in the world, with sophisticated social clubs, theaters, acrobats, storytellers, musicians, tea houses, organized banquets, restaurants serving an immense variety of foods, temples, schools, postal system and paper-printed money. The economy was the most developed in the world with joint-stock companies, an advanced iron industry and use of coal. The government provided social welfare, including hospitals and retirement homes as well as help for the poor. Technology developments included hydraulic clocks, uniform grid scale maps, movable type printing and a magnetic mariner compass. There was truly nothing comparable in Europe for another 600 years. Again, this flourishing has a moral component, as it is viewed as a time in which both society and leaders followed the precepts of Confucius on how to run a virtuous and harmonious society. It is this kind of past glory that the Chinese look longingly back to.

As we just saw, there are those who would like to go back to a time before the Industrial Revolution and the French Revolution; we can call them "deep" conservatives. And then there are those like American conservatives who would like to go back to the years following the American Revolution itself. Let us call them "shallow" conservatives. Interestingly, the modern revolutions that appear to "deep" conservatives as disruptive and ugly, form the very premise that "shallow" conservatives adhere to. Though the American Revolution arguably helped spark the French Revolution, both inaugurating political modernity, some conservative Americans regularly hark back to times closely following the American Revolution, to a Jeffersonian democracy that partially existed between 1800 and 1824, when the country was worked by honest, hardworking and independent yeoman farmers, where a limited small government prioritized getting land for people rather than looking mainly after the interests of merchants, bankers and manufacturers. Some American conservatives even look to more recent times, like the 1950s, a time seen as being composed of prosperous middle-class families that were disrupted by sexual liberation, women and civil rights movements, and antiwar protests. While European conservatives go back to a time before the French and American Revolutions, no American would like to go back to the restoration of the colonies under a British king.

Though deep and shallow might seem instructive temporal metaphors at first, conservatives often combine different time points depending on which events or historical processes they dislike. Thus, a conservative can simultaneously be in favor of a time before the Industrial Revolution, before feminism or gender nonconformity, or before the migration of Muslims or Mexicans. Conservatives pick and choose; they put together an imaginary mixture, a pastiche image of some past age before these disruptions, an illusionary time to which they would like to go back. Often, they will use violence and be disruptive and "revolutionary" in trying to reach that imaginary world again. Sometimes this endeavor of rolling back progress and reforms is successful. There are many historical examples of this. Reconstruction in the American South brought Blacks to relative political influence. This was rolled back by Jim Crow laws that enacted racial repression and lasted for another 90 years. This rollback worked effectively in separating schools and public spaces, discriminating in employment, restricting the vote, and terrorizing with lynching.

Many of the progressive achievements of the Russian Revolution of 1917 were rolled back by Stalin. The revolution decriminalized homosexuality, legalized abortion and instituted no-fault divorce. Beginning in 1933, Stalin recriminalized homosexuality, outlawed abortion and made divorce subject to court discretion. Yet another example is the introduction of Sharia law in the Iranian Revolution of 1979. The introduction of Sharia law in Iran made apostasy and homosexuality criminal behaviors and also put in place many restrictions on women such as not allowing them to choose where to live or apply for a passport without permission from males. After 1983, a law was instituted requiring wearing hijab in all public spaces. Undercover "morality police" enforced these dress-code regulations. Those who did not comply faced lashings as well as prison sentences of more than 20 years. In response to women comprising 50 percent of all higher education and 70 percent of science and engineering students, new laws have been instituted to use quotas to keep "too many" women out of higher education. In the United States, workers' movements and trade unions that had made great headway in collective bargaining rights and real wages were violently contained and then largely eliminated between the 1950s and 1990s. The 1950s and 1960s marked a time of dramatic decolonization and independence of third-world countries all across the world. This was a time when those countries tried to overturn their subjugation to Western capitalism and attempted to seriously engage in economic development for their huge rural and impoverished populations, populations that had been exploited for many years by Western colonial powers and local elites complicit with these powers. These progressive attempts have since been widely repressed and put in reverse, often quite brutally; for example, the CIA organized the military coup of Iran in 1953 that ousted the democratically elected Mohammed Mossadegh after he nationalized the Iranian oil industry previously operated by British companies. The overthrow of Guatemalan president Jacobo Árbenz in 1954, after he attempted land reforms that threatened the holdings of the US-owned United Fruit Company, launched Guatemala into years of brutal civil war. There was the ousting, in 1963, of João Goulart, president of Brazil, who advocated a platform of Basic Reforms (Reformas de Base), which included combating adult illiteracy, taxing multinationals and land reform. Such measures were taken in more than 30 countries in the second half of the twentieth century. Another way in which the autonomy of third-world countries has been undermined has been through loans by the IMF and the World Bank. These loans have been given on condition that the countries borrowing the money partake in structural adjustment programs. These include privatization of state-owned industries and resources, liberalization of trade, and a reduction in the government deficit. Amazingly, such loans cannot be spent on health development or education. They enforce austerity in the loaning countries. Ultimately, debt is used to ensure access and control to cheap raw materials while forcing developing countries to compete with one another to sell cash crops to the north. As third-world governments cannot decide their own economic policy, such loans are in fact a kind of financial neo-colonization. Thus, conservative attempts to roll back freedom and autonomy to workers, blacks, women, people from the third world, homosexuals, etc., are often successful.

Sometimes conservative measures or revolutions are unsuccessful. A good example is the case of Nazi Germany. The conservative project of making Germany racially "pure" again failed. But it is important to realistically assess why it failed. It was unsuccessful because this *particular* conservative project was expansionist. If the Nazis had attempted to purify Germany and stay within their borders, there is a good chance that the project would have been highly successful. Nazi racism came with German imperialism. It was only the latter that the Soviet Union and the US decided to fight against. Defeating Nazi racism was a byproduct of the war; it was used for propaganda purposes. This is especially clear to see in the case of the war that the US waged on Nazi Germany. At the time of the war, the South in the US was segregated by Jim Crow laws, which were in effect until 1965. Nazism was in fact inspired by Jim Crow laws. It specifically found valuable the US anti-miscegenation laws that prohibited whites from marrying blacks, Filipinos and Asians. When thinking how to racially define Jews, Nazis considered the American "one-drop" rule that stipulated that anyone with any black ancestry was legally black and therefore could not be married to a white person. However, they found the rule too strict and settled on anyone with three or more Jewish grandparents. American classification of race was harsher than that of the Nazis, and until entering the war, white Americans were not particularly anti-Nazi; in fact, a majority of the white population affirmed ideas of racial purity. Americans were also not above anti-Semitism. Major industry leaders like Ford endorsed the Protocols of the Elders of Zion and universities had quotas for including Jewish students. Nazi Germany also shared with the US an intense and violent hatred toward communists. For instance, in November 1919 and January 1920, American attorney general A. Mitchell Paler had 3,000 anarchists and communists arrested and 556 deported out of the US. The Nazi Party was built on by Frei-corps, demobilized soldiers from World War One, whose sole purpose was to crush leftist insurrections of the German Revolution of 1918-1919. Thus, the war on Germany was not a war on racism and anti-Semitism and most certainly not a war on the Nazi Party's treatment of communists that was mirrored by McCarthyism in the US. It was solely a war against German expansionism. We should always have this in mind when we think that reactionary projects are doomed from their conception.

Many liberals think that conservative revolutions and other reactionary projects are a kind of aberration that goes against the natural positive direction of history. Such a direction for history was first articulated by monotheism. Before monotheism, most cultures had a cyclical view of time and history. People construed time by following day and night, the cycles of the moon, the changing of the seasons and the movement of the stars. Thus, people thought of historical time as cyclical. It was the Old Testament that introduced the idea of a linear history going from creation to redemption. This idea was transformed and secularized in the eighteenth and nineteenth centuries and became the Western idea of progress. The idea of progress is the belief that the human condition is improving through the course of history and will continue to get better and advance. The narrative was already fully fleshed out right before the French Revolution. The French Enlightenment thinker Marquis de Condorcet (1743-1794) believed in the perfectibility of man, that through his senses man accumulates knowledge not only as an individual person but collectively as well, that the "course of this progress may doubtless be more or less rapid, but it can never be retrograde; at least while the Earth retains its situation in the system of the universe..." Like many optimistic enlighteners, Condorcet thought that the advancement of knowledge and sciences becomes indissolubly linked to the progress of "liberty, virtue, and the respect for the natural rights of man" and that both knowledge and "commercial intercourse shall embrace the whole extent of the globe." Theories of benign forms of globalization and progress have been with us since the very dawn of the idea of progress. French economist and statesman Anne Robert Jacques Turgot (1727-1781), who wrote perhaps the first book that articulated the idea of progress, *A Philosophical Review of the Successive Advances of the Human Mind* (1750), saw progress that manifests itself beyond the wars and bloodshed that captivate our attention in the present:

> Self-interest, ambition, and vainglory continually change the world scene and inundate the earth with blood; yet in the midst of their ravages manners are softened, the human mind becomes more enlightened, and separate nations are brought closer to one another. Finally commercial and political ties unite all parts of the globe, and the whole human race, through alternate periods of rest and unrest, of weal and woe, goes on advancing, although at a slow pace, toward greater perfection.[1]

The idea of progress is very persuasive. In fact, many best sellers in the past 20 years are basically a repetition of this doctrine. Narratives of progress are often simplistic in the way they tell history. As we saw in real history, technological advance, such as the invention of agriculture or of industry, involves a mix of great positives with great negatives. Agriculture allowed the creation of cities, of arts and sciences, but also of hierarchy, exploitation and slavery. The Industrial Revolution that created dramatic economic growth came with exploitation of wage labor and the degradation of the environment and global heating. The computing and internet revolutions have brought us an infinity of information and knowledge at our fingertips but created a small and all-powerful elite that controls the algorithms that "harvest" attention.

New inequalities and environmental destruction do not really go against the idea of directionality of history, merely against simplistic ideas of progress. One can differentiate between progress in the full sense of the word, that is, a notion that the human condition is getting better, and directionality, which is more neutral. For instance, the trend toward integration, mobility, hierarchy, interconnection, interdependence, communication and complexity seems one-directional. Many, of course, cite the fall of the Roman Empire as a reversal of these trends. However, this narrative is problematic on many different levels. It is true that on some counts, things in Western Europe did go backwards. The roads and aqueducts that ensured the effective and safe travel of people and water across the Roman Empire were largely gone. Nevertheless, the "dark ages" narrative is highly exaggerated. First, the Eastern Roman Empire existed and even thrived until 1453. Second, it is Eurocentric and provincial to measure progress and direction of history through the Western Roman Empire. While the Western Roman Empire was declining, the Muslim Empire and Chinese Empire were thriving. If we zoom out and view things from a longer time span, though empires may rise and decline, the ancient world definitely experienced movement from city-states to empires. Just like agriculture, the rise of empires took place independently in several places that have had little connection with one another: the Americas, Mesopotamia and the Far East. It seems that empire building was inevitable, and that there is a logic of expansion in empire itself. It's true that some empires, like those of Ancient China, chose to stay within the bounds of the middle kingdom and did not expand overseas; nevertheless, some empires like Greece and Rome were seafaring. It seems almost inevitable that at one-point empires like the Spanish and British would connect the world's major landmasses. Thus, there seems something almost necessary in the movement from the isolated civilizations before the beginning of the colonization of the Americas in the fifteenth century, to the tightly interconnected world of the nineteenth century, to the hyper-connection and mobility of today.

Another influential model of directionality was hinted at by

G.W.F Hegel and developed by Karl Marx and Friedrich Engels, who offered dialectics as the directionality of history. This kind of directionality manifests itself in several ways. Engels calls one such way that directionality manifests itself the law of transformation of quantity into quality. Just like water does not change gradually into steam but often looks to us the same at 40°C to 70°C, but radically different between 70°C and 100°C when it starts to boil. Processes in society and economy are underway even as things look mostly stable and repeating. Things brewing below can cause sudden change that creates a qualitative leap. These events or phase transitions give rise to new kinds of being with a new complexity. Life itself has made a qualitative leap from the prehistoric molecular soup to self-reproduction; agriculture and the birth of industry and democratic political revolutions were all such leaps creating qualitatively new kinds of societies. Political revolts or movements are a good case in point. For many years a population may seem docile, almost accepting its fate. There is no indication that anything is going on. Those who are seeking change may look at the population and reach the conclusion that it is "backward," politically uninformed, believes in ideas that oppress it, etc. Nevertheless, beneath the surface, a thousand injustices, pinpricks and injuries to dignity are taking place, leaving their mark on people. Then one event, often an event that is no different from others like it before, sets everything off. As I am writing this in 2020, the death of George Floyd by police has set off a new chain reaction whose results are to be determined.

Another way in which directionality shows itself is by a series of contradictions. With a passage of time, often an event or a statement draws a contrary reaction. For example, the Enlightenment's almost obsessive stress on the rule of reason and ideas drew a response from romanticism that stressed emotion and experiences. Modernism drew both from ideas as well as from dramatic experiences while, of course, presenting itself as a radically new kind of statement. A similar dynamic can be seen with the interplay of opposing forces in society. A good example is the way a dominant group interested in keeping the status quo stands in conflict with those who want to change it, leading to directional change. Let's take a specific example. Wealthy elites of Western European origins might find themselves responding to challenges to their rule from a diverse but overwhelming majority of the population. They might be challenged by their own workers, by those who they have colonized or enslaved, or by women or any coalition and natural overlap of the above. Each of these challenges has necessitated various forms of response in the attempt to keep dominance, thus creating a unique chain of events. Take just the short twentieth century as a case study. The century essentially opens with the Russian Revolution that challenges Western elites by the workers. Repressing this challenge explains the sequence of events of most of the twentieth century. It starts with the civil war in Russia that aims to contain and eliminate communism. Then Nazis weaken it substantially but fail to eradicate it. Then the US, the wealthiest and most powerful empire the world has ever known, represses it worldwide for more than 50 years through very hot wars, not cold ones, in Korea and Vietnam, covert regime change, and embargos and actual invasions in South America, the Middle East and Africa. Communism is more or less defeated by 1991 with the fall of the Soviet Union. No country in the world has been left untouched by this conflict. Nevertheless, in fighting communism the US had to change itself significantly, often creating a giant military industrial complex as well as repressive state apparatus not much different from those in the Soviet Union. It reached a new synthesis of big government and capitalism. Another overlapping example in the twentieth century is anti-colonial struggles. Of course, anti-colonial struggles have been with us since the start of colonization in the fifteenth century. For example, the Powhatan confederacy already resisted their colonization with the "terrorism" of the Jamestown massacre of 1622. While in general one can say that the colonization of most of the world was successful for several centuries, in the second half of the twentieth century, powerful decolonization movements challenged this dominance. India, Africa, the Middle East and the Far East have been decolonized. In response, Western metropolitans had to invent new ways of asserting control, mostly through debt; that is, the elite has to evolve as well as those who challenge it. Sometimes symbolic gestures are made by elites such as the waves of apologies that statesmen in Canada and Australia have issued to Native Americans and aboriginals. Sometimes demands are suppressed, such as Trump's criminalization of those who would like to topple confederate monuments. While it may seem that the dynamic is that of a going back and forth, it is in fact a directional spiral as those supporting the status quo and those challenging it adopt and change as a result of each other.

One can see this even more clearly with the feminist movement, its different phases and the different reactions that it elicited. The four waves of the feminist movement are women's suffrage in the nineteenth and early twentieth centuries, women's liberation in the 1960s, third-wave feminism in the early 1990s and fourth-wave feminism that began around 2012. Each of these waves responded to either accommodation or repression by those upholding the status quo. For instance, the adaptation of universal suffrage for women in the first wave meant that the movement moved to battle more broad and everyday occurrences of sexism and patriarchy in the 1960s. The fact that some of the demands were rejected and some accepted (for instance, wages for housework rejected while legal equality generally accepted) has meant that in the third wave, novel demands were articulated, such as freedom for those who are gender nonconforming, and the fourth wave was characterized by curbing sexual harassment with the #MeToo movement.

Thus, there are strong indications of directionality in history; even when things seem to go back to what they were, they never really do. The conservative idea of going to a golden past is strictly impossible; any attempt to do this would result in extreme destruction. For example, some conservatives would like to go back to simple preindustrial rural living. I find this vision very attractive as I think that living in or next to nature is important for human well-being. Yet any transition to preindustrial society with a world population of eight billion people will result in utter devastation. Without industry there would be no ability to provide basic food, health services, sanitation or water for the population. Billions will die horrible deaths, and life for the rest will be unbearable. Other conservative visions such as reverting to some sort of racial nationalism, though always possible, will be genocidal. The conservative take on the past is dangerous and cannot be implemented.

Not only conservatives look to the past for orientation; progressives of all kinds have done this as well. Already in the eighteenth century, Jean-Jacques Rousseau looked back to a time of greater equality before civilization. Extrapolating from colonial travel literature of the Americas, he saw hunter-gatherer life as more worthwhile than the life of civilized high society around him, where people were hypocritical and conniving. In the late nineteenth century, many different kinds of progressives and leftists were thinking of the past as well. In 1884, Friedrich Engels, one of the writers of the communist manifesto, wrote *The Origins of the Family, Private Property and the State*. This book is one of the most important works simultaneously for socialism and feminism, as well as what we would call Big History today. Engels's work uses Lewis Henry Morgan's description of the Iroquois Nation of North America and characterizes them as living in primitive communism. In this society, all able-bodied persons are engaged in securing food, and everyone gets a share in what is produced by gathering and hunting. These societies also partake in group marriage. This means that all those who belong to a certain generation are married to each other: all grandfathers and grandmothers are married to each other, all fathers and mothers, etc. The only people with whom one is not married or have sexual relations with are grandparents, parents and one's own children. Engels argues that state is characterized by a fierce egalitarianism, a primitive communism. Contemporary historical and anthropological studies largely corroborate Engels' argument. There are material as well as social reasons why these societies were egalitarian. Unlike grain that can be stored and therefore monopolized by a small elite, food that is hunted and gathered rots and is therefore shared. Another reason for egalitarianism is that while the impulse to dominate others exists, in hunter-gathering societies it does not really have effective sanctions behind it. Those who would want to dominate others cannot threaten them with organized violence administered by the police or army because these institutions do not exist. The strongest man can be killed by surprise by the weakest, and most certainly by a coalition of two or more people. However, in hunter-gatherer societies, things very rarely reach this point of internal violence. Social mechanisms of ridicule, done mostly by women and often ridiculing masculinity and sexual performance, and sophisticated "Machiavellian" coalition building, quickly put down those who would want to dominate. Authority is fluid in hunter-gatherer society. People are spontaneously listened to according to their ever-changing, ever-fluid reputations and group dynamics. Nor can one be sanctioned with withdrawal of livelihood, like the threat of being fired that hangs above one under capitalism; because resources are collected directly from nature by hunting and gathering, they are not provided by a wage from above.

According to Engels, the agricultural and herding revolutions inaugurate a turning point toward inequality. They create hierarchies between man and woman, master and slave, nobility and peasants, priests and followers. All of these hierarchies were ultimately enabled by surplus agricultural production and private appropriation of this surplus. Surplus enables the creation of a ruling class, soldiers, policemen and priests who are free from the need to obtain food. Surplus translates into private property; and the need to be sure that one's property is inherited by one's biological children has led to the control of women's sexuality, her appearance and in fact forcefully made women "disappear" from the public sphere. It is hard to overestimate the negative consequences of this development. We ourselves still suffer from living under a state that can extract taxes and draft our children, and threaten with police violence. Billions are deluded by religious institutions, and women have only recently attempted to recuperate from their being forced to be in the private realm, from the control of their bodies, and from double standards in sexual expression. It is to a past that came before these developments that some on the left miss. Nevertheless, this past is out of reach in many ways.

Thus, the left too has a past, though it is more out of reach. There are no continuing institutions from hunter-gatherer societies. The sharing, rituals, culture and way of life of hunter-gatherers is largely gone. This is in marked contrast to the situation for conservatives. The institutions of agricultural society are still with us, such as the church, the army, the police and the state itself. Though the "golden" and "pure" past is gone for conservatives as well, they can participate, admire and support very powerful existing institutions such as the army, police and the church; there is nothing comparable for the left to do.

The left needs to start from scratch, so to speak, and create novel institutions that may incorporate elements of the past but in general are innovative and thus very fragile. These have been conceptualized and attempted from the early nineteenth century to today. Early visionaries include Charles Fourier (1772-1837), who envisioned new voluntary communities called phalanxes in the countryside. Within a gigantic meandering house there would be 1,620 people living together doing various work in small groups. Robert Owen (1771-1858) was another early visionary; in 1824 he invested most of his fortune to create an experimental socialist community at New Harmony, Indiana. Ebenezer Howard (1850-1928) initiated the garden city movement in which communities are surrounded by agricultural greenbelts. Such voluntary experiments in intentional communities took place all through the nineteenth to the twenty-first centuries. Recent developments today include the ecovillages that seek environmentally sustainable communal living. Such projects attempt to take some aspects of the past (living from agriculture) and integrate them with modern living.

Another time in the past that the left is attached to is the heyday of the welfare state between World War Two and the 1970s, a time in which the state made significant concessions toward the working class in the form of universal health care, free education, minimum wage and labor regulation.

More characteristically, though, the left harks back not to stable times but to times of protest and revolution, viewing them as emancipatory, while conservatives stress their destructiveness and violence. The French Revolution, the Paris Commune, the Russian and Chinese Revolutions, 1968, the Arab Spring, Occupy Wall Street, the Ferguson Uprising, Yellow Vests, Black Lives Matter, etc., are not really states of being like suburban life in the 1950s or rural life in the village, but rather are states of transformation, states of becoming. These states can alert us to possibilities that we can seize in order to change the future trajectory of the world.

Longing for previous times is inherently problematic. When

one longs for the past, one usually takes some aspect of the past and conveniently disregards all the rest. Past times in recorded human history were never really good for everybody, only for a minority. For example, some Americans miss the time after World War Two and before the 1960s, a time that working people, blacks, women and Native Americans do not see as specifically redeeming. Even the privileged white elite did not live in the carefree mood that was ascribed to it later. The Cold War generated anxiety due to the specter of nuclear war and specific grievances about "losing" China to communism. There is also something distortive and non-authentic in yearning for some frozen picture of the past, since that past itself was not static; it was dynamic.

The distortion regarding the past can also sometimes be accompanied by a forceful attempt to make that past happen again. Trying to force a past can be just as violent as a revolution aimed at the future. Marx noted that history repeats itself "first as tragedy, then as farce" when he wrote of a French coup of 1851. In contrast, I would like to argue that the twentieth century teaches us that the attempt to go back to the past and repeat is not ridiculous but extremely violent. The most important attempt to reverse fundamental features of modernity was Nazism. The attempt to construct an invented past of a racially pure nation ruling over an empire proved catastrophic for all involved. As we mentioned earlier, we should understand that it was catastrophic because it led to an expansionist war against two superpowers, the Soviet Union and the US, not because it was an internally unviable political strategy. Mobilizing masses around national pride and external and internal scapegoats (Jews, Muslims, Soviet Bolshevism, the Chinese, immigrants, anarchists) is highly successful. It is, in fact, a strategy that is extremely dangerous and yet is spreading in our world today. It is important to see how this contemporary development took place. Racial nationalism could not continue unaffected after the defeat of the Nazis and the knowledge of all the violence that they brought to the world. These types of racial nationalisms had to reinvent themselves to suit a post-Holocaust world with a strong commitment to liberalism. It took not much more than 30 years after World War Two for it to reconfigure itself and find new winning strategies. Since the late 1970s, we have witnessed a resurgence of ethnocentric kinds of nationalism all over the world. Looking around the globe, one sees that more or less camouflaged racial nationalism has made a comeback. Such nationalism makes a disguised appearance in places that are committed to universalism, like France, England and the US. There it is articulated as an anti-immigration political platform and Islamophobia. It makes a more explicit appearance in Poland, Hungary, Turkey and Russia in which the government takes active steps toward reintroducing ethnicity and religion into politics. Indeed, one strategy of responding to the discrediting of racial theories and racial politics has been to reintroduce religion into politics in a way that will function just like race did in the past. A good example of this is the BJP of India, a party platforming Hindutva or Hindu-ness. The party first came to power in 1977, and since that time it has been less and less subtly calling for the marginalization of Muslims in India. This marks a dramatic erosion of the liberal socialism that was the hallmark of the largest democracy in the world.

Such trends are both empty of real ideas and dangerous. Especially since the state itself has grown in power through surveillance and policing capabilities. As an ideology, religious, ethnic and racial nationalism is first and foremost violent and dangerous to those it scapegoats. Symbolic violence and hate speech can quickly turn into real police violence, deportation, etc. More subtly, however, this type of discourse deflects, distracts and displaces real problems such as the degradation of the ecology and access to health care, education and work. This discourse is not like traditional religion – the opium of the people – but a kind of largely false fix, the cocaine of the people, providing a false sense of superiority and power over others and the invoking of "our" brave troops, policemen, generals and "our" great heritage.

What is "ours" and what is "theirs" of course depends today largely on the fault line between the West and the rest. In the West, a sense of identity is predominantly formed by the non-Western other, the Muslim, the Chinese, the Russian.

But in the rest of the world, identity politics and political legitimation flow from a kind of anti-Westernism. In the rest of the world, the conservative urge to go back to the past goes back to a time before Western colonialism and Western hegemony. I would not like to insinuate that the relationship between the West and the rest is symmetrical. It is not. Though the world has been mostly decolonized, most countries around the world stand under various pressures by the West. Almost all the countries in Latin America, the Middle East, north and sub-Saharan Africa, and Southeast Asia are debt dependent on the West. Those that have chosen not to play by Western rules, like Cuba, Venezuela and Iran, face economic embargos that slowly devastate their economy. Nevertheless, it often happens that an authoritarian regime legitimizes brutal repression through its struggle with the West. Doing this, the regime in places as different as the Middle East, Russia and China often invokes some glorious past before colonization and the rise of the West. When someone from China, for example, decries many of the things that I critique in this book, such as an exaggerated sense of individualism and materialism, and a false sense of freedom, he or she does so for different reasons with different aims. China is a great example since in many ways it is a country that concerns itself mainly with the future, and yet even there the past creates a pernicious backward.

Perhaps an extended personal story will clarify this best. I met Professor Fang at a conference in Madrid. He immediately showered me with presents and warmly invited me to visit his university in Hangzhou. Being hosted in China means lengthy lunches and dinners as well as incessant group photography. People are sensitive and patient and look after your every need – they "see" you in a way that people in the West usually do not. They ask whether you need Wi-Fi and suggest you go to the bathroom before a long walk. As their guest, you are given all kinds of honors; you will be sitting in a private room in the restaurant with a round table and a lazy Susan in the middle. You will be sitting at the innermost seats of the table (with your face to the entrance); to your right and left will be the most important people in the room. When toasting, your hosts will jostle to have their glasses be physically lower than your glass; when taking the obligatory group photograph, you will be placed at the bottom center of the picture. However, as much as they honor you as their guest, you are also part of a system of authority, hierarchy and control that is constantly marked in traditional ways. In any group meeting, one physically knows how important one is by the way one is sat and treated. This traditional hierarchy and control that ultimately stems from the social arrangements of agrarian societies has not only lingered on but has been exacerbated by the technological means of the modern state. Control by authority is persistently felt. Though I have experienced highly securitized countries such as Israel/ Palestine and the US, the security in those places pales in comparison to the securitization of China. Cameras are literally everywhere, including classrooms, and there are three different baggage checks in the airport – including a new invention, checking boarding tickets when you exit the airplane. When I asked Professor Fang about this, he told me that it makes him feel safe and that young girls can walk the street at night in China. This is the answer that was provided repeatedly – that authorities are looking out for our safety. The lack of criticism regarding securitization and loss of privacy is directly linked to traditional acceptance of authority. However, while in the twentieth century traditionalisms of the past were combated (sometimes violently in the Cultural Revolution), today they are reinvented in ways that are incoherent.

Over lunch, Professor Fang informed me that freedom is a Western invention. He told me of a dangerous trend of young people exposing themselves to Western media and becoming more enamored with Western individualist values. I asked him whether people don't feel frustrated under so much control and authority. He said that Chinese people don't mind being under authority and that many believe that those above them are looking after their interests. I asked him politely about the many times in which the Chinese people rebelled, from the Boxer Rebellion to Tiananmen Square. He was against rebellions, viewing them as wholly destructive. I had a feeling that a person like him would never have joined the communist cause in the first place and would be happy under the emperor.

He was very critical of the Cultural Revolution; every time we went past a Buddhist statue or Daoist temple he did not tire from letting me know the way that the Red Guards destroyed them. In contrast to such acts he affirmed a statement made by President Xi regarding the need for China to develop cultural confidence, that is, to be less beholden to the West and rediscover its classical Confucian culture. As he was talking, I was thinking that naturally those who feel or actually were under Western domination need to affirm and revive their own classical traditions.

Nevertheless, I came out of our discussion worried that "cultural confidence" will turn quickly into an instrumental use of tradition. Tradition will become a political tool – it will be used to unify people of great economic disparity within one national identity that is poised against various enemies and threats. This will be very useful for elites since in this way they don't need to face calls for democratization of power and wealth. Classical traditions of the past thus often mask and repress precisely those differences that have the potential to empower those who lack power. I have experienced this both in the Middle East and the US where Judaism, Christianity and Islam are made to falsely suture class differences and create convenient scapegoats and others. I have also experienced the attraction of religious traditions and their power to provide a sense of meaning and direction. However, we must remember how these traditions reintroduce other hierarchies, between those who authoritatively hold the tradition and those who don't, between men and women, and between insiders and outsiders. Let's try to grasp these traditions in broad terms and then evaluate what they can offer and what are their dangers.

Our most valued traditions were articulated in a very different time; they are answers to questions that were formulated 2,000 years ago, in what German philosopher Karl Jaspers called the axial age. The axial age took place between 800 BC and 200 BC, in which in a space of a few centuries, Confucius and Lao Tzu in China, the Upanishads and Buddha in India, the prophets Elijah, Isaiah and Jeremiah in Palestine, and Homer, Parmenides and Plato in Greece all appear on the world stage. How can we summarize such a legacy, a legacy from which our very culture is made and our identity constituted? One can see it as a new kind of solution to the perennial problem of insecurity and anxiety. In response to the sometimes-extreme vicissitudes of life in the ancient world, ones that include famines, wars, betrayals, and frequent death of children and close family members, axial age thinkers promised a new kind of inward security. This security seemed to bring a certain kind of detachment from the outer world and a focus on a new kind of inwardness or otherworldliness. In the Mahabharata, Krishna counsels detachment from thinking of worldly consequences, Buddha would like us to extinguish desire and focus on the characteristics of consciousness itself. Judaism requires single-minded devotion to the laws given by an otherworldly God as well as a withdrawal from the worldly joys of representation. These doctrines still have the power to inspire, and since we still often find ourselves insecure, unstable and disturbed for various reasons, in our jobs, relationships and health, we continue to find this kind of re-centering on God or mindfulness helpful. Yet, at the same time humanity has come to deal with insecurity by the techniques of civilization itself, by technology and government.

In the past couple of centuries, more and more people have been able to rely on food security, access to basic health care, stable government and relative confidence that their children will outlive them. These were enabled by the ever-growing power of industrial farming, health technology and expansion in the power of government to guarantee political stability. At the same time, these growing powers have created new systematic problems, the ecological crisis, pandemics, social inequality, meaningless work, disconnection and alienization between people. These problems are not likely to be solved by a turn inward toward God or consciousness. The texts of tradition give us little of import on how to reduce CO_2 in the atmosphere, how to manage heterogeneous societies, and what to do with surveillance and privacy, algorithms that make life choices for you, aging populations, bioterrorism and new diseases.

Moreover, often traditional solutions aggravate and confound contemporary problems. They encourage a particularistic worldview that is at odds with solving problems that we all essentially share, as well as playing into the hands of politicians who would like to buttress their legitimacy and power through the creation of various threatening others.

The particularism of traditional worldviews just does not make sense in an interconnected world; it lacks universality and generalizability. Ask an adherent of the axial religions, or a more modern nationalist for that matter, what she would hope for the rest of humanity, and one gets either a missionary response or something largely incoherent. Does a Russian orthodox nationalist or a Muslim fundamentalist expect 1.4 billion Chinese to join the Ummah or convert to Christian orthodoxy?

Often as an ersatz to having little relevance to contemporary problems such as growing inequality and environmental catastrophe, some traditionalists create a sense of coherence, drive and purpose through a belief that their way of life is under attack. For example, a white Christian nationalist in the US might think that his way of life is under attack from Latinos, Blacks, leftist professors, atheists, Marxists, Jews, feminists, Muslims, the Chinese government, gays, etc. From the perspective of the white nationalists, all of these, though they contradict each other, have come to challenge and undermine their identity and way of life. European nationalists share many on the list, perhaps with Muslims first. In fact, almost each country around the world today has its own list, a list of people who threaten to move the nation further away from its past greatness, a greatness that has in reality little relevance for today's world. The religious and national past seems to have little to offer us in terms of our politics, but what about the present?

The Present

Though past traditions exercise a growing pull on politics and thought, our present represents an incalculable force on the way we think and act. There are good evolutionary, existential, psychological and social reasons for this. We live in the present – sometimes what we do now decides our very survival. The present seems to be all we have (at any point in time); the past speeds away from us while the future is not here. The present is coded with the full sensuality of reality; we see, hear, smell, feel and taste the present. People around us at any given point in time also generate and exacerbate the importance of the present. We have a built-in sensitivity to the faces and words of people around us in that present. In general, we suffer from presentism. Our memory, both collective and personal, is highly distorted by the interests and concerns of the present. Human history, for example, is regularly written through the lens of the present. In the ancient world, histories were written of kings, empires and wars. In the nineteenth century, we related history by phases, the Stone Age, the Iron Age and the Bronze Age. We did this since material production was foremost in the heads of the newly industrializing. Today we have histories of gender, ecology, biotechnology, information and artificial intelligence.

Our own personal memories are highly distorted as well. If we are happily married, we tell stories of how we met and got together; if we have just divorced, we go back to the successes and failures of dating many years ago that are suddenly more relevant. If we change career paths, we will sometimes retell our whole life narrative to suit the new career path chosen. When looking at the future, all we can see are kinds of projections from the present. If we are in the 1960s, we think of the future either as technologically induced affluence in tranquil suburbia or a nuclear catastrophe; if we are in 2022, we think of ecological catastrophe, pandemic or displacement by AI. We extrapolate from the present; we think the future will hold only a kind of continuation of bad and good trends, while in fact the future will be a strange mix of continuation with the present, exacerbation of current trends, but importantly real surprises. Those who lived in the 1980s could not imagine the collapse of communism of 1989; those in the early 2000s could not see the Great Recession of 2008. Those living in the 2010s could not see COVID-19 coming.

What does all of this have to do with the ruling ideas? Ruling ideas exploit presentism in the interests of maintaining power for those who rule society. The present arrangement is self-evident and thus also their power over others legitimate. At any point in history the present is seen by most people as largely how things both are and, in a sense, should be. For example, if one lived in feudal Europe, the ideas propagated by the church were part of the fabric of the universe itself. The world, the seasons, human society and its orders all emanate from God. There is something awe inspiring and eternal about them. One feels part of a wondrous, mysterious, sublime yet meaningful and moral universe. All of these feelings and cognitions fix and stabilize the social world. Until a rupture by the hand of God himself occurs, everyone is in his rightful place in this universe. Virtue is knowing your place in the hierarchy, the great chain of being. This was precisely the central message in Confucius's China without the use of God: it is most important to fulfill one's duties as son to father and subject to emperor.

In the modern world, things cannot be as static as in agrarian societies. The Industrial Revolution and capitalism itself have inaugurated a dynamic rupture in human history. From that point on, change intensifies, and one cannot plausibly hold an ideology that celebrates stasis in a system that depends on growth. Thus, mainstream discourse celebrates innovation, disruption and change. And yet this change is limited; there is little innovation in social institutions or any deep change in culture. Capitalism believes in presentism; though everything is said to change, it looks at present institutions as eternal. Change is all well and fine in technology but not in the way we run business. The cutting-edge start up is as old as the chartered corporation of the Netherlands and England in the seventeenth century. The Dutch East India Company is considered by many to be the first modern corporation. It was the first permanently organized limited-liability joint-stock corporation. It is suggestive to learn that the first modern corporation was an innovation of colonialism. The model was quickly and highly successfully copied by the British in their East India Company. It is interesting to note that many futuristic dystopian narratives posit a multinational corporation that is in political control of a country; our present is thus projected into the future (as we will soon see). Interestingly, a multinational corporation that controls a country has already happened. The East India Company brutally exploited and terrorized India, a huge country with 20 percent of the world GDP, from 1757 to 1858.

We can see a continuation of this past as contemporary multinationals vie for world markets often with the help of governments and armies behind them. Radically innovative technologies are contained by the same institutions arranged according to rules that have been our present for the past 300 years. Silicon Valley may celebrate technological disruption, but it's just a disruption of one kind of corporation by another quite similar kind of social arrangement. The present social arrangement with its hierarchies and division of labor is deemed natural. What is the contemporary corporation? Those on the top of the pyramid are celebrated and invested with a kind of sacred aura, just like kings, royalty, bishops and popes were celebrated in the past. We cannot imagine something truly different in the future. We remain unable to imagine a future that is more egalitarian.

A similar phenomenon happens with national ideas. People take key aspects of their present national or religious culture and make them stretch indefinitely to the past and future. This is misleading in many ways. For example, if a Frenchman or a Russian thinks that Frenchmen and Russians existed in the Middle Ages, this is a kind of backward distortion. Whatever characteristics the people around you have today are made eternal. This is misleading in many ways. Serious writers on nationalism like Ernest Gellner, Eric Hobsbawm, Benedict Anderson and Elie Kedourie view national identity and nationalism as something that did not exist before 1780. In fact, the people before that time had mainly local identities as well as those that supersede nations, like being Christian.

Ruling ideas often make themselves strong by the sensuality, concreteness and solidity of the actual and present rather than with the ghostly presence of the past and the possible futures. A law court, a department store, a hospital, a school and a nation-state all seem to be solid – they are what exists. Yet they did not exist in the past and they can be transformed in the present. Their very seeming solidity is used to preclude alternatives. We naively accept them as the way of the world. We feel the weight of this dumb acceptance when we move through time and space and experience real differences between the ways in which people do things.

Many Americans, for example, are as used to private ownership of guns as they are to having cars. Just as almost none of us will call for abolishing automobiles because of car accidents, many Americans will be against abolishing private firearms because of mass shootings, police overreaction and suicides. For anyone coming from countries in which private firearms are illegal, Americans seem strange. Cannot they entertain the possibility of prohibiting guns? Are the people of Australia, Canada and Western Europe really less free because they don't own guns? Would it really be a good idea to introduce private ownership of guns to these places? Americans are captured by their present surroundings that may lessen by prolonged exposure to other countries. Similar reactions are likely to be given to student debt, health insurance and a host of other issues. People often find explanations to rationalize the present; even if they believe in the cause of change, they often think of it as impractical.

One of the ways in which we can free ourselves from presentism is by going to different places and reading about different times. Wherever differences exist, possibilities exist as well, and presentism seems to lose some of its ground for us. Differences, it is important to stress, cut across political lines; they are not just differences that we can agree are better or worse. Sometimes it's a choice between two bad things. For instance, China deals with inequality and resultant crime by pervasive surveillance. The question of whether this should be recommended to Brazil or the US, whether mass surveillance is more or less acceptable than mass incarceration, is a political, ideological and cultural question. What is essential is that the difference negates the narrow confines of presentism. Difference is not just a difference that arises from place but differences that arise from time as well. If you are affected by presentism and you live in the 1960s United States, you may think that women are cut out only for certain types of jobs. Present before you are women working only as secretaries, elementary school teachers, etc. This seems to be what women naturally do. However, if you flew over to the Soviet Union at that time, you would see many women occupying "novel" roles of engineers, doctors and party officials. The distortions of presentism are often used by elites to legitimize their rule and their privileges. There are millions of teachers, media personnel, journalists, presenters, actors and directors who are busy explaining that there are no real alternatives to our system that are not absolutely catastrophic, that the maximal change we can make is to include a token of a racialized minority member in the workplace, recycle our plastic and vote for a center-left political candidate. Many of us who face difficult lives as it is, find it hard to initiate change; we respond to blows and difficulties and pleasures that life provides without any kind of conscious planning. Both knowing different social arrangements and promoting initiative and discipline are needed in order to counter presentism with the space of the possible, a space needed in order to reshuffle the social deck. These possibilities were often articulated by thinking about the future.

The Future: Utopia and Dystopia

There used to be a future. At least an imagined future. During the Cold War, writers in the West imagined the future either as utopia or as totalitarian dystopia. Popular culture, especially television, had a very distinct future horizon. The children's series *The Jetsons*, for example, was first broadcast in the US in 1962. The Jetsons live in Orbit City in which all the homes and businesses are stationed above the ground on long columns. George, the husband protagonist, lives in Skypad Apartments, and his wife, Jane, is a traditional homemaker. He commutes to work in an aerocar and teleconferences regularly. Housekeeping is seen to by a robot, while George Jetson's workload is an hour a day, two days a week. The plot of the series follows the family as they complain and deal with various small frustrations and breakdowns of their technologies. At the height of the Cold War, a truly different future society could not be represented. The traditional family with its gender divisions is the focus of the show. No other political and social arrangements could be imagined. The future of the Jetsons is a continuation of the same. Yet though the future is just like the present plus technology, it could still be imagined, and was a largely positive future.

Another variation on confidence in a positive future was imagined four years later when *Star Trek* went on air. *Star Trek* imagined the future as a scientific adventure. Its explicit mission statement, narrated at the beginning of every episode, said, "Space: the final frontier. These are the voyages of the starship Enterprise. Its five-year mission: to explore strange new worlds. To seek out new life and new civilizations. To boldly go where no man has gone before!"

Existing beyond earthly politics, the starship Enterprise itself is an egalitarian scientific endeavor. It is a future in which people are freed from work as a necessity and do what they do in the name of furthering mankind's knowledge of the universe.

Turning from utopias to dystopias, it is important to stress how dystopias fundamentally changed in the second half of the twentieth century. From the 1930s to the 1960s, the most popular dystopias described a totalitarian future. From Aldous Huxley's

Brave New World (1931) to George Orwell's *Nineteen Eighty-Four* (1949) down to the present, several of the most prominent dystopias took this route. Still, in the late sixties we already see a forerunner of today's dystopia. Philip K. Dick's *Do Androids Dream of Electric Sheep?* (1968) takes place in a post-apocalyptic 1992 after "World War Terminus." The polluted, radioactive atmosphere leads to mass emigration to off-world colonies in order to protect human genes. Going off world comes with free personal robot servants – androids. The deteriorated Earth has a technology supported by a religion called Mercerism, in which everyone connects using virtual reality to worship Wilbur Mercer, a Christ-like figure who eternally climbs up hills and is crushed by stones. Philip Dick's narrative is one of the first times in the twentieth century that the future is described as a dystopia that is unrelated to totalitarianism. In the film's adaptation, the *Blade Runner* movies, it is even more apparent that what we get is a certain exacerbation of current trends: replicants, a market for genetically engineered animals and humans, the end of nature, and a degraded environment. This story can be one of the first that exemplifies the dystopia of unsustainable development. Narratives that show the future cannot possibly be like *The Jetsons*, a continuation of the present with better technology, a scientific adventure like *Star Trek*, or a kind of capitalist totalitarianism as seen in *Blade Runner*; all these variations on the possible future cannot be imagined today. These kinds of alternatives are gone.

Today we imagine the future as a kind of making extreme of the effects of techno-capitalism, mainly new and dramatic forms of inequality, as well as nature that is degraded or "strikes back" with catastrophe. New inequalities include genetically enhanced vs. not enhanced (*Gattaca*), urban center vs. districts (*Hunger Games*), human vs. robot (*Blade Runner, The Terminator*), man vs. woman (*Handmaid's Tale*), man vs. ape (*Planet of the Apes*) and man vs. alien (*District 9, War of the Worlds*). Science fiction was essentially created with the Industrial Revolution. It highlighted the close connection between technological development and the creation of inequality between rich factory owners and workers who were kept on mere subsistence levels. Since the depression of 1928, the two world wars and the use of atomic weapons have added a layer of world catastrophe that has been haunting our imagination. We are more and more aware that nature will not lie dormant for us to exploit indefinitely and will create catastrophes of its own. One can say that the future of the derailment of nature is already here. In an interconnected world, its effects become more and more extreme. The derailment of nature is presented in a series of various natural catastrophes like earthquakes, tornadoes, pandemics, rising oceans, floods, droughts and wildfires and with them millions of dead or environmental refugees who will intensify conflicts over resources all over the world. The very global interconnectedness of communication, production and consumption has, as COVID-19 has shown, created unique vulnerabilities. Future trends include stagnating or decreasing income, precarious work or unemployment, super-concentrated wealth, and environmental catastrophes.

It is telling that as Frederic Jameson once wrote, it is easier for us to imagine the end of the world than the end of capitalism. It is as if capitalism, like an undead zombie, can continue without the world itself. Both kinds of futures, the techno-optimist and eco-disaster, foreclose on the ability to imagine fundamental changes. We must release ourselves from a future that slides into dystopia by simply exacerbating current trends of poverty, inequality, surveillance and the disappearance of habitable nature, as well as from the implausible future that promises to just be a socially conservative technological utopia. Both of these futures are passive, futures that essentially happen by themselves without citizens trying to make an intentional effort to effect and build their world. They both entail a passive determinism, a political quietism that actively effaces the choices that everyone partakes in every day. These choices, how we work, what we eat, how we dress, and most importantly whether we protest and organize effectively will determine our actual future.

We need to free ourselves from a past, a present and a future imbued with ruling ideas.

Future generations living in an uninhabitable planet weigh like a nightmare on the brains of those presently living.

Chapter Nine

The Holy Trinity of Conservative Thought: God – Nation – Family

In 1917, members of the National Women's Party were peacefully demonstrating in DC, calling on President Woodrow Wilson to grant women the right to vote at the federal level. Thirty-three women were arrested. In prison, the women demanded to be treated as political prisoners. In response, the prison superintendent, William H. Whittaker, called his guard to throw them into cells with regular criminals. He also ordered their torture. Lucy Burns had her hands tied to the top of her cell, forcing her to stand all night. Dora Lewis's head was smashed into an iron bed, and she lost consciousness. Dorothy Day's head was slammed down forcibly into the arm of the iron bench. All three suffered severe wounds.

In 1905, Father Georgy Gapon, a Russian Orthodox priest, organized workers in order to foster among them a truly Christian way of life. He wanted to improve their working conditions without violence or disruption of the law. Father Gapon's respectful petition to the tsar asked for an eight-hour workday, fairer wages, improved conditions, an end to the Russo-Japanese War and universal suffrage. An overwhelming majority of the workers were Orthodox, believed in autocracy and were largely unpolitical. They believed that the tsar was the little father to the big father in the sky, and as they marched, they held religious icons and sang God Save the Tsar! At 11am, soldiers started shooting four volleys into the crowd, then Cossacks on horses started slashing the protestors with swords.

On May 2, 1963, about 700 black children protested segregation in Birmingham, Alabama. The children, who were trained in nonviolent protest, went out of their classes and marched to downtown Birmingham where, as blacks, they were not allowed to be. Hundreds were hit by policemen, arrested and jailed. The day after, when hundreds of additional children showed up again, Public Safety Commissioner Eugene Connor told firemen and police to assault the children with the use of fire hoses, police dogs and batons.

To understand conservative ruling ideas, we first have to understand what leads to their active deployment. I will argue here that they are mostly reactive ideas. Here is how the dynamic works. Some segment of the population makes a certain very reasonable demand, in fact a kind of self-evident demand that they should not have been forced to make in the first place. Slaves or serfs want to stop their subjugation; women want to vote; workers demand livable wages and job security; blacks want to be free to walk, eat and shop wherever they want; and environmentalists ask for a future livable world. The first reaction is shock and active punishment of those who make the demand.

Sometimes after a long and often violent struggle, some demands are accepted. Women are enfranchised, and blacks are desegregated. If they are accepted, conservatives play act as though they were originally for these measures. A conservative on American soil before the American Revolution would be for staying under the king of England; after the revolution, all of a sudden he will be for the Constitution. At one point in history, a Christian conservative will be outraged by the Protestant Reformation; a little later on he will espouse religious freedom. There are no real principles or a genuine concern for the well-being of people, only refusing to grant or even negotiate with people with various legitimate claims. If the demands for reparations for African Americans will be met in the near future, we can be sure that future conservatives will view them as self-evident in the far future. However, in the present, the conflict always rages on, and conservatives need to push back and repress reasonable demands. To cover a lack of principle or basic empathy to legitimate demands, and as they attempt to reassert arbitrary hierarchy and privilege, conservatives have always evoked God, nation and family.

God and Legitimacy

There are not many good arguments as to why a small elite should deny reasonable claims of an overwhelming majority, no wholesome reasons why certain people should exploit and rule over others. Nevertheless, for the past 10,000 years this has been the condition of humanity. How has such a social arrangement been justified and legitimized? For the majority of time in which such an arrangement lasted, that is, from the creation of city-states 10,000 years ago until roughly the French Revolution, some 9,000 years of human history, the answer has been religion. Why is religion so useful for denying the wishes and desires of the many and for legitimizing the power and privilege of the few?

The roots of religion are innocent enough and don't have anything to do with legitimizing hierarchy; as we shall see, religion has in fact been hijacked to perform this function.

The origins of religion lie in our cognitive, emotional and existential relationship with nature.

Humans were and still are vulnerable to nature. It is much easier both emotionally and cognitively to understand natural forces such as the sea, the rain, thunder, the sun and the moon by personifications. We are hardwired to think in terms of *persons*; we find thinking about persons, their motivations, their desires and their actions much easier than to think in terms of natural forces. It is easier for a child to understand a story about the sun and clouds having a fight than to understand low-pressure weather systems. It is not only easier to understand but also to generate a sense of agency and control. If rain is a god and I desperately need rain for my crops, then in contrast to a weather system, I talk (pray) or sacrifice to a rain god. I can feel that I possess a technique for influencing my environment and fate. Together, both the cognitive motivation, understanding the world in terms that I can understand, and the technical-emotional motivation, feeling a sense of agency and control due to having a technique that influences the world, make the creation of spirits and later gods irresistible. And indeed, gods and spirits have been created independently in every human civilization that we know of.

How have gods been hijacked to do the work of legitimizing tiny exploitative elites? Gradually. At first there were relatively nonhierarchical intermediators. The shaman in the village might be a person who is good at organizing the ceremony for the rain god. In the band or the village, the shaman might be respected, but there can be little doubt that he or she is essentially like you and me, maybe with some extraordinary capabilities but basically the same. As villages grow larger and larger, as we move from tribes of hundreds to chiefdoms of thousands, the shaman becomes a full-time professional, working in tandem with village chiefs, who are in charge of granaries, of collection grain and then of redistribution. Gods, though they continue to personify and provide the illusion of control over nature, start doubling as legitimizers of political authority. This development comes naturally as ritual becomes more elaborate and centralized. The chief who runs the granaries with a handful of officials also presides with the shaman/priest over the collection of sacrifices. Once chief and priest organize the ritual, they start in a sense to monopolize the connection with the gods and thus the sense of control and manipulation of nature that comes with this connection. There is a likeness between the role of rulers and priests as collectors and redistributors of agricultural surplus and their role as collectors of sacrifices used to intervene on behalf of the population with the gods who will then facilitate better crops and defend against enemies. We can view this as two kinds of circulation: circulation of grain and circulation that turns the sacrifices to the gods into favorable conditions. What is important is the monopoly on certain crucial nodes in this circulation. In the case of grain, it is the granaries that turn temporary value into value that lasts, this in contrast to meat, vegetables and fruit of hunter-gatherers that rot. In the case of the circulation of sacrifices – turned to godly favors, the priests monopolize the crucial node of the temple. It is in the temple that offerings turn into good intentions of gods to create a good environment for people, an environment that can produce grain and sacrifices. Those who own this node in the circulation, those who build and run the temple, the rulers and priests, win legitimacy.

As collections of villages turn into giant city-states, those priests and rulers become increasingly distant from the people. Using impressive architecture that evokes hierarchy and transcendence, massive rituals that monopolize the sacred, and police and army that monopolize violence, they can convince the population in a topsy-turvy image of the world in which the entire population is existentially dependent upon the ruler, rather than the actual truth that the ruler is totally dependent on them. If rain comes after sacrifices, the ruler appears as part of the sublime grandeur of the natural world, a dominant force in the universe itself. From the ruler's perspective, he has succeeded in harnessing the cognitive proclivities and emotional needs of the people in their relation to nature for his own legitimacy.

It is true that manipulating nature through the gods was not the only source of legitimacy for rulers. Often the ruler is presented as the one who smashes the people's enemies. In contrast to controlling nature, which the rulers cannot actually do, they can protect from external enemies. Though this might seem a wholly rational source of legitimization free from irrationalism, it is not completely so. First, it is the army that protects from enemies, not the ruler; second, rulers regularly appeal to gods in order to help them win battles and wars against their enemies. The outcome of wars is at least as unpredictable as nature; people have responded to this uncertainty with the creation of gods of war. If the ruler has a special relationship with this god of war, then, again, this ruler wins more legitimacy for whatever decision he takes.

Let's take Ancient Egypt as an example of how all this works together. Pharaohs of Egypt were divine all-powerful rulers; they acted as intermediaries between the people and the gods. The gods needed to be sustained by rituals, sacrifices and offerings. Crucial sacrifices and rituals (those that were felt to sustain the gods) could only take place in state-owned temples; that is, the Pharaohs controlled the space in which significant influence over the gods could take place.[1] Ancient Egyptian religious myth centered on the conflict between Ma'at and Isfet. Ma'at is variously translated as truth, harmony, law, morality and justice. Isfet means violence, disorder, evil and difficulty. The Egyptian Pharaoh's role is to uphold and create Ma'at, that is, to constantly be on guard against Isfet, and whenever there is a disturbance to reestablish order. Ma'at represents the cyclical order of the universe, the raising and setting of the sun, and the annual flooding of the Nile, etc. Various things could disturb this order. Sandstorms can cover crops; the Nile can fail to flood properly, causing famine; or flash flooding can suddenly ruin crops. Foreign enemies also threaten Ma'at, and the king is most often presented in reliefs as holding his enemies by the hair and preparing to smash their skulls with a mace. Death itself is a disturbance of Ma'at, and the pyramids are essentially a technology used to uphold Ma'at by making the Pharaoh immortal.

Being divine or being uniquely connected with the divine creates several advantages in terms of ruling over others. Some of these advantages were thrown into greater relief in monotheistic tradition initiated by Pharaoh Akhenaten (1352-1336 BC) as the short-lived monotheistic cult of Aten the Sun God. Monotheism made imperial sense in imperial Egypt. It unifies all the different cults under one all-powerful god. The cult took hold for a while but then ultimately faced a backlash. Nevertheless, it continued with what would become the Israelites, and resulted in a religious revolution of the ancient world. The capricious, vengeful God of the Old Testament is in one way a continuation of the Pharaoh (he smashes enemies); in other ways he is unique in being formless, he does not represent any natural entity.

From the point of view of rulers, monotheism is indeed very useful. A formless, transcendent God is allowed the utmost freedom. Claiming to be chosen by God and following God's words provides a ruler with maximal leeway, and almost any political action can be cast as His will; it does not need any further legitimation. In contrast to Dostoyevsky who said without God anything is possible, in reality it is the legitimization of God that makes everything possible: crusades, inquisitions, colonialization and suicide bombings.

However, let's start with a milder example, the story of King David from the Old Testament, as it is more representative of the sometimes subtle ways in which God does the work of legitimization for rulers. The King David narrative is essentially a story of a nobody who came from nowhere, that is, with no royal and hence "legitimate" background, who usurps the rule of King Saul. A neutral retelling of the story would make David a power-hungry thug. The beauty of the biblical God is that one can make the story of a gangster coming into power into something both mysterious and legitimate. The story starts with the delegitimization of King Saul. God disfavors him because he unlawfully offers a sacrifice and does not kill all of the Amalekites. These two reasons are so arbitrary that any perceptive reader would understand that they were invented after the fact in order to legitimize David's rule. In response to those "offenses," Samuel (Saul's personal prophet), who in a godless historical narrative could not be conceived of as other than a traitor to his king, anoints a son of Jesse of Bethlehem whom God in dramatic fashion, after showing all of Jesse's other sons, reveals to him. The nice thing about God is that nobody knows what he wants. David wins popularity with the people (in retrospect, one can always claim to have been popular with the people) and then flees Saul, who rightfully suspects that David would like to usurp him. Conveniently, in a private meeting with no other witnesses, Saul's son Jonathan (the rightful heir!) comes and confirms his loyalty to David as the future king of Israel. David has the opportunity to kill Saul in a cave in Ein Gedi and spares him, an event that again nobody witnesses. In short, the whole story is a concocted fairy tale designed to create legitimacy to a new line of David's house. In many ways, both subtle and blunt, from the beginning to the end, God's wishes, anger and will function similarly to secret meetings in caves that nobody saw; they are both just inventions that legitimize David's rule.

This type of legitimization narrative is highly effective. I myself read the story while doing an MA in literature and, to my great shame, can say that I did not recognize the main point of the story. I naively thought Saul was problematic and moody, and David was young, charismatic and charitable. And though I am an atheist, the will of God somehow also played its role in making me root for David. Was I thinking that the story was created merely for aesthetic enjoyment? That it's art for art's sake, the kind of thing the bourgeoisie invented more than 1,500 years later. Now, when I read the story again, I imagine the scribes who wrote it showing the story to David or his descendants as they nod their heads in approval.

God can subtly legitimize almost anything because no one knows what the will of God is, and the public can be made to believe a version of historical events in which God's will coincides with that of the ruler. There is no need for decisions to be constrained by the interests of the greater good, or even to give reasons for one's policy. Thus, rulers all over the world have orchestrated stories of them being elected by God to rule; sometimes God "tells" them to build churches or provide charity, sometimes to go to war, take taxes, conquer other people and decimate them, execute those who dissent, convert the natives, and burn the heretics. This principle is still directly invoked today in several countries including Afghanistan, Iran, Mauritania, Saudi Arabia, Sudan and Yemen. It is also indirectly used by leaders in countries with a Christian majority. For example, the repetition of the formula "God bless America" spoken by all US presidents, or the way Orthodox heads of church endorse Russian presidents, lends a kind of legitimacy to whatever they decide to do.

The idea of God is one of the most successful ideas in the world because it serves a double function. There are, so to speak, two gods tied into one idea: the god of legitimization (the political god) and the psychological/spiritual god. It is hard to resist the idea of a calming parental figure in the sky who created the universe and has a plan for you and is watching over you. A being that is like a parent who tells you to be good, who deliciously restricts both eating and sexuality (not to have sex before marriage or eating only Halal). A being that generates both shame for not complying as well as pride in compliance, inflicting punishment on the one hand but is also open to influence by talk (prayer) on the other.

The best metaphor to understand the relationship to God is sexual submission. This might seem outlandish at first, but I do believe that much of the pleasures of God are of a certain type of erotic joy that is unwilling to admit itself as such. Once we look at their interaction it is easy to see that the relationship between God and the believer is highly similar to those between a dominant and a submissive. Both the interaction and even the words used are almost identical. Submissives and believers are told to do service and degrading things; this might mean kissing shoes or prostrating oneself head down on a carpet in the direction of Mecca. They are both made to say self-effacing things to the effect, "I am nothing before you, I am just a worm of the earth, forgive me I have been sinful, you are the most important thing in the universe, you are so powerful, there is no one else but you, punish me and let me sacrifice things for you." Both God and dominants like to restrict masturbation; God does not like it when you waste your seed in vain. If the dominant does allow you to masturbate in front of him or her you might enjoy her telling you that you are bad and filthy. God's instruction in the Bible is of the same drift. In Deuteronomy 23:10 it is written: "If any man among you becomes unclean because of a nocturnal emission, then he shall go outside the camp. He shall not come inside the camp..." or Leviticus 15:16-18: "If a man has an emission of semen, he shall bathe his whole body in water and be unclean until the evening. And every garment and every skin on which the semen comes shall be washed with water and be unclean until the evening." Your God is likely to dislike pigs and your dominant might call you a disgusting one. The more adventurous male BDSM player might be emasculated or sissified, that is, his masculinity will be brought down in various ways, like wearing women's panties or a chastity device. The religious equivalent is circumcision, a subtle reminder that you are not fully a man, you are partially castrated. If you are a female heterosexual submissive, of course, the analogy works even better. Big Daddy in the sky thinks that you are a slut. He may ask you to cover your whole body and face with a black niqab. As one fully niqabed YouTuber said, "I feel close to Allah; when I wear the niqab, I can feel him around me, I can talk to him, I can practice and be of service to him, I feel at peace." Submissives describe subspace, the psychological result of an effective scene, as a feeling that only "my top exists." One feels high and "dizzy with joyful feelings"; most relate a feeling of floating or flying; and people become unable to talk and are surrounded with a kind of quietness. I would not like to reduce religion to just the erotic; clearly there is a layer of the metaphysical in which this dominant is also master of the whole universe and can overcome death as well as offer redemption, but at its emotional relational core, energy comes from an erotic dominant/submissive relationship. It is this kind of relationship that religious people look for, without admitting it to themselves.

It is not the philosophers', pantheistic God who is nature itself, or sophisticated theologians' God that died on the cross that most believers believe in. It is God as a sublime cosmic parental dominant that 99 percent of believers find peace in. It is this parental God that is one side of the coin of the political God used to legitimize authority over people. Thus, rulers have an interest in propagating the idea of God and people find much comfort and pleasure in it. A truthful spectator of human history can only be indignant that rulers all over the world for thousands of years have used a comforting and erotic mental prothesis in order to rule over and exploit humanity for their own power and benefit.

One has to concede that the idea of God or the sacred has sometimes been instrumental in liberation struggles, from the story of Moses to historical figures such as Thomas Müntzer, Gandhi, Martin Luther King Jr., Malcolm X and the movements associated with them. Sometimes, like the case of Thomas Müntzer in the sixteenth century, religion is the common tongue; one cannot speak about people's aspirations for freedom and equality without it. But if we think more deeply, do liberation struggles really need the idea of God? Does one need God to challenge slavery, colonialism, exploitation at work, sexism and racial segregation?

The appealing emotional core of the idea of God centers around its dominant parental erotic appeal. However, in contrast to a negotiated sex scene, it is problematic to go around the world with a vague notion that some dominant is both directing you but somehow also following your script. This belief, though pleasantly sedative (Marx compared it rightly to opium), thwarts various kinds of dark but necessary illuminations. Illusions can often hinder a truthful perception of the situation as well as subtly retard the thought of possibilities, and in this way helping the status quo and those who rule. Uncritical pleasure is a fictional authority that stands over you, looks after you, knows what you should do, has a plan for you, and in one instance may predispose you to think fuzzily and uncritically about real life authorities *who do not have your best interests at heart*. The whole emotional, existential, intellectual, relational attitude that religion inspires is that of submission and lack of effective action. Praying, keeping Halal or Kosher, or thinking that one is especially sinful will not change your fate; nor will it promote the common good. It does, however, predispose you to accept the authority of the community and ultimately its leaders without exercising reason.

The relationship to women and children prescribed by God's laws regarding divorce, abortion, circumcision, etc., exemplifies this blind acceptance of authority. If someone else can decide whether you can separate or not from your husband, have an abortion or not, are considered impure because of your menstruation, have to thank the maker for not making you a woman, and can cut a baby's penis following an order, all of this runs over the boundaries of playful consensual eroticism. If half of humanity is at the same time both unclean and poses an irresistible temptation, and should therefore be controlled in various ways – this is no longer an expression of sexuality but a repression of it that makes subjects compliant. Repressing one's own sexuality, with no real outlet, the whole catalog of sexual offenses, some like masturbation ones that generate *certain* transgression, serves to create subjects that learn to follow authority even if it goes against their intuitions and desires.

Subjects are not to question the repression of their sexuality; they are to repress their sexual feelings and, surprisingly, also put to the side their feelings of ordinary morality. For example, circumcision demonstrates clearly that one should put away one's usual feelings for babies and comply with cutting them in the flesh. In traditional Jewish Orthodox communities, this includes having a grown man suck the cut penis of an eight-day-old baby, in a rite called *metsitsah b'peh*, with attendant risks of transmitting disease. Since 2000, in New York alone, there have been 13 reports of infants contracting HSV-1, a type of herpes, and two of the babies have died from the condition. For my purposes it is important to stress how this ritual, just like the story of the binding of Isaac by Abraham, essentially teaches us that authority is beyond ordinary morality and human feeling. Violence against children is mandated again and again. For example, in Deuteronomy 21:18-21 it says:

> If a man has a stubborn and rebellious son who will not obey the voice of his father or the voice of his mother, and who, when they have chastened him, will not heed them, then his father and his mother shall take hold of him and bring him out to the elders of his city, to the gate of his city. And they shall say to the elders of his city, "This son of ours is stubborn and rebellious; he will not obey our voice; he is a glutton and a drunkard." Then all the men of his city shall stone him to death with stones; so you shall put away the evil from among you, and all Israel shall hear and fear.

Calling children who do not accept religious teaching evil, *rasha* is quite popular to this day. For example, I have been called evil several times in my own lifetime, by Jewish religious teachers in Modern Conservative Jewish day school. The word *evil* flies easily out of the mouths of the religious. Perhaps our culture's fascination with psychopaths, serial killers and Nazis instead of looking into the conditions that generate mass incarceration, immiseration and fascism also has religious roots.

God readily enjoins his people to get over their natural squeamishness about killing women and children. In Numbers 31:17-18, He says, "Now therefore kill every male among the little ones, and kill every woman that hath known man by lying with him. But all the women children, that have not known a man by lying with him, keep alive for yourselves." In fact, at several places, he admonishes leaders for not being genocidal enough.

Collective punishment of those with no responsibility abounds in the Bible. This includes visiting the sins of fathers "unto the third and fourth generation" and the commandment in Exodus 20:17 that rules out having certain thoughts and feelings: "you shall not covet your neighbor's house. You shall not covet your neighbor's wife, or his male or female servant, his ox or donkey, or anything that belongs to your neighbor." Since both envy and mimicry are natural to our species, this law amounts to the most unnatural thought and emotion control. In all likelihood this law was legislated as the ultimate tool for tyranny, as anyone at any time can be accused of this thought crime. There is a milder version of this. If one really internalizes injunctions against masturbation or coveting one's neighbor's wife and feels guilty about them, then this too opens a path to control and exploit others, for example, by selling indulgences, accepting donations or simply greater attention given to the voice of religious authorities that finds an echo within, a sensitivity that can be used by religious authorities in all manner of ways.

Self-repression is also a highly effective mechanism for steering attention away from society. More precisely it posits "bad" individuals and desires and then legitimizes social hierarchies as necessary to control these individuals. This type of ploy for social hierarchy and control found secular variants in Hobbes, who in this way legitimated the sovereign that prevents war of all against all as well as in Freud, who essentially legitimated the patriarchal father of the family as the one who prevents incest. However, regardless of the way in which Hobbes and Freud secularized this doctrine, it is the Bible that invented it.

The picture of an unruly human being that needs to be controlled by a society that is hierarchical, with God at the top, has been the predominant picture of the world in the West for more than 2,000 years. The very longevity of this picture encouraged seeing the social order as essentially fixed. The idea that the structure and hierarchy of human society is God-given and eternal, an idea that people in the Middle Ages entertained for almost 1,000 years, is now accepted by most as untrue. Change has been too rapid for us to sustain this belief. I would estimate that 95 percent of the world's population have grandparents who lived very different lives than they do, often in different places doing different things. This is certainly true for more than a billion people in India, China, Africa and the Middle East, who have only in the past 50 years moved from living as farmers in villages to living as various service providers in giant cities. This is certainly true for migrants, as the number of people living in a country other than the one they were born in has tripled since 1970; if we add both parents and grandparents who have migrated, the number becomes significant. People's occupations have also changed, and, of course, the communication technology of each generation (radio, television, cable, internet, mobile phone, streaming service, etc.) has changed how and what kind of information people consume.

Nevertheless, though change is relentless, many still have

inherited an essentially religious worldview in which the world in its most fundamental attributes has changed less. The most important changes have taken place in the past, specifically, the revelation of Moses, and the coming of Jesus and Mohammad, and there will be another important change in the future, the second or the original first coming of the Messiah, resurrection and judgment; however, until that time, the most fundamental aspects of society are static. Many secular people might at this point feel a slight sense of superiority that their sense of history is much more aligned with reality; they recognize change. Nevertheless, there are secular versions of this no-change doctrine. Believing in the eternal validity of a constitution, for example, is one such belief. It is reasonable that as society and the world change, the fundamental legal framework should change as well. There is no a priori reason why what people formulated at the end of the eighteenth century should be binding for all eternity. Another such belief is the vague sense that hierarchy and inequality are eternal, somehow etched into the essence of society. Sometimes this is given sophisticated sociological treatments such as sociologist Robert Michel's iron law of oligarchy, which states that rule by elite is inevitable, an iron law! Any organization, regardless of how democratic it started and aspires to be, becomes an oligarchy. Michel started as an anarcho-syndicalist believing in democratic organization of workers; he slowly drifted from the left until in 1924 he joined the Italian Fascist Party. However, one does not need to be a fascist to believe in Michel's iron law; many liberals hold it implicitly as well. The law itself is false; not only did humanity for 98 percent of its time on Earth live in egalitarian hunter-gatherer societies, but there have been numerous successful attempts at democratic organizing that stayed democratic. More than one billion people from 96 countries are members of co-ops that are run democratically. Some of these co-ops are models of democratic governance; in none of them can decisions such as firing workers or moving production to China take place. However, even without these existing examples, history teaches us that novel social formations arise all the time. For example, the corporation is only 300 years old.

Systems and their characteristics are alterable; all systems change and thus there are possibilities to change them. The idea of God usually does the work of legitimizing existing rulers who in turn would like their subjects not to think about other possibilities but to see current social arrangements as somehow necessary.

Nation and Race as Conservative Strategies

Often the nation presents itself as living in a world of enemies. Its policies are seen as a defense against unpredictable and dangerous opponents. National rivalries and wars have been extensive and, in many ways, devastating. Contrary to sanguine globalization forecasts that were made in the 1990s, such conflicts do not belong to the past. In fact, the forecast itself, which said that conflicts between nations are obsolete, that there will only be asymmetrical wars between great nations and terrorist or insurgent groups, was largely Eurocentric. The statement was made only a couple of years after an eight-year war between Iraq and Iran (1980-1988) that killed approximately two million people. Nor are such conflicts relegated to the past. At the time that I am writing this we seem to be facing a long-term escalation of conflict between the US and China. Nevertheless, I would argue that such conflicts as well as their corresponding nationalism, racism and imperialism are mostly articulated for domestic reasons.

We have Eckart Keher (1902-1933) to thank for the motto "the primacy of domestic politics." His most important work was his doctoral thesis "Battle Fleet Construction and Party Politics in Germany, 1894-1901: A Cross-Section of the Political, Social and Ideological Preconditions of German Imperialism." Before this dissertation, the most prestigious historians such as Ranke wrote histories in which state leaders looked after the national interests of the people. Such histories exemplified the primacy of foreign politics of the nation against other nations. Ranke shared with Bismarck the belief that society with its inner turmoil and conflicts should be subordinated to projecting strength abroad. The nation stood above all the particular interests of the groups that comprised it.

Eckart Keher was assigned by his largely famous conservative *doctorvater* historian Friedrich Meinecke to write a dissertation on reasons of state in the late nineteenth and early twentieth centuries. Keher chose to study the various groups that led to the decision to build the great German battle fleet during the years 1884-1901. He looked at the attitudes of different German classes, parties and status groups. His finding was that the naval bill passed largely for domestic reasons. The bill passed because of the unique needs of the old Junker aristocracy in coalition with the new industrialists. The Junker aristocracy wanted to keep tariffs on grain that would help them generate revenue from their large landholdings. Industrialists who opposed the tariffs agreed to keep them on condition that the government commission a great steel battle fleet; a significant proportion of this large commission would go to the industrialists themselves. The foreign "threat" to national shipping interests was used to get the masses to acquiesce with using state expenditure (generated from taxes) to essentially enrich the industrialists. Such domestic motivation for war repeats itself reliably most dramatically in the decision to invade Iraq in 2003.

If we step back from specific instances, we can ask what the fundamental use of the "national interest" by elites is. The idea of national interest has several functions. First of all, it covers up for the radically different and often opposing interests that elites and the majority of people have. By presenting their interests as national interests, elites can "stitch" together the chasm that separates them from regular people. More precisely, they deflect from the difference between them and regular people toward the difference between their nation and other nations.

On a psychological level, nationalism builds on the fact that familiarity breeds liking. For example, most people like the food that they ate as kids; they are used to the way their environment feels, to its day-to-day rituals, to connecting with family and friends, to national sports team and national entertainment; and they are most comfortable with their native language. The national idea builds on feelings of love of place and its people and personifies them with a name of the nation. These experiences and feelings are in a sense nationalized; they come to be seen as constituted by the nation-state. An expatriate British man who lives in China might miss British television, the soccer league, talking in English in the street, sitting in an English pub, etc., all of which will have a special place for him; he feels that he is attached to the nation.

However, attachment to the nation is made to go deeper. Often nations are conceived as eternal and extremely powerful and, as we saw, exceptional. Regular people take pride and vicarious satisfaction in things that they had no actual part in.

Germans may feel pride for being "Das Land der Dichter und Denker," land of poets and thinkers; Brits, Americans and Russians *today* feel pride that their respective national "we" supposedly vanquished the Nazis more than 75 years ago; and the Chinese may be proud to have the oldest continuous civilization. Billions around the world (including myself) feel joy as "their" team wins an Olympic sport or progresses to the next stage in the World Cup. Indeed, the main draw of nationalism is a vicarious feeling of power; this can be a subtle feeling of pride when a conational wins a Noble Prize or the more blunt enjoyment of participants in nationalist political rallies in which the leader invokes how powerful, exceptional and great the nation is.

Nevertheless, however great the nation is, every nationalist will also present his or her nation as a victim. This is not hard to do since most countries around the world have suffered either colonialization or invasion at some point. Thus, nationalists across India, Africa and the Middle East can rightfully point out that they have been subjected to colonial rule or are threatened by empire. An Iranian nationalist, for example, can quite reasonably be afraid that the US will conquer and devastate her country like it did Iraq. A Chinese or Russian nationalist can claim that the US is stationing nuclear arms all along their borders, and that they have been genocidally victimized by invasions from imperial powers in the past (Japan for China, Nazi Germany for Russia). These historical conditions make nationalism easy to use by elites who would like to efface the differences between them and the people. While in some cases this might be warranted, such as when a nation is colonized by various foreign powers, for example, Algeria, Vietnam, India, etc.; however, the minute that the nation is free from colonial rule, nationalism usually turns exploitative.

More inventive is nationalist victim discourse in the US, a place that has never suffered a serious invasion and is the most powerful country in the world. Donald Trump, for example, took pains to construct US workers as economic victims of China. He talked about trade agreements in which the US is disadvantaged and that had cost workers and ordinary Americans billions. The truth is, of course, more mundane. US workers are directly affected by their employers. If factory owners and management choose to cut production costs and leave for China, then their workers remain jobless. However, right-wing leaders all over the world use nationalist discourse to mask their preference to help owners rather than workers and conveniently project economic hardships on foreign countries. It allows leaders to present themselves as working for regular people while furthering the interests of economic elites. What is remarkable is that though the above analysis is objective to the extent that even conservative historians claim this was indeed the strategy used in many countries, from Hitler's Germany to Russia to China, still, to middle-class ears it will sound somehow too radical and conspiratorial for one's own country. The fact that many people both on the right and in the center *feel* that this analysis is too harsh; that it's too negative just shows how effective national feelings are. There is a general lack of acceptance of the collaboration between moneyed interests and power at the expense of people who work rather than own for a living.

As an intense form of reactionary nationalism, Nazism is a good lens to see what nationalism does and is at its most extreme. Liberal elites like to focus on the Nazi regime's murderous racism. In the West, one's main association with the Nazis has to do with extermination of the Jewish people. Yet any history textbook will tell you plainly that the origins of the Nazi movement were anti-communist. The Nazi movement originated with discharged World War One German soldiers who were used to crush socialist and communist uprisings in the Weimar Republic. A little later, German conservatives and business elites helped Hitler to power out of fear of communism and because he promised them that they would be able to keep their property. Nazism was first and foremost an anti-communist movement in the post-1917 world, a world after the Russian Revolution. To this day, a conservative historian like Ernst Nolte can unabashedly and quite correctly see Nazism as an important force that helped check and hold back the USSR Bolshevism from taking over Europe. In the twentieth century, one of the most important roles of reactionary nationalism was to counter communism.

Communism, unlike the Jews, posed a real threat to the status quo. The Jews in Weimar Germany were not a group with a coherent agenda. There were conservative Jewish bankers and merchants, Jewish communist revolutionaries, ardently German nationalist soldiers, bohemian artists, bourgeoise doctors and lawyers, and working-class immigrants from Eastern Europe. The most you can say about them as a group is that they have shown a tendency for immaterial production as well as a kind of modernizing tendency – as shown by the relative high percentage of Jews at the forefront of capitalism, science, arts and socialism.

Needless to say, there is nothing Jewish about capitalism, socialism, arts or sciences; all have been developed by non-Jews before Jewish integration into Gentile society. Even typifying Jews as somehow modernizing is not strictly true as many chose to remain traditionalist or Orthodox. Nazism arose not to battle or decimate the Jews but to win the hearts and minds of German workers *away* from socialism and communism. The Jews were just an expendable scapegoat, an internal enemy, that helped make German workers feel that they somehow had the same interest and the same enemy as their German employers did. Various disruptions whose source is capitalism itself, like militant worker movements and the financial crash of 1928, could be conveniently blamed on the Jews. There is nothing peculiarly German or even Nazi about this kind of scapegoat politics; it has been exercised to great effect all around the world. In the history of the United States we regularly see how poor whites are tethered to rich whites by inciting hatred toward blacks and natives. American exceptionalism and nationalism is regularly used to support the privileges of the status quo. More precisely, race nationalism is used regularly to reassert a status quo that is being challenged by those with less privilege.

"For things to remain the same, everything must change," is a famous quote from the historical novel *The Leopard*, set during the time of civil war and revolution in Italy in the nineteenth century. The hero, the nobleman Don Fabrizo Corbera, Prince of Salina, has to choose between upholding upper-class values and breaking with tradition in order to secure the continuity of the family line for his nephew, Tancredi. It is Tancredi who says the line. If anything from the old order is to remain, one must vigorously innovate. And indeed, conservativism must be highly inventive.

Fascism was the new conservative innovation of the twentieth century. Until that point, conservativism relied on a mixture of religious pity, the glamor of nobility, and money from the newly rich for material support. In the early twentieth century, conservatives faced a problem: how to maintain elite power in an age of mass mobilization. Faced with this irrepressible force of democratization and revolution of the early twentieth century, things had to change in order for them to stay the same. There was a need to appease the masses, to give them something, but this something could not detract from the power and wealth of those in power. Race and nation became this "something": a new kind of pseudo-nobility, a new kind of blue blood, that would not take anything away from the elite, but would let the masses feel superior toward "inferior" minorities in their own country and certainly over others of conquered lands. Race privilege formed the core content of the new conservative ideology. This core was supplemented by the outward form of socialist solidarity. In its outward form and political technology, the Nazis borrowed from socialist workers parties, the parades, youth organizations, political organization and proletarian dress. Thus, we have a new thing in the twentieth century – fascism, a conservative revolution in the name of the race/nation dressed up in socialist drag. While back in the middle of the nineteenth century, Marx correctly saw that socialism would be a formidable force in the future, no one could have imagined that fascism and reactionary nationalism would be such a potent force to counter it in the twentieth century.

Conservative strategy has to reinvent itself constantly since it is always challenged by progressive forces. Today, we are also witnessing several innovations in conservativism, and indeed some of them take their cue from the left as well. One such innovation is the adoption and even celebration of victimhood. Once upon a time, conservatives celebrated power, the glory of nobility, "joy through strength" of Nazism; they were adamant in telling the weak that they were simply resentful of the strong. Today, there is very little of this. Copying the liberal culture on college campuses, the New Right incessantly complains about being weak and feeling unsafe – a kind of snowflaky right. The Swiss, French and British alt-right proclaim a white genocide or white extinction. Anti-immigration protestors hold a sign that says, "Diversity is the code word for white genocide."

According to this ideology, the global liberal elite is colluding against the white population of Europe in order to replace them with non-European peoples. For example, in an interview on YouTube, French intellectual Renaud Camus argues that future European people will suffer a similar fate to Native Americans; they will be lucky to possess the rights to open casinos on their reservations.[2] British writer Douglas Murray writes that Europe is committing suicide by bringing in immigration and losing faith in its beliefs due to guilt over colonialism and the Holocaust.[3] Right-wing pundits in Europe regularly make the claim that each people have their own country, the Japanese have Japan, the Iranians Iran; only Europe is the country for everyone. Such claims are highly distortive. The claim, for instance, that Europe is the country for everyone is in fact a stunning reversal, a topsy-turvy image of history. In fact, for the past 400 years, the whole world, from South America to Australia, has been the country of Western Europeans.

One notices here that in Europe the right does not speak strictly in the language of old nationalism of the nation-state, but in the language of a new European identity. Things must change in order for things to stay the same. In order to keep racial privilege and hierarchy, it accepts the European Union, something *unthinkable* for every nationalist only 30 years ago. Right-wing nationalists no longer see themselves as German, French, Swedish, etc., but as "white" Europeans. In a sense, the name conservativism is a kind of misnomer for their politics; conservatives are both willing to accept change as well as instigate it as long as it helps with their power and privilege. In reality, there is nothing objective that they are trying to conserve, such as nature, culture or tradition. The only thing that they are trying to "conserve" is their own privilege and power. This manifests itself in the confusing logic of conservative argument, when conservatives in Europe want the king and nobility back while those conservatives in the US want those rich-white-men groups to be the only ones with power, a group that precisely deposed the king.

At the end of the day, it is difficult to argue in cognizant rational terms for arbitrary privilege of a particular ethnic or racial group. Motivation is usually a mixture of fear and greed – feelings that don't make for cogent argument. Yet at the same time we must remember that just as the motivation toward equality, the "fluid" of egalitarianism moves through our thoughts and feelings and ultimately comes to illuminate our politics, culture and society, so does the thought of inequality. There is a strange and almost ancient cohesion and appeal to the image of society with exploitable subjects at the bottom, and enemies to be killed, or negotiated with outside. Once such a society was ruled by nobles and the church, now it is ruled by the billionaires and politicians, but the way in which such societies treat those who work, the way its subjects are tethered to rulers, the way it compensates for this by drawing distortive pictures of an "us" and a "them" remains the same. It is willing to change much in order for things to stay the same. Thus, a French conservative like Renaud Camus often has no problem with the European Union; they don't want to get into a war with England or Germany like they did in the past; they don't really try to conserve the glories of France against the "great displacement"; they simply attempt to sustain and enhance the privileges of European citizenship, the currently relevant privilege.

Conservatives necessarily repress history and reality. France, for example, conquered Algiers in 1830 and kept it under colonial and exploitative rule for 132 years. During this time, the French in Algiers were not foreign migrant workers; they were the masters of the country. The majority of wealth produced in the land went to them and to France, the mother country. Currently, approximately 3.5 percent of the French population are Algerians, most of them doing menial jobs that French people of European origin would not like to do. It takes much distortion, even a certain inward ugliness, to pretend that France has kept to itself and is now being invaded by outside barbarian hordes that threaten Western civilization or something called Judeo-Christianity.

Conservatives like to evoke anxiety and fear regarding Western civilization. However, their use of the concept of Western civilization is empty rhetoric; it's not really about the West or about civilization. We know this because the very concept of Western civilization and its boundaries is quite contingent on its political needs. For instance, central Europe under the Soviets was definitely not the West and now it is. More interesting is the case of South America. By religion and language, it is definitely part of the core of what can be considered Western civilization, and yet a Christian person speaking Spanish who attempts to cross the border between Mexico and Texas is not treated as someone from the West.

More telling still is the political opportunism of the new hyphenated term Judeo-Christianity, used now almost everywhere. For more than 1,000 years, this term would have looked ludicrous. Are not the Jews the stubborn people who killed Christ, did not Pilate wash his hands and declare himself innocent of Jewish blood, did not the crowd say, "His blood be on us and on our children!" (Matthew 27:25, RSV)? Did not St Stephen say the following to the synagogue council before his execution?

> You stiff-necked people, uncircumcised in heart and ears, you always resist the Holy Spirit. As your fathers did, so do you. Which of the prophets did your fathers not persecute? And they killed those who announced beforehand the coming of the Righteous One, whom you have now betrayed and murdered, you who received the law as delivered by angels and did not keep it.

Judeo-Christianity, of course, did not exist after Christianity became the state religion in Rome in the fourth century. Intermarriage was prohibited, and conversion to Judaism was outlawed. In the fifth century, the edicts of Codex Theordosianus barred Jews from the army, civil service and legal professions. Synagogues were actively destroyed all through the fifth and sixth centuries. All through the Middle Ages, Jews experienced blood libels, accusations of host desecration, periodic expulsions from both France and England, forced conversions, and burnings. The Crusades decimated Jewish communities in Germany and France. Jews were often blamed for the Black Death. The inquisition in Spain forced either conversion or death or expulsion. Martin Luther wrote a short book, *On the Jews and Their Lies*, which calls on his Christian brethren to perform pogroms against them. In many periods, the more authentically Christian you were, the more you hated the Jews. This history goes on up to the Holocaust.

From the Jewish side, things don't look much better. Judaism is a "tribal" counter-religion that was based on a strong antagonism with its surroundings, whether Egypt or Canaan and then Christianity. It developed laws and moral codes specifically designed to differentiate and reject interaction with surrounding peoples. Specifically, the relationship with Christianity is based on a vehement rejection of Jesus and Christianity. In fact, some scholars claim that we should not look at Judaism as a religion that existed prior to Christianity, a parent religion, but as a sister religion, that both were born together. It's not only that Christianity explicitly articulated itself in the rejection of many of the attributes of Judaism (e.g., legalism) but that Judaism articulated itself as a rejection of Christianity.[4] Thus there is a great fault line, a border between Judaism and Christianity that cannot be ignored. And yet today many use in a seemingly unproblematic way the term Judeo-Christianity. What is the reason for that?

For Jewish conservatives of America and Europe who finally have a full and legitimate seat at the table, the term indicates that they have, so to speak, "arrived," that they are part of the elite, no longer strangers or minorities but a central part of the "Western" tradition. For non-Jewish elites, the term Judeo-Christianity constitutes a facile denial of the violent anti-Judaic past. Most importantly for both the term marks a new alliance against the Muslims who are not part of Judeo-Christianity. The latter, of course, is the most important use of the term. The fact that Islam in various ways is just as important for Western culture (without Islam, there is no Plato in the West, for instance) is also conveniently repressed.

Aside from the opportunism of Judeo-Christianity, the very concept of Western culture and identity is finally belied by the fact that Christianity itself, the supposed core of Western identity, comes from the Middle East.

Perhaps some will retort that the core of the West is not Christianity, that in fact what distinguishes it are the ideas of the Enlightenment, of progress and equality. Certainly, one can argue that the Enlightenment originated in Europe; still,

239

it has certainly not remained exclusive to the West. The Soviet Union, China and Vietnam adopted communism, heir to the Enlightenment, an ideological system most energetically bent on both progress and equality; and, of course, they are seen as the antithesis of the West. Of course, liberal democracy is also not exclusive to the West, as India is the world's largest democracy.

The incoherence of the concept of the West reveals that its true purpose is not to describe any real tradition or past entity but simply to keep and strengthen the privileges of Anglo-American capitalists and their allies in Western Europe above everyone else. This is clearly shown by the contradictory way in which the other is represented. Sometimes the other is a fundamentalist Muslim, sometimes a communist, sometimes she is black, sometimes a Jew or homosexual. In fact, the only thing that these "others" have in common is that they may challenge the supremacy of a tiny but powerful group of rich men of Western European origin. However, saying I want my tiny group to be on top of the world is pretty arbitrary. Like the way royalty of olden times used to impress on the masses their legitimacy through pomp and circumstance, grandeur, glamor and opulence of mansions, palaces, coronations and processions, today talk of Western civilization serves to legitimize a tiny ruling elite using a hodgepodge of things that people are impressed with such as the Bible, Greek philosophy, classical music, French novels, the art of the Renaissance, and science and technology. These really quite disparate and conflicting achievements have little to do with one another.

Even more unintelligibly, they are sometimes tied together as if a distinct national genius is at the source of all these very different achievements. This is indeed a core ruling idea that has no basis in any kind of reality. Every existing nation-state is in fact an amalgam of achievements and traditions taken from the most diverse sources. The Ancient Greeks did not invent writing, the Hebrews did not invent monotheism, and the US did not invent liberalism or even the main principles of its own Constitution. Needless to say, African universities teach relativity theory, Thailand pasteurizes its milk and Russians listen to hip-hop.

Though the idea of a nation or a race as a distinct autonomous entity with a distinct culture is clearly false, we must acknowledge the profoundly satisfying emotions associated with the nation. Most of us lead fairly limited lives filled with small concerns and anxieties; will I get a promotion, will my apartment be devalued, can I get my children into a good school? At the same time, we are called by nationalist discourse to be a part of a great nation: a nation that for some (Chinese, Indians) stretches from time immemorial and is associated with a sublime highly sophisticated and refined culture. Newer nations such as France, Spain, England and the US. have been rulers of the modern world whose empires and influence covered the whole world. A nationalist can feel a sense of pride that a co-nationalist has won a Nobel Prize or a gold medal in the Olympics as if this is partly her achievement. The nation has the effect of lifting you up from everyday frustrations and finally serves as an antidote to death. Like your children, the nation will live after you, giving meaning to your life.

Family

In day-to-day life there are very few things that are more important to most people than their family. In a largely alienating world of computer screens, offices, hotels and airports in which most of our work relationships are both interested and hypocritical, where we have to censure ourselves and tread carefully, it is with family members that we feel deep feelings of love and commitment. Yet we must also think about the societal role of the family and our ideas around it carefully. Almost all societies have ideas that support the family. In many places like China, the Middle East and India as well as some parts of Europe, these ideas stand in the background, often not forming an explicit ideology, while in others such as the US and Russia, they are front and center.

I recently had what was for me a surprising discussion with a graduate student who works in our department whom I will call Benjamin in the interests of anonymity. Benjamin is a student of political science and an aspiring writer. He is the distant inheritor of an American firm that produces whiskey. He tells me that the family fortunes peaked around 1910 and went down from then on due to over-fertility (at one point the family had 20 children). Ugly bickering between the siblings ensued, as well as the proliferation of new types of whiskey that cut into their market. He sees it as his job to bring the family back into wealth and greatness by writing a best-selling book that will help the family get back on track. When I asked him what his political views were – he laughed and said,

"Monarchist, though philosophically anarchist."

"What do you mean?" I asked.

"Monarchist," he said, "because people are idiots; they like to look up to these arbitrary people." Anarchist because he hates to cede to government of any kind.

"Why should people be rewarded according to which family they were born to, rather than their merit?" I asked.

"I believe in meritocratic families," he said.

"You know there are billionaires involved in petroleum who would exacerbate a worldwide environmental catastrophe in order to provide their children with half a billion dollars, say, and not 'just' 60 million."

"I would prefer more power for my children than the good of humanity!"

I did not really know how to answer this. I finally said something like this:

For a young man of twenty who has just left your family to become independent, you are obsessed with family. Why not surround yourself with people you choose, not those whom you happened to be born with? Writers, artists and revolutionaries have always left their families in order to pursue lives with elective peers. With peers you can argue, compete, collaborate, get high, have sex with and fall in love. Many writers who came from affluent families rejected their comfortable life for a more exciting one. Expressionists, Symbolists, futurists and Dadaists are unimaginable without their groups. If you are interested in politics, then you must essentially leave the family. Take any political figure from Napoleon to Martin Luther King Jr. and Gandhi; their family was largely irrelevant – there were hundreds of families very similar to their family of origin. Nor did achievements flow to artists or scientists from their families or later on to their children. Statemen and artists could not reproduce what made them great in their children, nor could they replicate anything that made them influential. In general, it's very hard to reproduce anything truly original and worthwhile in one's children.

I don't think I won him over, but I do think he was listening and what I said was interesting for him; coming from a conservative milieu he had never heard anything similar. I continued to think about his extreme family values. I wondered to myself what does taking family values hyper-seriously and exclusively look like. What kind of people take family values to their logical conclusion? After a bit of thought, royalty, the Mafia and business dynasties like the Waltons came to mind.

It is good to start with royalty, because it's the oldest, and till today the most venerated form of family worship. Royalty presents the essence of arbitrary privilege based on family. It is a social order in which one's family quite arbitrarily seizes up the resources of many thousands of individuals and justifies this through God's will as part of the natural order. It is the most extreme symbol of a fundamental inequality. A royal person essentially says to all of us who are not royalty, "You are worth much less than me *not* because I worked or studied harder, have shown more leadership or even business acumen, but quite arbitrarily – you were not born to the right family." Royals have cared mainly about their own rule; historically they have ruthlessly pursued power and wealth at the expense of both their own peasants and by conquering other peoples. Yet through their brilliant rhetoric of glamor and their use of religion, they succeeded in winning people's love and admiration.

Seemingly opposite, at least as far as our feelings are concerned, is the Mafia. Unlike the legitimacy and respect that is afforded royalty, the Mafia provides protection through violence that is outside the law. Nevertheless, they are similar to royalty since there are no ethics, laws or principles that come above the interest of the family; just like royalty, they will murder and steal in the name of the family line. With the Mafia and gangsters, we have a more complex emotional relationship. We feel a mixture of both seeing them as people who are lower than us (criminals, etc.) but at the same time, especially in Hollywood, seeing them as the embodiment of the courage, cunning and resilience needed to fulfill the American dream. Often in the Mafia films of Francis Ford Coppola and Martin Scorsese, we will see alternating scenes of murder and violence and festive family occasions like marriages or baptisms. These films resonate so much with us since in an exaggerated way this is how most of us, gangster and non-gangster alike, believe and behave in our society.

The ideology of the family allows one to occlude the moral character of many things that we do in the world, under the excuse of "I am supporting my family." To understand the family as a conservative ruling idea for most of us, we must take the familyism of the Mafia and royalty and tone it down. For royalty in the past and the Mafia up to the present, the family legitimates even murder; for us it legitimizes extreme competition, total egotism, and complicity in corporations or institutions that clearly harm the world, all in the name of doing the best for our children. Admittedly, a person who is responsible and loving toward family members is better than one who is abusive and does not even care for anything but himself or herself. Nevertheless, all too often this responsibility and this love get translated in our society to an all-out effort to use whatever means available to ensure that one's child will be upwardly mobile.

Society constrains us in our options; most of us do not have much wealth, nor own a business that our children will inherit. This means that they will work for a wage. Given that they will have to work for a living, middle-class parents are fearful of working conditions and the life of the working class as they push their children to professions that can provide them with an adequate salary as well as autonomy and a modicum of status and respect. Such professions are much sought after; they are highly credentialed and therefore require academic success. This being the situation, hyper-parenting that seeks to ensure social mobility for one's children becomes almost mandatory.

Yet a society of individuals looking out only for their own families is a bad society. It fundamentally represses an orientation toward various public goods, including knowledge, culture and social justice. All over the world, from South Korea to the Middle East, those towns and villages that are politically organized around extended families (Clans or ʘamūla) by definition suffer from nepotism. But they also suffer from lack of public spaces such as parks, libraries and pools, lack of public health facilities, and lack of public education; sometimes even sidewalks are lacking. There is no "public" to pay for them; all value is sucked into a couple of households. These societies embody the ideal that Margaret Thatcher valorized: "There are individual men and women and there are families and no government can do anything except through people and people look to themselves first…There is no such thing as society."

Positing only individuals and families as the only thing that exists makes little sense. Families and especially individuals depend on a larger society that functions. It also does not make emotional sense. The most individualist culture in the world still creates films in which the whole audience, conservatives included, roots for the good guy who usually aims to save something more than himself or his family. When they vote, they presumably vote for someone who looks for something beyond his own private power interests. Our most popular television shows and romantic comedies have protagonists with lots of close friends, social media promises friendship, while the fact of the matter is that people are more isolated than ever. Being thrown back for ultimate purpose and meaning on one's family alone means that you live in a society where the underlying motives for true free association have been fundamentally repressed. For free association is very much pointless if there is no common good, with nothing but yourself and your family to associate.

However, there is another major function of family besides separating people and legitimizing pursuit of self-interest under the mantel of familial altruism. This, of course, has to do with the way human beings are "produced." It is widely observed from the nineteenth century to today that children growing up in various alternatives to the family such as institutional care (orphanages, etc.) are physically stunted, with lower IQs and a variety of personality characteristics that make them bad workers. These issues include rebelliousness, excessive fantasizing, lying, stealing, difficulties in learning tasks, acting out, and lack of impulse control in sexuality and food. Children benefit from growing up in a long-term relationship in which authority is articulated together with love and affection and in which intellectual and moral development are supported. Though there are alternatives to the family, for example, a similar loss of IQ and stature was not seen in Kibbutzim in Israel where children did not sleep in the same house as their parents and grew up together in a children's home; in the West, at least a consensus formed that the traditional family is the best and, of course, the most cost-effective way to create functioning and industrious people. These observations lead to a stress on the benefits of growing up in a traditional family both as a genuine concern for well-being and development as well as an interest in creating human beings who are productive in society and do not burden its various institutions and taxpayers.

From the perspective of having a pliant workforce, it is important to socialize human beings in a way that will make them on the one hand accept authority, but on the other be able to take upon themselves both responsibility and initiative. Abilities such as these are fostered in an environment that both directs and controls behavior but does so in a way that is perceived as both empowering as well as providing incentives for creativity and enterprise. Since working-class people also have an interest in creating human beings who are not stunted, there is an overlap of interest regarding the family. It would seem that the family's stability would be secure. Indeed, right after World War Two there seemed to be a compromise within capital, labor and government that saw the creation of a stable, family-oriented middle class, mainly through providing family wages for working men. However, these arrangements were soon undermined.

First, middle-class feminists rightfully challenged women's economic dependency on men as well as their consignment to the private sphere away from power and influence. In the late 1970s and early 1980s, this coincided with the implementation of neoliberal policies that extended the power of employers over employees that had the effect of controlling the workforce through short-term contracts as well as precarious kinds of labor. While in the 60s a factory worker could in the span of a decade transition to a middle-class lifestyle, since the 1980s, this was no longer possible. Like many such "unholy" combinations, progressive gender politics as well as detraditionalization intertwined with conservative economic interest. More precisely, the system recuperated from broad demands for change in the 1960s by selectively accommodating, transforming and rendering either innocuous or useful many of the demands for more equality that came in the 1960s. The ultimate development of combining stagnating wages with the demand for equality for women was the breakup of the traditional nuclear family.

While in the past a two-parent family was almost a universal institution instantiated in all classes and ethnic or racial minorities, it is now a kind of privilege afforded to the upper middle class. Under a "paternal and caring" attitude, conservative ideology jumped at the chance of reviving an age-old trope of the lower classes as suffering their bad fate because of their immorality. Already in 1837, German writer Georg Büchner had the bourgeois army officer reprimanding the working-class barber Woyzeck for having a child outside the church while the doctor who does experiments on him tells him that he pissed like a dog in the street. Things are not as blunt in contemporary think tanks and academic magazines, but the drift is essentially the same. First, traditional marriage is shown to be better for children and men. Children from traditional families do better, are more upwardly mobile, and men are healthier, live longer and are less likely to commit suicide. The implicit argument is the old Protestant idea that if you are doing badly in life, it is because of a moral failure. On the surface level, you are led to believe that those who are poor lacked the integrity, foresight and impulse control to build a family that would have been beneficial for their children's and their own life prospects. More implicitly, one is subtly invited to imagine that the lower classes are debauched and overly sexual. Sometimes this approach is presented with a kind of false sense of commiseration. In so many words, conservative pundits, like conservative sociologist Charles Murray, seem to say, "Your way of growing up has caused you to be unable to create family life, or you were simply born into a race with a biologically lower IQ, unable to use rational control over its desires." This lower IQ, which translates into lack of control, in turn increases your chances of unwed pregnancies and thus fractures the traditional family.

Sexual morality, biological intelligence and race – this is all heady and exciting stuff. What it serves is mainly to displace the origin of social ills like inequality and unemployment from history and the economic system to either morality or biology – "above" and "below" the social world proper. It is convenient for elites to present the social problems of poverty in this way. However, it just takes a minute of thought to see that morality and biology have relatively small roles in global inequality. If you were born on a Native American reservation, a favela in Brazil or a black inner city in the US, this has relatively very little to do with your biology or morality and, of course, everything to do with colonial history. Family values are just another weapon in ideological class warfare against the poor.

Most importantly, family values are a way to privatize social ills. If there is a youth unemployment problem or a housing problem, let thirty-somethings go back to living with their parents. If there is a problem with care of the old and sick, let them too be taken care of by those of middle age. Conservative writers do not tire of stressing how extended families are to take care of those who cannot take care of themselves. They also want to push back any idea or practice that would make people less dependent on their families. Finally, the assertion of family values is a covert attempt to maintain various forms of soft patriarchy, or more precisely to keep the work of reproduction of the whole society, that is of childrearing, education and housework, private and feminized as well as unremunerated.

God-nation-family usually work as a combo. They seep into each other. The nation is often imagined as an enlarged family, and this nation is conceived as under God. There is a kind of alliance between transcendence "above" and private biological reproduction "below"; both work in concert to deny the social and the immanent. They anchor the status quo in things that seem to transcend the ultimately arbitrary arrangement of society. Even for those who do not strictly believe in the God-nation-family triad, it subtly works in the background to anchor reality and preclude thinking of other social arrangements or even other ways of being an individual. It forms kinds of hidden coordinates with which many construct the meaning of their lives. However, these coordinates are not neutral; they serve to subtly legitimize a status quo that is bad for almost everyone.

Chapter Ten

A Short History of the Modern Critique of the Ruling Ideas

Early Modern Heroes: Reason and the People as New Sources of Authority

We saw before that one of the most important critics of ruling ideas of ancient times was Socrates, but who were his successors, and what can we learn from them? As can be imagined, critiquing ruling ideas in the Middle Ages was not popular. How did ruling ideas rule in the Middle Ages? First, we must not fall into modern self-smugness and self-compliancy and imagine a special despotism in the Middle Ages from which we are free. *All* societies propagate their own ruling ideas relentlessly; they also police and repress ideas that go against the ruling ideas. Additionally, in almost all societies the majority of people sincerely believe the ruling ideas. A minority that does not believe in them is afraid of stepping out of line by expressing views that are contrary to them. In the US, a country that enshrined free speech and free assembly in its constitution, arguing against the draft in World War One or discussing communism in the 1950s would get you fired from your job, expelled from the state or imprisoned. In general, the control of speech in the United States is part of a general disciplining of labor. The main sanction is losing your job, which in the US often means also losing your health insurance. There are various, though constantly changing, hard lines of free speech. James Damore, for example, was fired from his job at Google after writing a memo in which he said that in his opinion disparities between men and women in tech are not only due to oppression and sexism, but to the biological tendency for women to be more interested in people than in things. Marc Lamont Hill was fired from CNN after speaking in the UN meeting marking the International Day of Solidary with the Palestinian People. Lamont Hill focused his speech on human rights abuses in the occupied territories. He ended his speech with the words, "We have an opportunity to not just offer solidarity in words but to commit to political action, grass-roots action, local action and international action that will give us what justice requires and that is a free Palestine from the river to the sea." The Anti-Defamation League claimed that the phrase "river to the sea" is a dog whistle for the destruction of Israel. Regardless of what we think of what James Damore or Marc Lamont Hill said, it is clear that in the context where one's livelihood, health care, etc., is threatened, claiming that one has some abstract right to free speech is illusionary. One can be sure that criticizing the board or trustees or shareholders or in fact anyone above you in an American firm is very likely to get you fired. There are, of course, important differences regarding freedom of speech between the US and totalitarian regimes. In the US, even if you do use racist terms or undermine Israel's right to exist as a Jewish state, you will not be sent to a gulag. In other societies there is not even a law to appeal to in order to protect free speech. In many countries, such as North Korea, Egypt, Saudi Arabia, Vietnam and Iran, margins of political self-expression are extremely small. At the most extreme, you can be sent for reeducation for expressing the most mundane criticism of political leaders, or the way society is run, criticism that is wholly acceptable in the US. That being said, if one examines the World Press Freedom Index, the US figures at number 45.[1] Thus there are 44 countries with more freedom of speech than the US.

When we think about critiquing ruling ideas in the Middle Ages, we should think in terms of the risks and dangers of critiquing ruling ideas in totalitarian or authoritarian regimes. It is true that the state was not as powerful or efficient in the Middle

Ages; nevertheless, societies in the Middle Ages bear striking similarities to totalitarian regimes in their sensitivity to any divergence of opinion. The Inquisition, for example, functioned very much like secret police and had some of the same methods of using informants, keeping records, surveillance and torture. We should not think that the Inquisition is something limited in place and time to Spain in the fifteenth century. Images of the Spanish Inquisition burning heretics, Jews and "witches" are likely to distort for us how truly long and prevalent the phenomenon was. The Medieval Inquisition started around 1184, but it was only formally abolished more than 600 years later in Spain in 1825. In Early Modern Europe, the time that we are depicting here, the Inquisition was alive and well, collecting information and burning both heretics and witches. On top of this, the Reformation and Counter-Reformation created a tense atmosphere in which diverging from official ideology and belief amounted to political betrayal.

Due to the threat of violence and death, critiquing ruling ideas has had two tracks to it. One is explicit: those who undertook criticism of this kind were often executed or tortured or lived away from the reach of the church. The other was a very subtle philosophical critique that was either ignored by the church or dealt with without extreme violence. Let's start with the stories of one of each kind, an explicit priest and a subtle philosopher.

On April 4, 1600, Christovão Ferreira, a Jesuit intent on being a missionary, took a ship from Lisbon to the East. The ship successfully reached Goa, and the following year he continued his journey to Macao, the furthest outpost of the Portuguese empire. Ferreira continued his theological studies at Macao. In 1608, he was ordained a priest; on May 16, 1609, he left Macao and sailed for Japan. On account of dense fog, the voyage took longer than usual, but ultimately they reached shore on June 29, 1609. As was customary, he was immediately sent to study Japanese at the seminary, which he learnt quickly. At the time, the rulers of Japan decided to curtail Christian presence in the land. In 1613, a census of the various religions in Japan was ordered. At the beginning, it was masked as a census of all religions in Japan including Buddhism, but later it became clear that it was a preparation for the government's repression of Christianity. In Western books and films (Scorsese's *Silence*, for example), this repression is often represented as pure cruelty, forgetting that Japanese rulers knew the role the Catholic Church played in the cultural and physical genocide of civilizations in the Americas. It was clear to Japanese leaders that the destruction of the temples and rituals in Central and South America had disoriented the population, undermined their trust and support in their own leadership, and were conducive to the West in conquering them. Indeed, in light of the truly dramatic difference between the fate of Japanese civilization and the civilizations of the Americas, the rulers showed appropriate judgment and foresight.

An order was issued to dismantle the churches and to ask the Christians living in Japan to renounce their religion. Ferreira was forced to go undercover, moving from house to house and endangering the people who housed him as it was decreed a crime to hide a priest. He was ultimately caught and tortured by being hung upside-down within a pit three feet into the ground. Wooden boards were then closed to the side of his body, and thus he experienced total darkness and the feeling of being upside-down with mounting blood pressure in his head. Ferreira recanted his belief in Christ after five hours.

The government furnished him with a small house and a widow of an executed Chinese merchant. Ferreira's name was changed to Sawano Chuan; he wore Japanese dress and lived like a Japanese. He was asked to act as an interpreter of Portuguese and Spanish documents.

Ferreira's faith was probably not the strongest since he quickly made many persuasive arguments against Christianity. In 1636, the same year that Descartes wrote *Discourse on Method*,

Ferreira composed a small book called *Kengi-roku* (*A Disclosure of Falsehoods*). The book opens thus:

> Viewing the world around we see that everything is endowed with its own nature and merit: bird or beast, insect or fish, grass or tree, earth or stone, air or water, each one has its natural quality and merit. All this is the work of Natura. Man stands at the head of all existence and Heaven has endowed mankind with the natural facilities of charity, justice, propriety, sagacity. Therefore, mankind discriminates between good and bad, as well as aspires after equanimity [extinction of emotion]."[2]

In this short book, Ferreira argued that God did not create the world, that original sin, Hell and Paradise did not exist; that the story of Christ was made up, particularly Mary's virginity, as well as the story of the three kings and resurrection; that such events were absurd inventions; and that the Papacy is immoral and exploited the masses through indulgences. It was also dangerous since it regularly excommunicated. Confessions and sacraments were a trick. Religion in general was argued to be an invention to ensure power over other men.

Such direct attacks on the basic tenets of Christianity were not possible for anyone living in Europe at the time. For those wishing to continue to publish or just to live, criticism had to be much more subtle. The critique of ruling ideas in Europe was not by direct confrontation with church doctrine, but by subtle shifting of the foundations of knowledge and politics.

Though a brilliant mathematician, Rene Descartes tired of learning from books. He decided to learn from the world itself, and thus he took on war as a profession. In 1619, he was a mercenary, stationed with the Bavarian army in Ulm. It was winter at the time, and the snow arrested his journey. He described himself as undisturbed by cares or passions at the time, and he found himself alone, shut up in a warm room with time and leisure to occupy himself with his own thoughts. Having traveled widely and seen the variations in human beliefs he was preoccupied with the uncertainty of knowledge. On November 10, he had three dreams. In the first dream, he is walking in a street that he does not know. Suddenly he sees a ghost. Terrified, he tries to run away but feels a great weakness on the right side of his body. He makes an effort to stand up, but a strong wind suddenly spins him like a top on his left foot. In his second dream, he hears a sharp explosive noise; he wakes up immediately and sees that sparks from the fireplace scatter in the room. He discovers that the noise he heard was a dream after all. In a third dream, he sees a book on a table; he realizes that it's a dictionary and he is not interested, but then he sees another book, a poetry anthology. He comes across a Latin verse saying, "Which path in life will I choose?" A strange man appears and presents a poem that begins with "What is and is not." Suddenly the man disappears. Desecrates took these dreams as telling him that he must choose a life path that will determine what is true and what is false among the confused combination of reality and illusion. The Anglican bishop William Temple wrote that Desecrates's dreams were the most "disastrous moment in the history of Europe." They mark the beginning of Rationalism, the belief that ordinary reason is the chief source of knowledge. In his *Discourse on Method*, Descartes describes the personal characteristics that allow him to search for truth. First, he stresses that his mind is like anyone else's; he is a mental everyman:

> I have never fancied my mind to be in any respect more perfect than those of the generality; on the contrary, I have often wished that I were equal to some others in promptitude of thought, or in clearness and distinctness of imagination, or in fullness and readiness of memory. And besides these,

I know of no other qualities that contribute to the perfection of the mind; for as to the reason or sense, inasmuch as it is that alone which constitutes us men, and distinguishes us from the brutes, I am disposed to believe that it is to be found complete in each individual.

Thus, it's important that the search for truth will not depend on any extraordinary mental facilities but on things that we all share. This might seem harmless enough, but it is radical nonetheless. Implicitly it will claim that one does not need to be special, one does not need the charisma of a prophet or to be chosen by God to reveal truth.

After doubting truly everything, the whole of reality and all of his beliefs, Descartes famously reaches "Dubito ergo cogito, cogito ergo sum" (I doubt therefore I think, I think therefore I am). This thought does not lead him to any belief system that is significantly different from the one institutionalized around him. He distinguishes between mind and body, proves the immortality of the soul and the existence of God. Thus, with very small variations, he reconstructs the very ontology and belief system that was socially accepted at the time. His books set out to prove the ruling ideas of the time (the existence of God, the immateriality of the soul) on firmer ground. It might seem that the whole exercise of radical doubt is somewhat pointless if at the end you get the same belief system as at the beginning. But then one does not notice that Descartes slyly legitimized doubt, as well as put reason as the foundation of all belief, under the guise of strengthening the core beliefs of the church. In his new system, the very existence of God and the immortal soul rests ultimately on the solitary and rational thinking self. While seemingly buttressing the worldview of the Middle Ages, he in fact reverses it. Instead of faith and revelation, reason and self-evident truths become the foundation. While many in the church might view the tract as largely harmless, in fact what it

ultimately means is a new dependence on the thinking self and
what this individual self considers undoubtable. If it should
be the case that other new things become self-evident to this
self, then the very fact that they serve as a new foundation will
topple everything that comes atop them.

Explicit arguments against religion, like the ones Ferreira
made, grew in the seventeenth century, but in fact it was the
implicit arguments and the new rational foundations given
that proved most devastating to the old regime. This was made
very clear by the way in which the use of reason as foundation
moved from the realm of metaphysics to that of politics.

About 15 years after Descartes composed his famous books
in which he used reason to prove the existence of God and the
immaterial soul, Hobbes used reason to legitimize the existing
authority of kings. In his book *Leviathan* published in 1651,
Hobbes did something similar to Descartes, only in the realm
of politics. The king's authority was traditionally legitimized
not by reason but by divine right. The monarch is not subject
to the aristocracy, the will or interest of the people or the laws.
The monarch derives his authority directly from God's will.
Though today this may sound both highly arcane and despotic,
we should remember that religion and sacred histories help
legitimize many rulers and governments around the world
even today. In contrast to sacred sources of authority, Hobbes
attempted to legitimize the authority of the king by rational
argument. He imagined a state of nature with no sovereign, a
state of nature in which the legitimate use of violence was not
monopolized by the state; in short, a state of war against all in
which anyone can use violence on anyone else. In such a state,
even the weakest man can kill the strongest. Such a situation
entails radical insecurity for everyone. As a result of reasonable
self-interest, all would agree that it is better to relinquish one's
own use of violence and give the right to use violence solely to
the sovereign or the state, which can then enforce and protect

against the private, arbitrary and widespread use of violence.

Hobbes' idea became a cornerstone of legitimizing rulers and states in general; since the nineteenth century, it itself became one of the main ruling ideas. Till today, much of the media reports on any political demonstration as an intimation of the state of nature that must be crushed before it rears its ugly head. Regardless of this reactionary and repressive legacy, it is important to notice that like Descartes, Hobbes moves legitimacy itself from Heaven to Earth, from the divine to rational self-interest under the state of nature. Once the first premise of political argument became the character of the state of nature and not God's will, it was then relatively easy for Jean-Jacque Rousseau to come and claim that the state of nature is wholly different and much more positive than Hobbes imagined it, and draw revolutionary conclusions. But where did Rousseau get his positive state of nature?

In late August 1683, Louis-Armand de Lom d'Arce, a French aristocrat who became an army officer because of the insurmountable debt of his father, mounted a small warship from the seaport La Rochelle in western France. One month later, he reached Quebec. Louis-Armand was sent to help wage war against the Native American tribe of the Iroquois. During his time there, he witnessed various atrocities and what we would now consider war crimes. Several Iroquois who had been under Christian missionary tutelage were captured by the French; they were tortured by the Algonkin allies who took pleasure in maltreating those Iroquois whom the missionaries segregated from the general Iroquois population. Louis-Armand interceded and hit some of the young tormentors who reached for their weapons to kill him. He was only saved by the Canadians who told the Algonkin that he was drunk. Louis-Armand was asked again to go on an expedition whose sole purpose was to destroy villages and crops of the native population. He was then asked by the governor to build a fort on the upper lakes and to take possession of this vast region in the name of the king. It may be the case that, in the name of reason, Louis-Armand was critical of Christianity to begin with; nevertheless, it is also clear that his unbelief as well as his critique of Western civilization was deepened, both by the behavior of the colonizers and by experiencing the life of Native Americans. The first sentence of the second volume of his "New Voyages to North America" published in 1703 is, "The Savages are utter Strangers to distinctions of property, for what belongs to one is equally another's."[3] Their life, he goes on, is unaffected by money, which they call the "French Serpent." He then provides their viewpoint on Western civilization:

They'll tell you that amongst us the people murder, plunder, defame, and betray one another, for money...They think it unaccountable that one man should have more than another, and that the rich have more respect than the poor. In short, they say, the name of savages which we bestow upon them would fit our selves better, since there is nothing in our actions that bears an appearance of wisdom...They brand us slaves, and call us miserable souls, whose life is not worth having, alleging that we degrade ourselves in subjecting ourselves to one man who possesses the whole power, and is bound by no law but his own will...Besides, they value themselves above anything that you can imagine, and this is the reason they always give for it, that one is as much master as another, and since men are all made of the same clay there should be no distinction or superiority among them."[4]

Louis-Armand devotes many pages to their resistance to Christianity. It is clear that Louis-Armand uses their persona in order to critique Christianity, a critique that he may have had before getting to know them; however, it is also clear that meeting with them has powerfully demonstrated for him a society that lives perfectly well without Christianity. Louis-Armand writes:

> The word *Faith* is enough to choak them; they make Jest of it, and allege that the writings of the ages are false, superstitious…They plead, that a man must be a fool who believes that an omnipotent being, continued from all eternity in a state of inactivity and did not think of giving being to creatures till within these five or six thousand years; or that at that time God created Adam on purpose to have him tempted by an evil spirit to eat of an apple, and that he occasioned all the misery of his posterity by pretended transmission of his sin. They ridicule the dialogue between Eve and the serpent, alleging that we affront God in supposing that he wrought the miracle of giving this animal the use of speech, with the intent to destroy all the human race. To continue their wild Remonstrances they say "Tis a thing unheard of, that for the expiations of Adam's Sin God should put God to death to satisfy himself; That the Peace of the World should be brought about by the incarnation of God and his shameful death; that his disciples should be ignorant Men that fear'd to die. This they say is still the more unaccountable, that the Sin of the first Father hath done more harm than the Death of the latter hath done good, the Apple having intail'd Death on all Men, whereas the Blood of Jesus hath not sav'd one half of them […] That this religion being divided and subdivided into so many sects, as those of the French, the English etc. It can be no other than a human artifice: for had God been the Author of it, his Providence had prevented such diversity of sentiments by unambiguous Decisions."[5]

Louis-Armand continues to write on natives' derision at the doctrine of the incarnation of God. That the Divine Word has been "shut up for nine months in the bowels of a woman," that

Paul contradicts himself constantly, that the first Christians were simple and superstitious folk, that the scriptural "Many are called, but few chosen" is cruel and unnatural. After supplying many powerful arguments against Christianity, Louis-Armand writes:

> Such, Sir, is the obstinacy and prepossession of this people. I flatter myself that this short view of their notions may divert you without offense. I know that you are too well confirm'd and rivetted in our most Holy Faith, to receive any dangerous Impression from the impious Advances. I assume myself that you will join with me in bemoaning the deplorable state of these ignorant Wretches.[6]

This is one possible way in which religious and political authority was challenged at the end of the seventeenth century. The encounter with the natives has intensified criticism of every authority, both religious and political. Of course, such critique could not be articulated directly, on pain of death, and yet dozens of writers and intellectuals undertook it.

What is no less important for our purposes is the way Louis-Armand characterizes the life of the natives. Again and again while describing different facets of Native American life, Louis-Armand stresses their egalitarianism, also between the sexes:

> The savages never quarrel among themselves, neither do they reproach or affront one another; One man among them is as good as another, for all are upon the same level. They have no disorders occasion'd by a girl or a wife...The girls indeed are a little foolish, and the young men play the fool with them not unfrequently; but then you must consider that a young woman is allow'd to do what she pleases; let her conduct be what it will, neither father nor mother, brother nor sister can pretend to control her. A young woman say

they, is master of her own body, and by her natural right of liberty is free to do what she pleases.[7]

Louis-Armand stresses that true equality allows for sexual relationships that are not distorted by power:

> You must take notice, that forasmuch as the savages are strangers to *Meum* and *Tuum*, to superiority and subordination; and live in a state of equality pursuant to principles of nature; they are under no apprehension of robbers or secret enemies, so that their huts are open night and day.[8]

A young man visits the tent of a young woman, who uses a simple gesture to let him know whether he is wanted or not: "If she blow out the light, he lies down by her; but if she pulls her covering over her face, he retires; that being a sign that she will not receive him." Native Americans are incredulous that:

> Europeans, who value themselves upon their sense and knowledge, should be so blind and so ignorant as not to know that marriage in their way is a source of trouble and uneasiness. To be engaged for one's Life time, to them is matter of wonder and surprise. They look upon it as a monstrous thing to be tied one to another without any hopes of being able to untie or break the knot...Tis allowable both for man and woman to part when they please. Commonly they give one another eight days warning; sometimes they offer reasons to justify their conduct, but so the most part the usual plea is, that they are sick and out of order, and that repose is more proper for them than the fatigue of a married life.[9]

Louis-Armand goes on to describe how the savages go by the

mother's name, that is, their matrilineal kinship system. That there are types of women who will not marry, these women are called *hunting women* as they join the men in the hunt. He claims that they are too independent for marriage and too careless for bringing up children and too impatient for staying indoors the whole winter: "Their parents and relations dare not censure their vicious conduct; on the contrary they seem to approve of it, in declaring as I said before, that their daughters have the command of their own bodies and may dispose of their person as they think fit; they being at their liberty to do what they please."[10]

Louis-Armand describes the way in which the Jesuits try to repress what we would consider freedom and equality:

> The Jesuits do the utmost to prevent the lewd practices of these whores, by preaching to their parents that their indulgence is very disagreeable to the great spirit, that they must answer before God for not confining their children to the measure of continency and chastity, and that a fire is kindled in the other world to torment 'em for ever, unless they take more care to correct vice. To such remonstrances the men reply, *That's Admirable*; and the women usually tell the good fathers in a deriding way, that if their threats be well grounded, the mountains of the other world must consist of the ashes of souls.[11]

Louis-Armand depicts the health of the "savages." He relates that they are well built, with robust and vigorous bodies, of a "sanguine temperament, and admirable complexion"; it is surprising to him that they are so healthy as they "Weaken themselves by violent exercise of dancing, hunting, and warlike-expeditions, in which they have frequent returns of heats and colds in one day, which in Europe would occasion a mortal distemper." He even tells that among the Illinois Illinesse tribe, "there are several hermaphrodites, who go in a woman's habit, but frequent the company of both sexes. These Illinesse are strangely given to sodomy, as well as other savages that live near the river Missisipi."[12] Even the pressure and hierarchy of what we now call compulsory heterosexuality is missing among the natives.

Louis-Armand's *New Voyages to North America*, published in 1703, was one of the most successful books in the early-eighteenth century, a best seller. It, and books like it that describe the Native Americans with an eye to criticizing Europe, were a major influence on Jean-Jacques Rousseau.

Rousseau uses the burgeoning accounts of the life of Native Americans to exemplify the state of nature and to argue that this life is in fact much more equal and noble than life under absolute monarchs and the nobility. He therefore uses the Hobbesian premise that authority should be legitimized by rational interest of the population. However, he uses it for the exact opposite purpose of Hobbes. While Hobbes legitimated kings, Rousseau undermines them. Rational interest as a foundation to power makes Rousseau posit something he calls the "general will" as a determinate factor of legitimate political authority. Ultimately Rousseau's ideas led to the overthrow of both Church and king in France and subsequently the establishment of people's republics in much of the world today. Early modern philosophers created a new rational foundation for metaphysics, that which exists in the world, as well as a new basis for the political order. With the American and French Revolutions, this has led to the creation of new kinds of societies based on Enlightenment ideas codified in political constitutions based on "self-evident" truths rather than on religious revelation.

Virtues and Problems of the Enlightenment

Here is the beginning of a constitution. I have left out the name of the country:

The Republic of X shall be a democratic republic. The sovereignty of the Republic of X shall reside in the people and all state authority shall emanate from the people...All citizens shall be assured of human dignity and worth and have the right to pursue happiness. It shall be the duty of the state to confirm and guarantee the fundamental and inviolable human right of individuals. All citizens shall be equal before the law, and there shall be no discrimination in political, economic, social or cultural life on account of sex, religion or social status. No privileged case shall be recognized or ever established in any form. All citizens shall enjoy personal liberty. No person shall be arrested, detained, searched, seized or interrogated except as provided by Act.

Here is another constitution:

Y is a democratic federal law-bound state with a republican form of government. Man, his rights and freedoms are the supreme value, the recognition, observance and protection of the rights and freedoms of man and citizen shall be the obligation of the State. The bearer of sovereignty and the only source of power in Y shall be its multinational people. The people shall exercise their power directly, and also through the bodies of state power and local self-government. The supreme direct expression of the power of the people shall be referenda and free elections. No one may usurp power in Y. Seizure of power or usurping state authority shall be prosecuted by federal law.

Which countries are these constitutions from? Such language can come from about 150 countries with such constitutions, in this case X is South Korea and Y the Russian Federation. Whether deeply implemented or not, the political ideas of the Enlightenment have had a profound influence around the world. This is very explicit in all the countries that enshrine Enlightenment values in their constitutions. Political legitimacy is said to flow from the people; where political measures are presented as done in the name of the people, where the law presents itself as impartial and protects individuals' rights, the ideas of the Enlightenment have taken effect. Historically, these ideas were first implemented by the American, French and Haitian Revolutions, then by the revolutions in South America that took place from 1810 to 1820 and then spread to southern Europe, were fought for in the spring of nations in 1848, and spread throughout the world after decolonization. The initial sequence of trying to implement these ideas, lasting from 1765 to 1848, sometimes called the age of revolution, has used Enlightenment ideals to either defeat feudalism or weaken it substantially in the most powerful countries of the world economy. By the mid-nineteenth century, Enlightenment ideas became ruling ideas themselves, and increasingly came under criticism. Their problems are perhaps clearest in the country that implemented them first, the US.

While entertaining guests or even having a solitary dinner, Thomas Jefferson would use a panel on the side of his fireplace, put in an empty wine bottle and then pull out a new one. Guests were astonished, until they learned that the panel covered a dumbwaiter that a slave in the basement would pull and replace the bottle. Though as framer of the Constitution, and famous for the radical "all men are created equal," he could also write to the then president, George Washington, that he was making a good 4 percent increase on the natural procreation of slaves: "I allow nothing for losses by death, but, on the contrary, shall presently take credit four per cent, per annum, for their increase over and above keeping up their own numbers." Thomas Jefferson, who was among the Founding Fathers, is the one most appreciated for his striving after equality. He was not merely "stuck" with slavery; he saw slavery as the future of economic development.

On his plantation, Monticello, young boys aged 10-12 would be whipped brutally to get them to work in his nail factory. In order to control his slaves, Jefferson created a hierarchy, with laborers at the bottom, then artisans, managers and, on top, household staff. Great George Granger, who worked as a foreman, had to persuade the boys by any means possible to do the job. In the winter of 1798, he refused to whip them. A letter was sent to Jefferson (who was living in Philadelphia at the time) that "insubordination" has "greatly clogged" the operations at Monticello. A new foreman, Gabriel Lilly, was found, who whipped them mercilessly. Lilly, for example, would not let James Hemings, one of the nail boys who was sick with high-fever, rest from work. He whipped him so hard (the boy could hardly put his hand up) that a white worker sought to intercede with Jefferson to protect the boy. Jefferson wrote that Lilly is the best man for the job: "Certainly I can never get a man who fulfills my purposes better than he does." [13]

Much has been written on the particular hypocrisy of Enlightenment ideals in the US, but we must remember that the bluff of the Enlightenment that claimed universal freedom and equality has been called in other places as well. Words similar to Jefferson's "all men are created equal" were uttered in France in 1789.

In 1789, France's National Assembly ratified the "Declaration of the Rights of Man and of the Citizen." Its first two articles said the following: "Men are born and remain free and equal in rights. Social distinctions can be founded only on the common good." And "The goal of any political association is the conservation of the natural and imprescriptible rights of man. These rights are liberty, property, safety and resistance against oppression."

At the same time, there was the exclusion of women, more than half the population in the said rights proclaimed by Enlightenment revolutionaries. In 1791, two years after the "Declaration of the Rights of Man and of the Citizen" was put into effect, playwright Olympe de Gouges wrote "Declaration of the Rights of Women and the Female Citizen." The declaration opens with the following lines: "Man, are you capable of being fair? A woman is asking: at least you will allow her that right. Tell me? What gave you the sovereign right to oppress my sex?" Of course, no answer was pending from the mainstream faction of French revolutionaries at the time. Olympe de Gouges was executed in the Terror for suggesting that the people will decide through a plebiscite among a republic, a federalist government or a constitutional monarchy. This went against the law of the revolution, making it a capital offense to publish anything that might suggest reestablishing the monarchy. Though her execution had nothing to do with her demand for equal rights for women, nevertheless, it was used as a warning for women. The radical Pierre Gaspard Chaumette, an ultra-radical Enragé who wanted the working poor to have access to a radical redistribution of wealth, reminded a group of women wearing the revolutionary symbol of the Phrygian bonnets of "the impudent Olympe de Gouges, who was the first woman to start up women's political clubs, who abandoned the cares of her home, to meddle in the affairs of the Republic, and whose head fell under avenging blade of the law." That being said, he was unusually sexist for the Enragés, who regularly appointed women as speaker representatives in the national convention and who possessed revolutionary proto-feminist leaders such as Claire Lacombe and Pauline Léon. Nevertheless, rights were ultimately denied to women by the assembly.

Blacks and women were not the only ones excluded from supposedly universal rights; so were the workers and the poor. The Constitution of the US as well as other constitutions based on the Enlightenment were built in such a way as to exclude and marginalize those who were not wealthy. In fact, one can say that only wealthy white men (a tiny fraction of the population) possessed full rights even in Western democracies. For example, in 1815, only 11 percent of adult males had the vote in England, and one had to have at least 50 acres of land in order to vote in the US.

Clearly, many laws explicitly discriminate against the poor, as Justice Felix Frankfuter famously said, "The law, in its majestic equality, forbids the rich as well as the poor to sleep under bridges, to beg in the streets, and to steal bread." Whole legal arraignments serve the interest of the rich and punish and repress the poor, from employment laws that strongly favor employers not workers, banking laws that favor banks over debtors and those who cannot pay their mortgages, land laws that favor big landowners, criminal laws that rule long sentences to poor people selling petty amounts of marijuana but are very lenient on fraud and insider trading, to laws related to holding elections in which only rich people or those who directly serve their interests can win elections and hold political office. The legal system in fact works directly to counter the stated aspirations toward freedom and equality written in the constitution. These later aspirations could not have been seen by those who suffer under the system as more than hypocrisy.

Then there is the critique of the Enlightenment in the name of the marginalized, of the mentally ill and incarcerated, a criticism perhaps brought to its culmination with the work of Michel Foucault who showed how the Enlightenment pathologized, medicalized and essentially silenced the mad while transitioning to a deeper control and punishment of those who were incarcerated.

Some Enlightenment conservatives attempt to make light or marginalize the violence, subordination and exploitation that natives, slaves, workers, prisoners, inmates and women suffered. Many fight for natives, racial minorities, workers, prisoners, inmates and women to have the same rights as those given originally only to rich men of Western European origin. They claim that what the Enlighteners said was correct; it just needs to be extended. Their ideas were so brilliantly universal that they mandated their own extension. These two reactions of defending the Enlightenment are possible. However, no such strategy exists with the Enlightenment's relationship to nature. Global warming, the disappearance of nature, pandemics and other ways in which nature strikes back deeply challenge the ideas of the Enlightenment on many levels.

The Enlightenment had the effect of canceling the ethical and physical limits of human activity in regard to nature and paved the way for an intensified regime of control and exploitation. Enlightenment thinkers sought and succeeded in finding ways of describing nature that intensified man's power over it. This is not to say that feudal traditionalism was benign and non-exploitative toward nature. In the history of man's exploitation of nature, an extinction of animals that goes back to hunter-gatherers, it has been demonstrated, for example, that many species of megafauna both in the New World and Australia have been decimated precisely at the time that humans migrated into these areas. Nevertheless, the Enlightenment and the Industrial Revolution brought man-made devastation of nature to an unprecedented level. From the point of view of the Enlightenment, nature exists solely as a resource; it has become disenchanted, quantifiable and mathematized, its qualitative characteristics wholly negated. The determining attitude toward it has evolved into getting the most resources out of it, and creating machines and techniques that speed up the use of nature.

Still, while criticizing the Enlightenment, we must remember that it is the Enlightenment that first enabled any kind of systemic critique of society and the ideology of this society. It created a public sphere in which problems facing us can be discussed collectively. It broke the intellectual monopoly of the church, a church that monopolized one's worldview and one's redemption and that served to legitimize the rule of an oppressive and exploitative society.

Roots of Today's Critique

During the nineteenth century, critique not only tried to hold up the Enlightenment to its own universal words regarding women, working poor, slaves, etc., but also continued its criticism of the ruling ideas of religion that still held strong sway over the majority of the population. The tradition of critiquing ruling ideas, the tradition that we still draw from today for everything from representation of race and gender in the media, disability-oriented criticism of representations of sports, to postcolonial critique of area studies in universities, comes directly from the nineteenth-century critique of Christianity. It comes under intellectual attack, as a totalizing belief system that requires complete allegiance and complete rejection of alternative belief systems. Intellectuals and indeed the reading public gained acquaintance with other religions, such as ancient polytheism, Native American spirituality, Buddhism and Confucianism for their own sake (not as heralding Christianity). Christianity was suddenly estranged. In comparison to animism, as well as ancient polytheisms, it was perceived as almost totalitarian, penetrating society, culture and people's psyche to a much greater degree. A more thorough and deep critique of Christianity was called for than was provided by the old critics of religion in the ancient world. When challenging religion, ancient sages and poets such as Lucretius were content to show that the natural world can be explained by natural causes and rules, that the gods did not create the universe, did not intervene in the world and do not care about human affairs. Though they understood that religion is often based on fear, they did not elaborate on the psychological motivations for religious belief nor on its political and social effects.

A deep understanding of these motivations had to wait for the three master thinkers of the nineteenth century. It is in the nineteenth century that the complex interplay between social power relations and ideas suddenly became apparent in a new way. Marx, Nietzsche and Freud became masters of explaining how power relations influence religious ideas. Their theories have created a new way of critically understanding why we believe what we believe in general. For them, belief is predicated on a social situation that allows a certain message to be found persuasive and thus deeply internalized. All three are powerful narrators of the coming into being of belief. All three were critical of naive realism that states that belief corresponds in some unproblematic non-mediated way to reality. In fact, naive realism, thinking that your beliefs somehow correspond unproblematically to reality, is itself one of the most distortive ruling ideas, an idea that precludes one from critical self-examination, as well as societal examination that is fundamental for having less distortive, more truthful ideas. The stories that they tell are complex and multifaceted, any honest analysis of our ruling ideas must in one form or another incorporate several aspects of these three stories.

Marx's and Nietzsche's narratives are big macro stories, stories about human beings in general or at the very least stories of the long arc of Western history; Freud's story is a micro story, a story of the individual in a family. Though Freud historically comes last of the three, it perhaps makes sense to start with him. What is the context, the concrete situation in which we acquire our fundamental beliefs and ideas according to Freud? The situation, of course, is of being a child who is totally dependent on his parents. With this utter dependency comes identification and an intense kind of love that has little to do with the objective characteristics of the parent, and much to do with utter dependence. A good expression of their own feelings and knowledge of this total dependency is the intense fear that young children feel when images of their parents' deaths come to mind. Children's love for their parents is laden with existential insecurity. Parents often focus on the difficulties, failures and problems of educating and socializing their children; they rarely see how much influence the relationship with their children had on not only their personality but also, more crucially for our purposes, the ideas that they hold about the world. The genius of Freud, however, was to tie both the *difficulty* and *great influence* in shaping behavior in one narrative.

For Freud, children are unruly in general and sexually unruly in particular. They are not driven mainly by a thirst for knowledge, but by their desires and fears. We might naively think that ruling ideas are imparted in a kind of scene in which a parent holds forth on a certain topic like a lecturer and the child imbues this teaching. Freud would likely think that such a scene does not lead to any kind of true internalization. Ruling ideas, or as Freud calls them, the superego, are deeply internalized only in a series of events that touch the child's desires and fears deeply. This series of events can be dramatized, condensed to a scene in which a child is rebuked for illicit behavior or desire. Freud's formulation, in fact, includes a much more diverse array of desires than the famous scandalous sleeping with one's mother. It is quite amazing that we still feel scandalized and incredulous with this formulation, though even a cursory look at adult sexuality will certainly reveal lightly camouflaged fantasies of domination by various paternal figures.

In any case, for Freud a child is a cauldron of desires, a polymorphous being, seeking enjoyment in any way he or she can find. The fact that we may have resistance to this formulation reveals more about our needs to keep children "pure" and asexual rather than something about children themselves. Even if the sexuality of children is minimized for the old reasons of Victorian prudery, or for the new reasons of fear of adult sexual response to the child's sexuality – it is extremely hard to deny that children are highly motivated by enjoyment and pleasure. In a way the most taxing and difficult job of every parent is moving them from a sense of enjoyment to a sense of duty.

Many parents will readily admit that in this endeavor they will use either various punishments or even more effectively various fears. It is, for example, well known that tiger moms get superior performance out of their children by threatening them with downward social mobility: "You will work at McDonald's if you don't study hard." Often fathers can be much more volatile and use physical punishments; it is this that Freud called castration anxiety. It is under *threat and fear* that the child chooses to quickly internalize parental ideas and values. It is as though the child, overpowered by parental authority, gives up his own point of view on the world and joins the parents' perspective.

Sometimes these parental ideas and values cause problems later in life (superego pressure and self-deprecation); in that case Freud suggests that we revisit, in therapy, the scene, so to speak, in which these ideas and values have been internalized. Such a dramatic revisit is needed, since even if one suffers under them, these ideas and beliefs are likely to seem self-evident and based on objective reality. By examining their formation in personal history, Freud creates a distance between the ideas and the persons. Though in large part one's identity and self were created out of these early identifications, we can yet, as autonomous adults, critically appraise them. One's freedom to criticize and revise these ideas depends on seeing that they have nothing to do with truth or correspondence to reality and everything to do with one's early weakness and dependency on caretakers.

It is the connection between weakness, lack of power and ideas that was the focus of Nietzsche's philosophy. At the very center of Nietzsche's philosophy stands a critique of culture that has developed its ruling ideas as a kind of defense against weakness. Nietzsche is a master of showing how seemingly disparate ruling ideas are a problematic compensation for lack of power. His main targets are Christianity; Greek philosophy, especially Plato; German idealism, especially Kant; and modern science. What could all of these different belief systems have in common? Nietzsche sees all of them as resulting from a kind of resentment. What is this resentment, and how does it create ideas? Resentment is a kind of projection of the pain and hatred that accompanies one's own sense of weakness onto external circumstances or onto those in authority. In his book *Genealogy of Morality*, Nietzsche writes the following:

> It is not surprising that the lambs should bear a grudge against the great birds of prey, but that is no reason for blaming the great birds of prey for taking the little lambs. And when the lambs say among themselves, "These birds of prey are evil, and he who least resembles a bird of prey, who is rather its opposite, a lamb –should he not be good?" then there is nothing to carp with in this ideal's establishment, though the birds of prey may regard it a little mockingly, and maybe say to themselves, "We bear no grudge against them, these good lambs, we even love them: nothing is tastier than a tender lamb."

Plato, German idealism, Kant and especially Christianity partake in justifying the weak, of equating weakness with goodness. Even science in its quest for impartiality and objectivity does this. Objectivity and even truth as an attempt to convey reality are orientations for people who are not powerful enough to pursue their will in the world. Nietzsche describes a world in which normative and justice claims are essentially self-justifications for weakness and failure. They are a way of discounting as bad the true virtues of those who achieved power and rationalizing as good the position of weakness that one found oneself in.

I believe that this position is ultimately untenable and that very few people can hold it consistently. Those who hold it usually use it as a tool against those they have power over, but rarely would they agree with it regarding those who have power over them. In the end, only a tiny elite can hold them consistently, as there are very few people who do not have a "bird of prey" over them. Thus, in response to demands for social justice made by women and blacks, a white male conservative working-class person in the US might think to himself that women and blacks should not make justice claims, their position in the world is justified, and they are undeserving. Women simply have a different set (implicitly inferior) of skills and tendencies; blacks were emancipated more than 200 years ago and yet they cannot be "moral," hold their families together and take responsibility for their condition, etc. This is what this person sees when he looks "below" at the "lambs" beneath him as lacking what he falsely considers his exclusive virtues as a white man (hard work, self-control, etc.). However, when he looks "above" at urban professionals, he will talk about the fact that he creates real value with his hands while they do empty and harmful jobs and have the temerity to look down at him. If he looks farther up, he sees a corrupt government coercively taking his tax dollars. His entire political worldview is in fact just an extended statement on why it is just that he should be above certain kinds of people and unjust that he be under other kinds of people.

Rarely does such a worldview extend to himself; rarely will he say that those making more in finance or higher echelons of government are simply doing work that is more valuable, that they are there because they deserve to be. There has been an ongoing discussion on the relationship between Nietzsche and Nazism; however, regardless of the position, few are willing to say that in occupied Europe during the 1940s, Nazis were simply superior to others and that one should not discount their greatness, and simply learn to live under their rule. Nor are people willing to say that because whites held more power, they have rightly enslaved blacks. Few are willing to acquiesce that legitimacy lies only with power. People would like to say that the Nazis and slave holders were wrong not just because they ultimately lost a war. In short, most of us do not hold Nietzsche's philosophy consistently, and those who do hold it are just opportunistic with it.

So, what can we learn from Nietzsche? Not that inequalities are justified, but that we cannot let the truth of injustice preclude us from willing what we want to achieve. Complaints and talk of injustice as well as promises of compensation in the afterlife or at the end of history can sometimes be like a kind of distortive idealistic mist; they entail all kinds of secret enjoyments that are essentially bad for you and make you sick and preclude you from action in the present. This is not only true in the conservative sense of saying to yourself "concentrate on what you can do for your own success and leave history and politics alone, etc.," but also in the sense of active political engagement with the world. Revolutionaries from George Washington to Vladimir Lenin often do not wait for the theoretically right moment to make revolution. Famously, most Marxists around Lenin reiterated that Russia was not prepared for proletarian revolution. They wanted to abide by the sequence that first one needs a bourgeois revolution like the American and French ones and the development of capitalism and industry before a communist revolution can take place. In contrast, Lenin looked at the concrete situation strategically and assessed that precisely because the middle and owning class are so weak and undeveloped in Russia, a revolution can take place. In short, he was unwilling to wait for the end of history and sought to seize current opportunity. For him there was the will for revolution and the reality of the current situation.

Nietzsche encourages us to cut through all resentful representations; these representations, though true on the macro level, are not real for the immediate situation and person.

For the person there is just his or her will and what can be done in the current situation.

In seeming contrast to Nietzsche, Marx starts with precisely an opposing analysis of the origins of our ideas. In Marx the lambs often rave and extol the virtues of the birds of prey. Not only do they think that birds of prey are good, but they think of themselves as bad and cheap.

There is a scene in Georg Büchner's play *Woyzeck* written in 1832 that foretells some of Marx's most poignant analyses of ideas. In the opera version of the play, composed by Alban Berg, Woyzeck, a poor barber, is shaving the captain, who lectures him on the qualities of being a "decent man." He criticizes him for living an immoral life, for behaving in a hurried fashion, telling him that he looks "so restless! It does not befit a decent man." He then goes on to say that we have "south-north wind." When Woyzeck says, "Jawohl, Herr Hauptmann" ("Yes, sir, Captain"), he makes fun of him and tells him that he is utterly stupid. He then tells Woyzeck that he is a good person but has no morals since he had a child "without the blessing of the Church." Woyzeck answers that "God our father will not scorn that poor brat, because no priest said Amen over us before he was conceived. The Lord said: "'Suffer the little children to come unto Me!'" The Captain replies, "What's that you say? What kind of curious answer is that? You make me quite confused! When I say, 'you,' I mean you!" Woyzeck answers, "We poor folk. You see, Captain, it's money, money...Those with no money...Just try bringing up children in a moral fashion without it! We are flesh and blood, too! Yes, were I a fine gentleman with a hat, a watch, and an eyeglass and could speak eloquently, then I would be virtuous too! It must be a fine thing, to be virtuous, Captain. But I'm just a poor fellow! The likes of us are damned in this world and the next. And I believe that if we went to Heaven our task would be to help the thunder!" The Captain answers, "All right! All Right I know that you're a decent man.

But your thinking burdens you. You always look so restless. Your discourse has strained my nerves. Go now, and don't run so! Walk slowly down the street and keep to the middle. And I repeat: go slowly, nice and slowly!"

Those who are oppressed and exploited partake almost completely in the ideals of those who exploit and oppress them. For Woyzeck, virtue exists only for those who are able to afford it. Those without money cannot be virtuous. The world of the play is not so different from the world that we know, in which billionaires parade as compassionate philanthropists, while those who are poor or oppressed often find themselves either competing fiercely with others over bad paying jobs or internalize what those above them call them and even come to think of themselves as lazy or criminal.

Many of us doing work that is either dull or even hurtful for society and strengthens its hierarchies, can sigh with Woyzeck and say that it must be fine to be virtuous, to be able to concern yourself with charity, with alleviating world poverty, with engaging people with their spirituality. But of course, we cannot. Nor do we regularly think that the charitable virtues of the rich are problematic in any way. It is also telling that for the Captain, Woyzeck's words are both confusing and straining; those in power find the authentic speech from those who suffer under them confusing and straining. They simply want their interaction to legitimize hierarchy; authentic truths must be shut out.

The Captain's admonition to be slower reminds us of the arbitrary way in which particular attributes of the bourgeoisie, attributes that they have by virtue of their social position, are used to admonish those under them. For the Captain, a "gute mensch" is a person who can do things slowly. A Captain whose physical work is done for him can indeed "go slow," be gallant. The Captain's admonition to "go slow" hovers between two meanings. First, going slow is the privilege of those who don't need to do physical work; it is the virtue of doing things gracefully and slowly like nobility. This virtue is used to feel superior over those who need to work fast. However, there is also something paradoxical about the admonition to go slowly, since it's clear that those who toil under the Captains of this world are required to work quickly and efficiently. "Go slow" does not let Woyzeck exercise the virtues of efficient work; it asks him to do the impossible and shames him in the process. This is not unlike the way the West often treats Chinese manufacturing, demanding that Chinese goods be dirt cheap and be quality work at the same time, or the way in which people in France or Germany speak of shoddy Arab labor. The play shows the whole arbitrary regime that aims at exploitation and control.

Control is the theme of another scene in the play. Woyzeck comes to the doctor; the doctor is mad at him because he peed in the street, "pissed against the wall like a dog!" We learn that the doctor gives him three pennies every day in order to eat only peas. Woyzeck tries to defend himself and says that "but when nature calls." The doctor answers thus:

> Superstition, odious superstition! Have I not proven that the bladder is subordinate to the will? Nature, Woyzeck! Man is free! In man, individuality is transfigured into freedom! Having to piss Pah!

This is a condensed study of the work of ruling ideas. Woyzeck, who is under compulsion to put his body under experiment in order to support his family, is being told that the will is everything and that individuality entails freedom. Doing precisely what the doctor wants, that is only peeing when one is allowed, is transfigured and transformed and discussed under the values of freedom and individuality. The built-in hypocrisy of the ruling ideas of the professional class are shown here in full effect – they want you to do precisely what they want, and feel free at the same time.

Büchner notices the hypocrisy in those ideas as early as 1837. Perhaps with even more foresight, Büchner critiques science from a class perspective. Science is presented as a thoroughly bourgeois activity that oppresses people in the name of personal careers of scientists and knowledge that is useful only for elites. Büchner's critique comes 30 years before Marxist critique of bourgeois economics and 120 years before Foucault wrote about the scientific discourses that oversee punishment and mental illness.

Though Büchner prefigures much in Marx and Engels, all of them critique the ruling ideas from a class perspective. First, one is likely to forget that the subtitle of Marx's *Das Capital* "Kritik der politischen Ökonomie" means a critique of existing economic theories of his time. In a sense, Marx is engaging in science studies, criticizing the social sciences of his time from a class perspective. However, Marx and Engels' more fundamental contribution to the critique of ruling ideas came from other writings. One of their most important conceptualizations of ruling ideas is that they create an inverted consciousness. Marx and Engels often use the metaphor of camera obscura: "If in all ideology men and their circumstances appear upside-down as in a camera obscura, this phenomenon arises just as much from their historical life-process as the inversion of objects on the retina does from their physical life-process." This kind of language was mainly aimed at idealism and monotheisms, which view things as originating from the top (God) to the bottom instead of from the materialist bottom to the top. Marx and Engels simply follow scientific explanation, which posits material as antecedent and prior condition to consciousness. The world existed in its full materiality long before any type of consciousness was formed on it. Marx uses consciousness in a different way than what this concept means in everyday life or in Anglo-American philosophical discourse. Consciousness is not simply being aware of your surroundings, of having subjective experience. Consciousness in Marx's use is the sum of our conceptualization of both the natural and social world around us. It is the result of our intercourse with others that takes place as we produce and reproduce the social world. For Marx, consciousness is not some ephemeral sublime thing; it is part of sociability and practical life. The production and reproduction of ideas and conceptualization are part and parcel of the general production and reproduction of society. Idealism was criticized because it severed the connection of conceptualization and ideas to life and presented them as wholly independent and primary. It is not consciousness that determines existence but social being [gesellschafliches Sein] that determines consciousness.

Where does the illusion that consciousness is primary come from? Marx sees its historical origins in the agricultural revolution or more precisely we would say today in the urban revolution, when humanity created cities 10,000 years ago. These cities had priests, lawmakers, judges and officials who relied on an extensive division between intellectual and manual labor. It is the former, those who engaged in intellectual labor, who could imagine themselves and their creations as prior and superior to the material reproduction of society. What allowed priests, lawmakers, officials, etc., to think that the spirit is primary, that God and law come before society, is the fact that they had others following their orders and building and sustaining their material world. It is their position within the social edifice that allows certain conceptions to occur.

One can elaborate on Marx's account and say that this belief ultimately pervaded the whole society, both because it is precisely priests and officials who monopolize the means of propagating ideas in society through their control of temples, royal decrees and writing in general and because they have made the ideology of consciousness emotionally comforting to the masses. In the face of death, the complete annihilation and disappearance of yourself and loved ones, the belief in a soul is soothing. It is also reassuring to know that the core of oneself is not the material body that is so vulnerable to hunger, sickness and violence, but a spiritual and eternal entity protected by a god. Intellectual elites were in the business of generating self-serving ideas that nevertheless bring psychological comfort to the masses.

Marx stresses that ideas that serve the ruling classes are always made to seem universal. The belief in the soul served priests more than it did the peasants since a priest gets his power and wealth from "administering" souls, being responsible for their salvation. However, this is also true to the ideas of the bourgeoisie. Ideas that valorize free trade, property rights, entrepreneurship, hi-tech, grit, higher education, health and fitness might seem available to all, but in fact benefit a small elite much more. To see that this is so, just imagine how these ideas look to a slum dweller who lacks a toilet or even to the cleaning lady. In every age, particular class interests get translated by intellectuals in institutions such as churches, universities and think tanks, into the language of universality.

Marx distinctly moved beyond the critique of priests and their ideology that was the staple of Enlightenment criticism and unmasked the ideology of bourgeois Enlightenment intellectuals themselves. For example, the idea that the state and nationalism can emancipate human beings is criticized as illusionary, since just like religion, emancipation through the state is alienated and done in a roundabout way. The citizen exists in the abstract realm of the law; in the rare times that he or she gets to vote, the real person meanwhile is not an equal citizen but is often a subjected worker or a greedy capitalist. Thus, according to Marx, bourgeois revolutions have created a split subject, a subjected worker or an egoistic private greedy individual on the one hand and an abstract, equal, juridical person that does not possess real individual life but an unreal universality. In a sense, man has alienated equality, and free association with other men, from himself to the largely imaginary realm of the state.

To understand more deeply the way in which Marx saw this type of alienation, we have to take a short detour through Hegel. Hegel told world history as a story of the self-realization of God or spirit. This spirit is motivated by wanting to become self-conscious, of fully knowing itself. In the process of this self-discovery, it externalizes and alienates itself into the mind of man, similar to the way in which God materializes himself in his son Christ. Man initially thinks that the world is objective and material, other than spirit. Coming to know the world as spirit means overcoming the otherness of the material world. It means that spirit achieves absolute knowledge that the whole of creation is spirit. There is both a process of alienation and a reaching of a higher stage as this alienation is overcome. Both have been taken from Hegel and used by Marx. But Marx could not learn to use them until they were adopted by another thinker – Ludwig Feuerbach.

Hegel's story is essentially a religious story. Its main protagonist is not humanity but God or spirit. Ludwig Feuerbach ingeniously turned the story upside-down, translated it into a story in which humanity is center. According to Feuerbach, it is not the case that God first alienates himself through materializing in man and then through man overcomes this alienization, but man first alienated himself through projecting his best qualities (love, compassion, etc.) onto God, and he will overcome this alienization when he reabsorbs these qualities in himself and society. One can use Hegel's description of history by turning it "right side up." Marx takes this formulation and applies it to new domains, to the political sphere and then to economics. In his "On the Jewish Question" he essentially claims that just as humanity projects its ideals of love and compassion on a transcendent deity, so it projects its own social power and ideals of equality unto the state. Humanity will ultimately have to repossess, take the power that has been externalized to God and state back to the people. Marx then extended this analysis of alienization from the political sphere to the economic. In capitalism, the worker is alienated from the means of his work as well as from its results. The worker is alienated from the means because he or she does not own the means of production. A worker in a factory does not own the machinery needed to produce the product that he or she produces. Such a worker comes to the factory, essentially sells his or her time and receives a wage. What he or she produces is not their own, but is sold for profit in the market. Such an analysis is still perfectly correct for all workers working in factories in China and the rest of the world producing the seeming infinity of commodities with which we surround ourselves. The professional who may be reading this book might think that such an analysis, though true, has little relevance for his or her own work-life. However, it takes very little thought to see why alienation is as true in a factory as it is in an office. In a corporation, the dominant workplace in the post-industrial world, one essentially works to increase shareholders' profits. Fundamentally, the workplace is designed to maximize shareholder profits while minimizing workers' wages. Now sometimes professionals may receive a small number of shares in a company, but these are usually token gestures. Almost none of the people working in a corporation are major shareholders. It is the latter, together with upper management, that make all the decisions in a corporation including what to produce, how to produce, where to produce and with which people. Professionals are more or less interchangeable and disposable parts of the process of production. The board of trustees can easily decide to move your whole production to another country with new employees. The hierarchy of any corporation means that you compete with other employees for promotion or even not to get fired. If you are fired, you will be competing with many unemployed people for another job. This competition is another source of alienation from others who are in the same situation as you are; it suppresses companionship and basic solidarity. In many senses, you are fundamentally alienated from your work. It is often the job of HR and your bosses to hide this fact from you, by team-building exercises, mandatory fun and company team vacations. You are then even alienated from your own emotions as you are called to signal that you are energized, a team player, and full of ideas and initiatives for making the company great.

The next major advancement in analyzing how ruling ideas work in the Marxist tradition comes from Althusser. Althusser's main contribution to the way in which the efficacy of ruling ideas work comes from the concept of interpellation. Like Freud's drama of castration, Althusser condenses a long socialization into one scene. As mentioned in the first chapter this scene works the following way. You are walking in the street and a policeman is calling, "Hey, you." You turn around slowly and say, "Who, me?" At that moment you have been interpellated. In a sense, the language of the state apparatus of the police creates a subject. The example is ingenious as it shows the dominance of signification (the signifier "hey, you") over what is signified, one of the predominant themes of French theory in the late 1960s.

While in the first chapter I stressed that this interpellation creates individuality, I would like to elaborate which individuality and which subjectivity it is. With the example of the policeman, the individual who emerges is quite "thin," he or she is simply the subject of state authority.[14]

Althusser brings another, richer example.[15] He quotes several lines from Exodus 3 that form a complex example of interpellation; it might be good to quote the context more fully:

> Now Moses was tending the flock of Jethro his father-in-law, the priest of Midian. And he led the flock to the back of the desert, and came to Horeb, the mountain of God. And the Angel of the LORD appeared to him in a flame of fire from the midst of a bush. So he looked, and behold, the bush was burning with fire, but the bush *was* not consumed. Then Moses said, "I will now turn aside and see this great sight, why the bush does not burn."
>
> So when the LORD saw that he turned aside to look, God called to him from the midst of the bush and said, "Moses, Moses!"
>
> And he said, "Here I am."
>
> Then He said, "Do not draw near this place. Take your sandals off your feet, for the place where you stand *is* holy ground." Moreover He said, "I *am* the God of your father – the God of Abraham, the God of Isaac, and the God of Jacob." And Moses hid his face, for he was afraid to look upon God.
>
> And the LORD said: "I have surely seen the oppression of My people who *are* in Egypt, and have heard their cry because of their taskmasters, for I know their sorrows. So I have come down to deliver them out of the hand of the Egyptians, and to bring them up from that land to a good and large land, to a land flowing with milk and honey, to the place of the Canaanites and the Hittites and the Amorites and the Perizzites and the Hivites and the Jebusites. Now therefore, behold, the cry of the children of Israel has come to Me, and I have also seen the oppression with which the Egyptians oppress them. Come now, therefore, and I will send you to Pharaoh that you may bring My people, the children of Israel, out of Egypt."

At this point in the biblical story, Moses is essentially a refugee from Egypt, with no particular mission. The interpellation that God does is detailed and rich. Let's for a minute ignore the story of Moses in Egypt before these events, and take him as a person who is just tending his sheep, almost an empty subject. When Moses says, "Here I am," he essentially becomes a subject extensively embedded within a great sacred-biological chain stretching from the past to the future. Not only is he embedded in this chain, but he is an essential revolutionary link. Though he is interpellated by one authority, he is called to undermine another authority. This is, however, a relatively rare occasion in which authority (God) calls on one to undermine other authorities (Egypt). It is for this reason that Exodus forms the most pivotal event in the Old Testament.

What is important for our purposes is to realize that interpellations are very rarely a "Hey, you" of the policeman; they are often elaborate discourses that produce and then reaffirm the subjectivities they address. Any message constructs an idealized subject who receives this message. An environmentalist TED talk creates someone who is concerned about the environment, who sees herself in a link in the history of environmental protest or at least concern, a person whose actions even in a small way are meaningful for the fate of the planet. A *Wall Street Journal* article creates a person who is enamored with CEOs and aspires to be like them even in very small ways. A Hollywood action film creates childlike spectators who are impressed with the strength and determination of their hero, filled with simple suspense regarding the events. A documentary on World War Two creates people who are sure that they are on the right side of history and that Hitler was a radical otherworldly evil. The speeches of politicians or of "our president" who address us in the name of our great nation, its history and future, create nationalist subjects.

Interpellation has proved to be an immensely fruitful concept, taken up by a wide variety of thinkers such as Stuart

Hall, Alain Badiou, Judith Butler and others. One theme that has emerged from these thinkers is the ways in which interpellation could fail or not be wholly successful from the perspective of authority or what amounts to the same thing, the way in which interpellation is resisted. Stuart Hall, for instance, offered three possibilities of different receptions of a hegemonic or culturally dominant text. One option is to be interpellated in the way that the text intended. When someone reads with admiring eyes a *Wall Street Journal* article on the exploits of Elon Musk or an admiring article on a new film with Brad Pitt, we have a hegemonic reading or decoding to a culturally dominant text. The reader is interpellated as a deferential fan who affirms just like Moses did, a whole set of belief systems about individualism, success, fame and the American dream. Another type of reading goes midway in affirming the message. Hall calls it negotiated reading of a dominant-hegemonic text. We often selectively accept and reject aspects of the text. For example, in the US when minorities, workers and women listen to hegemonic messages, they might affirm universal rights while rejecting market fundamentalism, nationalism and militarism. Finally, there is an oppositional reading of the dominant-hegemonic text. This book is essentially just that, an extended oppositional reading of the main ideas that we live under. But such oppositional readings are not as rare as we might think; they are not reserved to Marxists, anti-colonialists or radical feminists. One can hear such oppositional readings in satirical shows that usually poke fun at politicians' appearance on television and their speeches, such as when comedians make fun of presidents and prime ministers.

In a similar way for Judith Butler, it is impossible to oppose interpellation directly since it is through interpellation that the subject and his or her agency is constituted in the first place. For Butler, resistance can only take place through a kind of satire. It is a resistance in reproducing the interpellation's call faithfully, by exaggeration. For example, drag men who masquerade and perform as women or women as men essentially answer positively the call for compulsory heterosexuality. The participants are not challenging the norms that make people pass as either men or women. Men performing as women use all the stereotypical, society approved "props" that signal womanhood, such as long hair, painted fingernails, lipstick, long eyelashes, earrings and handbags. Butler argues that such exaggerated performances denaturalize and highlight the conventional nature of gendered norms, and in such a way problematize the original heteronormative interpellation though never simply refusing it.

However, one can argue that there are more straightforward ways of refusing various interpellations, especially when a space is formed of choosing between different identities. Bertrand Russell could refuse his early interpellation and write a book like *Why I Am Not a Christian,*"and Shlomo Sand can write *How I Stopped Being a Jew*, and David Horowitz can describe how he turned from being part of the Trotskyist International Marxist Group to writing *Why I Am No Longer a Leftist* in 1986, which explains why he advocates voting for Ronald Reagan. More importantly, perhaps, groups can decide to refuse interpellations together.

A good example is provided by Ashwin Desai in his book *We Are the Poors: Community Struggles in Post-Apartheid South Africa*; the context of this refusal takes place after liberation from apartheid when the African National Congress (ANC) government adopted neoliberalism with attendant policies of deregulation and privatization that were harmful to the poor communities of South Africa. In contrast to the promises that the ANC made, only 3 percent of the land has been redistributed and often the land that has been redistributed was given to commercial farmers and not to landless peasants. The specific events that Desai concentrates on happened when the local council of the ANC in Chatsworth tried to push poor people from their neighborhoods by water cut-offs and impending evictions. Most of the people in those neighborhoods were, in fact, Indian. When the ANC attempted to evacuate the community, it met fierce resistance in the form of squatting and demonstrations wholly stopping its evacuation attempts. Angry at this unexpected setback, one ANC member mobilized race, and began rebuking those who resisted as "Indians" who were trying to maintain their privileges against the poor black majority. However, the crowd responded by shouting, "We are not Indians, we are the poors." Those who were black in the crowd shouted, "We are not African, we are the poors." The crowd refused the interpellation that was to separate them according to race.

In a no less dramatic way, the 2011 Occupy Wall Street movement decided to reject various interpellations as white, black, men, women, straight, gay and immigrant and chose as their slogan, "We are the 99 percent," highlighting the rapidly growing economic inequality in the US and the pauperization of the middle class.

One of the most basic interpellations that is starting to be resisted is the call to see oneself as a master of nature, an ancient understanding that man has of himself since the agricultural revolution. The Bible puts it pithily: "Be fruitful and multiply; fill the earth and subdue it; have dominion over the fish of the sea, over the birds of the air, and over every living thing that moves on the earth" (Genesis 1:28). We are currently learning to resist such interpellations of ourselves, to resist seeing ourselves as wholly separate and having dominion over nature. We have been defining ourselves through our mastery of nature for more than 2,000 years. We casually say things like "Don't be an animal" when someone is violent, though no animal is as violent as us. We made celebrities of people who dominated nature like Rockefeller and Ford; our most successful enterprises like Amazon are machines for accelerating the devastation of nature. Activists, intellectuals and others are thinking of how to resist this interpellation. No master thinker or philosopher has emerged; rather today a truly collective effort is being made.

Resisting the human-supremacist interpellation, we can learn from the whole history of critiquing ruling ideas. The most pernicious basic idea is that of the great chain of being that traditionally was articulated as God – angelic beings – humans – animals – plants – minerals. The chain was already disrupted by Spinoza, who melded God and nature together as one, thus turning transcendence into immanence. We could definitely use ideas from Spinoza, Rousseau, the Enlightenment, Feuerbach, Marx, Nietzsche and Althusser in order to battle anthropocentrism. Spinoza showed us that we are an integral part of creation, not something above it; Rousseau showed that there is no great reason to be proud of our civilization, and that hunter-gatherers lived in many respects a more fulfilling life than subsequent generations. From the Enlightenment we are to learn how to extend the rights and the political enfranchisement of beings. The Enlightenment logic extended rights to slaves, to women and to the poor and will eventually extend these rights to animals and the natural world. Certainly, there is a long tradition that looks at technology critically as a creator of inequality. However, perhaps most important for us today is simply to resist and contradict simplistic interpellations. Becoming both subsistence farmers, "Going back to nature," as well as techno utopists, "Let's die on Mars," will not work as imperatives. There is no going back to nature with eight billion people, and terraforming Mars to become a hospitable planet is an imaginary endeavor for creatures who cannot even sustain their amazingly hospitable planet Earth.

To summarize, the history of undermining ruling ideas has much to teach us today. First, in various permutations, religion still figures in many parts of the world, especially the

Middle East and South Asia as an ideology that helps augment the legitimacy of exploitative and corrupt elites. The same intellectual weapons that were used against feudalism can be retooled today and reverse the trend to religious fascism in the Middle East and South Asia. For a whole set of issues, the Enlightenment call for reason is still unheard. We do not rationally run our economies, nor is our relationship with nature reasonable. We can use the Hegelian-Feuerbachian idea of alienization to help us understand how the very best parts of ourselves (like creative work, friendship and sociability) find themselves pitted against us in our workplaces and in our social media. We can certainly still mobilize the three masters of suspicion, Marx-Nietzsche-Freud, to look at the way our ideas do not result from some truthful correspondence with reality but are dependent on relations of power. Finally, we can look at the often-creative ways in which people resist their various interpellations, from simply gentle correcting of other people regarding what they suppose your identity is, to forcefully declaring new collective affinities.

Chapter Eleven

The Work of Patching Up: Being Fooled and Fooling Yourself

Patching Up Reality

Truman from the film *The Truman Show* (1998) is the unknowing star of the 24-hour reality television program, with hidden cameras following his every move. His entire life takes place in Seahaven Island, an artificial town, with actors used for everyone he knows including his mother, his wife and his best friend, and colleagues at work. The construction of an artificial reality is not perfect. There are various kinds of accidents that take place. Truman falls in love with the "wrong" woman during high school, and production staff forcibly rush the woman off the set. A spotlight falls from the "sky," a radio channel describes his movements precisely, and a rain shower falls on him alone. An actor used previously for his father who was "drowned" and disappeared by the decision of the director, suddenly shows up on the set and is whisked away.

These accidents and glitches in the presentation of reality are covered up by what Truman is told directly or indirectly. The radio says that an airplane began to shed parts to cover for the fallen spotlight. A newspaper says that they are cracking down on homeless people to cover for the sudden appearance of the father. His mother grows very sick after the "wrong" woman is whisked away, in order for him not to pursue her. The radio tells him that they have picked up a police frequency to cover for the surveillance-like talk.

What we can learn from this is that the control of belief and thought is not something static; it constantly needs to overcome problems with the official way in which reality is represented. Just like Truman, there are both small and large anomalies in our own world that are explained or repressed. These problems have to be marginalized or papered over. They are explained away, and effort is taken to distract and move the conversation away from them. If the problem cannot be ignored, both the state and the media intervene to secure the status quo. A good example was the financial crisis of 2007-2008, in which the government intervened to bail out the banks. The press followed the bailout with a concerted effort to reassert the ruling idea of *individual* fiscal responsibility. The media actively denied that there was a systemic problem and divided bankers into good and responsible bankers and bad and irresponsible bankers, and responsible lenders and irresponsible lenders, thus inculcating the idea that those who lost their homes are responsible for their fate. Another example is the outright denial that the COVID-19 pandemic and recession was related to our violent and exploitative relationship with animals, and that there are no fundamental changes that need to be made in light of it. Though it is impossible to deny the systemic nature of environmental degradation, pollution and global warming, the best efforts are undertaken to deny the consequences and the radical measures needed to be taken in order to avoid further catastrophe.

In many places around the world, the state incarcerates an extremely high percentage of the population. This is true especially for the US that comprises only 4 percent of the world population and yet has 22 percent of its prisoners. Other countries with mass incarceration include Russia, China and Brazil. Such high incarceration rates are obviously a striking anomaly; they signal that life in their respective societies is highly problematic. We know that it's a societal problem rather than a moral one since the same human nature exists in the Netherlands and Germany, and while the US incarceration rate is 693 per 100,000 residents, it is only 76 per 100,000 in Germany and 69 per 100,000 in the Netherlands. Thus, certain societies generate crime and then punish it, creating dreadful lives for the people who live there.

A related abnormality that has largely been repressed relates to the historical domination of the West on the rest of the world. In the colonialized countries of Africa and the Middle East from South Africa to Algeria, all through the twentieth century colonization was so cruel and dehumanizing that ordinary people were willing to commit suicide in order to contest their colonization. From the perspective of colonizers, these were seen as anomalies to be ignored, repressed or explained away. Either one does not talk about prisoners and those participating in violent liberation movements in polite company or one disqualifies them curtly on moral grounds, explaining their actions as things that bad people, criminals and terrorists do.

Perhaps the most decisive anomaly that will determine our future is global heating. Given that it's a natural catastrophe, not a group of people with interests that can be silenced, disparaged or ridiculed, the strategy has been to sow confusion regarding the facts themselves and generate a "debate" about the causes of global warming. If things are being debated, then nothing needs to be done.

Problems in the functioning of society and the world contest and challenge the status quo all the time. In response, the patching up of false-reality-making never sleeps. A whole range of well-funded institutions are vigorously busy adopting the ruling ideas to challenges and changed circumstances, lulling people into acquiescence and denial. Every country has a multiplicity of often somewhat overlapping as well as conflicting institutions whose complicated work is reaffirming the ruling ideas in the face of events that go contrary to their logic. Such institutions include much of the news media, government spokespeople, corporate public relations and think tanks.

A good example in the US is *Fox News*, which chooses a variety of strategies in maintaining the worldview of the elite among the masses. As an illustration, let's take a police shooting.

A police shooting is a dramatic, violent event and likely to get ratings; therefore, Fox reports on it. The event repeats itself because of mutually reinforcing societal characteristics such as widespread gun ownership, poverty and racism. Again, if you think these events have to do with the characteristics of the people involved, you have to ask yourself why such events don't exist in Europe or, for that matter, South Africa. Every year, usually more than 200 people are shot by the police in the US. At the very least, the systematic and repeated nature of police shootings challenges norms of gun ownership, as well as use of violence by the police. More widely, it challenges inequalities of race and class. Given this problem, Fox needs to get to the complex work of both presenting and neutralizing all of these challenges.

One of the main strategies can be called privatization of responsibility, or re-personalization. Here, instead of acknowledging the fact that systematic violence cannot possibly be accounted for solely in terms of the judgment and ethics of the agents themselves, Fox goes into the minutia and largely irrelevant forensics research to examine the relative responsibility for the shooting: the black teenage boy vs. the police officer involved.

Russel Brand has rightly called *Fox* a context removal system. The interesting thing about context removal is that the actual outcome of the legal theater taking place is ultimately irrelevant. If it's the police officer's fault, then he is a bad apple that must be cast aside; if it's the boy's fault, so much the better; then we can all rally around law enforcement agents who defend our interests and property. What is crucial is precisely to efface the structural problems and reinvoke and refit the ruling idea that life outcomes are only a result of decisions taken by individual actors around a certain event, the idea of personal responsibility. For those who watch a report of a police shooting on *Fox News*, it is very easy to get caught up with the drama of personal responsibility. Like children watching a magician, audiences are diverted by a highly engaging moral tale with victims, villains and judges. Like a sports event, we can discuss and analyze and disagree; however, this whole theater diverts us from thinking of the preconditions that allow this event to happen so regularly. This personalized theater itself is like a brain infection that does not let one think. We are thus captives to the way that things are represented even while we discount them.

To be critical, a person needs to discount and refuse most of what is presented while attempting to reconstruct a different reality almost from scratch. Truman and *Fox* viewers share something in common; they need to effortfully reject the world as it is represented to them and use clues to model a more truthful world almost from nothing. Nor are people who read more liberal papers or even those who read opinion pieces in the best journals necessarily better off. At the very top of the intellectual chain, many of the leading intellectuals of a country, its most sophisticated think tanks and its most prestigious journals will be engaged in a quite complicated form of argument that is still highly distorted. In fact, the complexity of their argument is usually due to the fact that they are aiming at legitimizing a blatantly unjust status quo. Given their complexity, sophistication and persuasive power, how is one to identify them?

The Trajectory of Fighting against Injustice: An Optimistic Reading

One first needs to conceptualize that for many political and moral issues we are, so to speak, in the midstream of their career, in a kind of arrested development. Let's imagine that we are in the 1830s in the United States, reading about slavery. For the past 50 years there have been calls to abolish slavery on the principle that human beings are fundamentally equal.

If you open a newspaper in the North at that time, you would get a range of opinion. A respected editorial states that many slaves are better off than workers in industrial factories in the North who are fired when they are sick or aged. In contrast, the article argues, in the South, owners take care and protect slaves when they can no longer work. Political "realists" will tell you that one needs to reform the institution of slavery, make slaves' living conditions better. Other articles will point out that if you abolish slavery, there will be a widespread economic catastrophe, the cotton economy will collapse, tobacco crops will dry in the fields, and unemployment and chaos will hurt whites and blacks alike. Critics of abolition point to the French revolutionary terror and say that abolition will create violent mob rule with unforeseeable consequences. James Thornwell wrote in 1860: "The parties in this conflict are not merely Abolitionists and slaveholders, they are Atheists, Socialists, Communists, Red Republicans, Jacobins on the one side and the friends of order and regulated freedom on the other." They point out that slavery always existed, especially in the most exulted societies of Greece and Rome. The Bible supports slavery, and though many slaves existed in the time of Jesus, he never spoke badly of the institution. The apostle Paul actually returned a runaway slave Philemon to his master. Slavery also helps the blacks themselves as it makes them Christian. It will hurt everybody including the slaves themselves to be freed as they will starve to death.

The people propagating these views saw themselves as upstanding and morally responsible citizens. They were often the most respected people in society: professors, business owners, judges, etc. If you suggested that such views and the people who held them were immoral, you would be met with violence and hate. The people who held these views saw themselves as upstanding and morally responsible citizens, and they represented at one point the views of the large majority of the population.

We see a similar kind of argument regarding women's right to vote. Since it is well argued, it would be good to include such an argument in full; here is an argument opposing women's suffrage written in 1911 by J.B Sanford, chairman of the Democratic Caucus:

> Suffrage is not a right. It is a privilege that may or may not be granted. Politics is no place for a woman, consequently the privilege should not be granted to her. The mother's influence is needed in the home. She can do little good by gadding the streets and neglecting her children. Let her teach her daughters that modesty, patience, and gentleness are the charms of a woman. Let her teach her sons that an honest conscience is every man's first political law; that no splendor can rob him nor no force justify the surrender of the simplest right of a free and independent citizen. The mothers of this country can shape the destinies of the nation by keeping in their places and attending to those duties that God Almighty intended for them. The kindly, gentle influence of the mother in the home and the dignified influence of the teacher in the school will far outweigh all the influence of all the mannish female politicians on earth. The courageous, chivalrous, and manly men and the womanly women, the real mothers and home builders of the country, are opposed to this innovation in American political life. There was a bill (the Sanford bill) before the last legislature which proposed to leave the equal suffrage question to women to decide first before the men should vote on it. This bill was defeated by the suffragettes because they knew that the women would vote down the amendment by a vote of ten to one. The men are able to run the government and take care of the women. Do women have to vote in order to receive the protection of man? Why, men have gone to war, endured every privation and death

itself in defense of woman. To man, woman is the dearest creature on earth, and there is no extreme to which he would not go for his mother or sister. By keeping woman in her exalted position man can be induced to do more for her than he could by having her mix up in affairs that will cause him to lose respect and regard for her. Woman does not have to vote to secure her rights. Man will go to any extreme to protect and elevate her now. As long as a woman is woman and keeps her place she will get more protection and more consideration than man gets. When she abdicates her throne, she throws down the scepter of her power and loses her influence. Woman suffrage has been proven a failure in states that have tried it. It is wrong. California should profit by the mistakes of other states. Not one reform has equal suffrage effected. On the contrary, statistics go to show that in most equal suffrage states, Colorado particularly, that divorces have greatly increased since the adoption of the equal suffrage amendment, showing that it has been a home destroyer. Crime has also increased due to lack of the mothers in the home. Woman is woman. She can not unsex herself or change her sphere. Let her be content with her lot and perform those high duties intended for her by the Great Creator, and she will accomplish far more in governmental affairs that she can ever accomplish by mixing up in the dirty pool of politics. Keep the home pure and all will be well with the Republic. Let not the sanctity of the home be invaded by every little politician that may be running up and down the highway for office. Let the manly men and the womanly women defeat this amendment and keep woman where she belongs in order that she may retain the respect of all mankind. J. B. Sanford, Senator 4th District.

This is a relatively late document, a rearguard action against the fight for the vote. What is interesting is the force with which these arguments were made and their mobilization. In the 1880s, anti-suffrage activists joined together in several places and eventually became known as the Massachusetts Association Opposed to the Further Extension of Suffrage to Women.

It is important to look at who is making these arguments against giving equal rights to blacks and women. Those making these arguments were men of accomplishment, professors of elite universities, economists, doctors, etc. What they said would sound commonsensical, prudent and smart to the people of the time. Many of us who read such a thing today are either offended or bemused and more than slightly complacent. We would say to ourselves, "Look at how backward people were back then." We pat ourselves on the shoulder, "Such a thing would never fly now, we have advanced so far!"

It is important to notice, however, that each such issue has a kind of career. At the beginning, exploitation, inequality and suffering are deemed natural; there is little to discuss. Those who are antislavery or for the equality of women – abolitionists and suffragists – are at first seen as simply bizarre, distasteful and repugnant. They are on the strange "crazy" periphery of society. Later, when political movements arise that support their arguments, an army of lawyers, intellectuals, judges, policemen, newspapers, teachers, government and literally armies and police forces are up against them. This is the time to repress these demands both by appeal to commonsense and by violence. This is a crucial point. Sometimes a movement will push through to victory like advocates for women's vote and legal equality. Sometimes movements will make partial gains but ultimately lose, like the workers movement in the twentieth century. There are currently many movements whose claims are contested. Many readers who hear such claims will find them offensive. They threaten one's way of life just like claims for the release of slaves threatened the South.

Environmentalism is a good case in point. Environmentalists

who would like to prevent the catastrophe of global heating, slow down the extinction of species and keep the indigenous population on their land are derided by mainstream politicians and conservative media. Activist Greta Thunberg was called "the mentally ill Swedish child" by Michaels Knowles on *Fox News*. Another Fox anchor, Laura Ingraham, compared her to a 1984 movie called *Children of Corn*, in which children are enticed to murder adults. British Prime Minster Boris Johnson called environmental activist group XR "nose-ringed," "hemp-smelling" "crusties." Name calling by the media and politicians is not innocent; it is actually a form of hate-speech, creating an atmosphere in which environmental activists are criminalized. Since 2000, more than 1,000 environmental activists have been killed. Each year more than 100 environmental activists are murdered throughout the world. In South America, "kill teams" of two men riding on fast-moving dirt bikes, one driving, the other using a gun, murder community leaders who speak up and organize against deforestation and displacement of natives.

The very reasonable changes that need to take place, going off fossil fuels, not eating beef, restricting air travel, bringing fewer children into the world, consuming less plastic, etc. – these are things that cut deep into our desires, that threaten our identities. Each of these demands will be ridiculed, contested and violently fought over.

Another related movement whose claims are contested is the animal rights movement. Regardless of whether you use animal products or not, it is incontestable that animals suffer and that man's relationship with them has been one of violent exploitation. Though one may feel that the morality of one's lifestyle is directly threatened by the arguments for animal liberation, one's answer is basically of the type of why women should not get the vote or slaves should not be freed. People say really the same things that we have seen before: humans have always eaten animals, not eating them will disrupt whole industries and put people out of work, lions eat animals, we are predators too, animals don't think, animals don't feel, they don't use language, they are not special like us, and plants have feelings too. Sometimes more sophisticated defenses of the way humans treat animals will be expressed. One can, of course, patiently answer each of these. Lions would die from not eating meat, not so humans; humans are special, but plants and animals are special too and do amazing things like breathe under water, fly in the air or turn sunlight into energy. Plants don't have neurons and therefore have no feelings. One would not make an unemployment argument, often made when the meat industry is threatened, regarding those who operate a concentration camp, so why make it toward a slaughterhouse, etc.? However, ultimately all the arguments against animal liberation are just ways of saying I enjoy the status quo regarding animals, and I would like to keep it that way.

Another contested conflict has to do with indigenous rights. Indigenous rights belong to peoples who have been conquered and colonized. The United Nations Declaration on the Rights of Indigenous Peoples includes their right to self-determination, right to be free, to be on land, or the right to land reparations, and a right to the protection of their culture through practices of language, education, media and religion. When voting for the resolution, 143 countries voted for it, while only four countries voted against (Australia, Canada, New Zealand and the United States). When making claims regarding European colonization and the need for various kinds of reparations and new accommodations with native populations, one meets a bizarre array of all kinds of arbitrary justifications. Early justifications now sound implausible to us, "We are making them Christian and their soul now can get to heaven." Yet justifications for modern-day debt bondage in terms of the need for austerity and balanced budgets, as well as "structural adjustments in the economy" that the IMF and World Bank formulate, sound eminently reasonable to contemporary readers. We have the classic fear argument: if "we" give autonomy to the natives, there will be chaos and bloodshed. We should have the courage to examine our beliefs regarding the environment, animals and natives and see that all our ideas that are used to combat claims for equality are ultimately both nonsensical and immoral. Yet doing that is especially difficult for people with education and power.

The Educated Class and Ruling Ideas

In many ways indoctrination is more thorough as one moves up the social ladder. In contrast to working-class people, the livelihood of those higher up the social ladder depends on propagating and believing the ruling ideas. Thus, nurses, handymen, truck drivers, personal and home health aides, construction workers, gardeners, and waiters and waitresses, though often in thrall of many illusions (usually religious or nationalist), can nevertheless potentially believe in whatever they want to believe. Their job does not entail believing in ruling ideas, their job is socially necessary; old people need taking care of, houses need to be built, cars need to be fixed, garbage needs to be collected. Their work itself is compatible with all kinds of beliefs. Their problem with discounting ruling ideas is mainly a problem of exposure; conventionally religious, nationalist, sexist or racist ideas are mostly what is available to them and what compensates them for the difficult conditions of their life. The world tells them essentially that they lack worth, that they can be made to do anything and be pushed around. The ruling ideas of religion, racism and nationalism come to compensate for this.

Religion tells them that a benign being is watching over them and that they are part of a supportive community (in contrast to their isolated and solitary work). Racism (for whites) tells them that though they are pushed around, they are part of a dominating civilization and that they personally are worth more than blacks, Arabs and Indians. Sexism (for men) tells them the same thing regarding women; nationalism tells them that they are part of a great nation that is superior to other nations. However, all of these beliefs are a compensation for their existence of low pay, low status, humiliation and precariousness. Their work itself, the things they actually do, has relatively little to do with ruling ideas.

When we move to the professional class, things are different; advertising agents, social media professionals, economists, PR agents, film and television industry staff, software engineers, and university professors all have an intense relationship with ruling ideas. For these people, beliefs, ideas and work are tightly interlinked. Examples include PR specialists, telemarketers, corporate lawyers, marketing gurus, lobbyists, those who write for in-house magazines and television channels that provide good spins on senior executives, and those who supervise people whose work needs supervision. All of these are intimately connected with essentially conservative ruling ideas and not coincidently they are what anthropologist David Graeber calls Bullshit Jobs.[1]

Graeber argues that contrary to common opinion in the efficacy and effectiveness of capitalism, many bullshit jobs are created simply out of the elite's will for social control of those under them. They are created by a feudal-like system in which hierarchies are created simply in order to upwardly redistribute wealth to managers and then to those who are called to validate them. This process has happened in many different industries, from banking to entertainment. A good example is the way deans in universities have surrounded themselves with people, often 20 or more, who clearly do not participate in either research or teaching. There is little for these people to do other than usurp faculty governance and think of initiatives either unrelated to research or teaching or that actually have a deleterious effect on these two core activities. For our purposes, it is important to notice that these new bullshit jobs usually validate themselves using ruling ideas. For example, positions like associate dean for academic initiatives and curriculum, or editorial director for the school of liberal arts magazine, create content and events that are largely about validation through ruling ideas such as lean-in feminism or token diversity.

Graeber claims that most people doing such jobs know that their work is largely empty and serves no real purpose; they know their job is bullshit. I suspect that this claim has to do with the overwhelming response Graeber got for his book, a large but self-selective group of people responded enthusiastically by basically writing back to him saying, "Yes, my job is bullshit" but I suspect that the overwhelming majority of people with such jobs do not think this way. It has been experimentally shown again and again in psychology experiments around the world that many people rationalize even the most stupid and meaningless tasks given to them. A simple reaction to this lack of necessity of one's work is a greater need to explain to oneself and others what precisely one does most of the day; people are very good at various forms of rationalization and self-deception.

There is a nagging, perhaps even innate, need for people to feel good about themselves, to feel that what they do is meaningful and contributes to the general welfare, despite years of propaganda trying to instill in them an ideology of radical individualism, greed and competitiveness. Thus, people of the middle class are much more prone to revise their ideas and thoughts according to their behavior, in what is called cognitive dissonance. Cognitive dissonance theory simply states that if there is a discrepancy between attitudes and behavior, it is attitudes that will change. For example, if subjects in an experiment go through an exceedingly boring and meaningless task, for example, filling in boxes on countless pages and then ripping them apart, internal pressure toward consistency will cause them to revise their beliefs; they will then believe and tell others that they did the task because it was interesting. Cognitive dissonance is the modern version of Pascal's famous injunction in which he said that in order for us to believe in God, "We must kneel, pray with the lips, etc., in order that the proud man, who would not submit himself to God, may be now subject to the creator."

Engaging in behaviors that are effortful, repetitive, stressful or boring creates a strong need to revise belief in accordance with them. People know that they are working because they have no other way to survive without selling their time for money, but people often need recognition and meaning, and ruling ideas come and fill in the vacuum that is created by a purely instrumental and alienated working life. For the professional class, some ideas that provide meaning are related precisely to the fact that they are not the working class. In contrast to the way they perceive the white working class, professionals pride themselves on diversity, inclusion, anti-racism and anti-sexism; in some countries they also pride themselves on their anti-nationalism. It would be wrong to see these ideas, as did French sociologist Pierre Bourdieu, only as a way of differentiating oneself from the working class; they are not just a matter of middle-class taste, of going to Whole Foods rather than Walmart. They provide meaningful narratives of progress; we are very progressive and not racist or sexist as people used to be; once we were narrowly national, now we are global and worldly.

Thus, the middle and professional classes have more than one reason to be beholden to ruling ideas. They are responsible for propagating them; they are the ideas that create both legitimacy and meaning for what they do. There is a growing army of people in university departments of economics, business and political science, in well-funded think tanks, and at elite journals and policy centers who depend directly for their livelihoods on propagating ruling ideas. Think tanks and many departments of economics, for example, do the slow work of showing how less government intervention or some kinds of mild reform can deal with a host of difficult problems such as global warming and rising inequality.

These institutes are in the business of de-contestation. Something has come up that contests the status quo, and these institutes work to de-contest it. Official reality-making never rests; it is busy creating plausible representations of reality for all of us to consume. One should imagine that most of what we are presented with as reality is better thought of as the kind of message delivered by spokespeople, official and nonofficial. Sometimes the "official" version of reality becomes contested and then communications channels go to great lengths to de-contest it. Other times the very repetition and incessive staging of pseudo-reality gives us a clue that it is staged.

The official view of the world is often reproduced by parental figures and loved ones. Parents explicate the world; they provide signification and meaning. Parents' beliefs are often deeply internalized. Parents might think that this is not so since they find themselves arguing and repeating themselves endlessly to their children. Yet if we zoom out of these conflicts (which are in any case more about duty vs. pleasure, that is, these conflicts are more about behavior than about belief), we can easily see how different communities reproduce their beliefs very efficiently. Liberal, Muslim, environmentalist or conservative parents regularly produce children with similar ideologies and identities. It is rare to find converts to Jainism among the Amish, or Bahá'í converts among Ultraorthodox Jews. The example of Jainism and Bahá'í is of universal religions that can accept anyone. Needless to say, someone born to Anglo-American parents in the US is very unlikely to become an Iranian nationalist, though if you think about it abstractly, nothing precludes anyone in the US from identifying with the aspirations of the people of Iran. People are likely to identify with their parents' beliefs regarding politics, society and suitable people to marry as well as worthy professions.

There is, in fact, quite a limited range that children conform to even when they leave their parents' beliefs behind. A student with conservative parents in the US or Europe may turn liberal due to a university education, but ultimately the spectrum of possible beliefs is limited; they will probably not turn Zoroastrian, Sufi, Nazi or pagan. There is a strong discrepancy between what we feel about our beliefs and their actual source. The reality is that one is thrown into the world arbitrarily. We pick up our beliefs and an identity from caretakers and peers who we had no say in choosing. We could have been switched at birth and have grown up with a wholly different set of values. Yet on the emotional level we don't feel that our identity is historically contingent but that it is somehow essential.

Often, we change our beliefs to accommodate our change of place, job, spouse, etc. The sources of the life change are often arbitrary, and in some ways it's clear that belief changes are self-serving and inauthentic. Let's say we are 14 years old and dating a boyfriend. His parents relocate because of a job, and we convince ourselves that this person is not worthy of our love in the first place and that we are better off without him. Or the opposite can happen; the loss of the loved one can create idealization or overvaluation. This is clearly a case in which anyone watching would say that we are being inauthentic, we are letting our situation, our particular interests, effect our beliefs. The person we were in love with did not change, but we distort our beliefs to fit our emotional interests. This is a relatively clear-cut case of self-deception. Other relatively clear-cut cases of self-deception are when one judges one's workplace in a self-interested manner. Let us imagine a statistics graduate student who has fairly leftist views. Before getting a job, this person is critical of the policies and effects of both the pharmaceutical industry and social media giants like Facebook. Entering the job market, she sends her CV to many places that she considers do positive, socially beneficial work. She gets no response. She sends her CV to both big pharmaceuticals and to Facebook. She lands a job at one of the big pharmaceutical companies. After a year, her views on pharmaceuticals change. She stresses the big R&D budget that these companies need in order to develop drugs, or maybe she lands a job at Facebook and stresses the way in which the platform helped with the Arab Spring. While these facts were known to her before and had not discounted her negative estimation of these companies, after she becomes one of its employees, they assume a new significance, arguably not because she learned something new in the workplace but because it's more emotionally convenient to feel positive about one's workplace.

Sometimes such people become those who enforce the rules in their institutions. They become what are called minions. We are all inside an oppressive system; however, not all of us serve it with the same enthusiasm. Philosopher Isabelle Stengers and publisher Philippe Pignarre give the minions a more precise definition:

Certainly, those who we are now calling minions are subjected – everyone who is "inside" is subjected, even bosses – but one must also say that minions, at all levels, from the boss to the secretary, work on the construction of this inside, that they do not limit themselves to applying or following rules, but take pains to apply the rules with loyalty that is to say, with certain inventiveness. And they do this even when it is a matter of apparently routine situations. Because what we call the "system" never functions smoothly; leaks have to be stopped up, escapes blocked, the signification of the rule has to be extended, a situation that is slightly out of the ordinary has to be brought back into line, definitions have to be made to evolve, undoing any possibility of evading them. We all say "we have to," but the minion says it a little differently, affirming the legitimacy of this "we have to" by saying "yes" to it, by eventually finding ways to better enforce it. Minions are enforcers.[2]

They suggest that minions (those who truly believe and enforce the ruling ideas) are known by their reaction to social protest. They feel the opposite of joy toward it, and wait for government to intervene and restore order. How are minions created? How do ruling ideas become hyper-operative in them? Stengers and Pignarre describe it like a "dark" initiation toward a form of knowledge that separates people from their former values and commitments that they now view as a weakness that one should separate oneself from. It is followed by a negation and contempt for those with a beautiful soul who still believe. Minions would like all of us to become minions by sneering and saying, "you still believe that..."

Minions are those who more enthusiastically contribute to defending and promoting the status quo at work and society, and help create a space in which articulating true alternatives is penalized.

Nationalist Intellectuals

Things get a bit more complex when one goes beyond complicity with the workplace toward collusion with the nation-state. Let's take the example of right-wing nationalist thinking. A nationalist person from England or the US may think that it's good that his state will promote religious education in schools, but will look at such promotion in the Middle East or Russia as dangerous indoctrination. A historian like Niall Ferguson waxes lyrical on the benefits that the British Empire brought to those who were colonized; yet most conservative historians are indignant about German empire building in World War Two or Russian empire building in Crimea. When facing claims of inconsistency, nationalists often argue that given that they see themselves as American, Russian or German, it does not make sense for them to generalize. They are meaningfully attached only to their own identities. Thus, they cannot make meaningful general claims that pertain to all people.

This leads directly to a lack of fairness. We can use John Rawls's concept of original position in order to see this. Rawls posits a situation in which agents are called to determine the basic structure and principles of society. However, this choice is made from behind a veil of ignorance. Participants in this discussion do not know their own particular characteristics in the future society. Thus, they do not know their ethnicity, social status, gender and their conception of the good. Rawls made the claim that under these conditions, participants will fear being those who are worst off in society and thus will promote principles that maximize the conditions for those who are worst off. Under these conditions, no one is likely to choose a state that furthers a certain religion or ethnicity since there is a good chance that one would belong to a minority and suffer from such policies.

We can, of course, envision that the veil of ignorance should pertain to nationality as well, that is, a veil that precludes us from knowing which nation-state we are born into. Not knowing which state one is being born into, one is likely to want to generalize principles that maximize the well-being of the worst off. For example, given that colonization and occupation are both exploitative and humiliating to those who suffer under them, those in the original position are unlikely to choose a world order in which colonization and occupation take place. In some sense certain kinds of nationalism are precisely similar to the example of someone justifying his quite arbitrary workplace. Many nationalists find themselves having to lie or downplay the bad things that their country has done as well as to lie about the good things that others have produced. For example, a nationalist in the US downplays the fact that Japan had already surrendered after the first atomic bomb and that the second had been totally superfluous, killing 50,000 civilians and only 150 soldiers, or with the genocide of Native Americans, they also play up the original American nature of the Constitution, whose basic provisions flow from the English philosopher John Locke.

Another form of the dynamic of self-deception has to do with achievement and class. People are much more likely to view what they have achieved as a result of solely their own efforts than as a result of the socio-economic position they were born into and the opportunities that came with that position. Conversely, they are likely to attribute failure to circumstances rather than to their own actions. This kind of distortion and self-deception is often reinforced by our society and culture. For example, in the US the belief that success is based on your actions and that circumstances have little import on achievement is reaffirmed by parents, teachers and a constant barrage of rags to riches stories in the media. Such belief has been drilled into American society for centuries. For example, writer Horatio Alger, who wrote the best-selling novel *Ragged Dick*, created a surge in these rags to riches stories. *Ragged Dick* is the story of a 14-year-old shoe shiner; he smokes and drinks and sleeps on the street but wants to turn a new page. He does not steal under any circumstances; he is helped a bit by various patrons and opens a bank account that slowly accrues money. Nevertheless, his real turn to fortune comes when he rescues a drowning child; the appreciative father gives him a new suit and a position in a mercantile firm. Alger continued to write more than 100 books of this sort, propagating the virtues of fiscal honesty and hard work and abstaining from smoking and drinking. Upward mobility is cleverly a combination of virtue plus luck, thus anyone reading these stories who is already working hard but not advancing (the majority of the exploited population) could still wait for the break of success to come.

Thus, for more than 150 years, Americans have been barraged with stories of success. While an analysis of the reality of this promise of mobility remains outside the scope of this chapter, today at least 25 countries are more socially mobile than the United States. Clearly the belief that the US is especially mobile is a false belief. From the perspective of the elite, any belief that proves beneficial for the elite themselves and has emotional potential for the self-deception of those who are ruled will be encouraged. Thus, individual grit, stamina, personal innovation, competitiveness, will-to-power, etc., are propagated constantly as the main values of society. They are embodied in America everywhere you go; they penetrate everyday life to a greater extent than Soviet or Nazi propaganda did.

Racist Suture

Though not obvious at first, racism is closely related to both nationalism and individualism. Especially during and after Western colonialism, it marked the nation on the body of the individual. Racism has proven beneficial as a ruling idea in many respects. First and foremost, it justified colonization and slave labor; yet at the same time it appealed to poor whites' false sense of self-worth. Though they are poor, they said to themselves they are still not black. In turn, this enabled the elite to take a class of people who could have been potentially threatening to the status quo (poor whites) and suture this class to the interests of the elite. While suturing helps poor whites feel they are part of the elite, this does not completely work, since poor whites do feel that they are *not* part of the elite in myriad ways and develop strong resentment toward this elite. Thus, to this strategy of racism toward those "below," we must add racism to those who are "above."

Imagine the situation from the perspective of even a mildly anti-Semitic poor white person. He looks at the news that reports on crises and scandals of people like Bernie Madoff, the Lehman Brothers, Mark Zuckerberg, Harvey Weinstein, Lloyd Blankfein and Jeffery Epstein, all of them Jewish. Some of these people are said to have caused the financial crisis, some control the communication and media industry, others sexually harass or traffic young white girls. Often, he reads these stories through a conservative lens. This means that the narrative is told as the moral failure of an important individual. Rather than looking into the system that created such men, we are captivated by the rise and fall of an ambitious person, a "gangster," who went too far in the pursuit of the American dream. Sometimes this person is made into a moral monster. These are the mainstream interpretations of people like Harvey Weinstein or Bernie Madoff. However, there is always the chance of politicizing their Jewishness or "taking the red pill" as the alt-right calls it, which then aggregates their actions and sees them as stemming from a corrupt and corrupting Jewish race. In this narrative, one deceives oneself by thinking that one is not superior to another race but that one is a unique victim of that race. Thus, instead of recognizing correctly that one is a victim of a capitalist system that perpetuates harm and crisis on all kinds of people, one exonerates the system itself and scapegoats a certain race.

Experience has the potential to liberate us from the ruling ideas that elites would like to instill in us. However, experience is often weak in comparison both to the frameworks and schemas provided by media, politicians, TED talkers, motivation gurus, CEOs and other figures of authority, as well as our own needs to deceive ourselves. Experience is deeply influenced from schemas, frameworks and ideas. We use them to make sense of experience, to categorize and predict the world, and to give it meaning and emotional resonance. Ideas can also powerfully discount and repress experience. A good example are workers and employees in the US who experience extreme work insecurity (they can be fired at any time), exploitation (sometimes making an unlivable wage) and absolute dependency on their employer (they have no other source of income as well as being dependent on their employer for health insurance), yet due to a strong ideology of personal agency and the American dream, they discount all this experience as immaterial and believe that the system that employs them is just, that they have reached a "free" agreement with mutual benefits with their bosses.

Ideas can sometimes override interest and experience. Many Soviet soldiers who spent time with Nazi prisoners overwhelmingly opted to go back to the USSR though what awaited them there was an interrogation by the NKVD and a likelihood of being sent to a gulag. Their ideological commitment made many communists willing to risk this. Many faculty members in universities have suffered by the new ability to report them for almost anything in the university and by the kangaroo courts, with no due process, whose results often mean the destruction of a faculty member's career and life. They are also aware that these reports, procedures and denunciations have substantially weakened their position in the university and have handed over power to administrators, and indeed the administration has used this tool repeatedly to get rid of whoever they do not want. Nevertheless, they think that feminism and anti-racism is best served by these procedures. It is interesting to note that they do not advocate either within university or without for free childcare (this is provided for faculty members in many European universities), or adequate parental leave. This is the power of ruling ideas. They have the power to steer and neuter even the most emancipatory ideals. Ruling ideas can take any experience and any value and distort it to their own purposes.

Ideas can supersede suffering and can dominate over experience. Most people use reality to reaffirm their preexisting notions, discounting evidence that suggests otherwise. For example, there are many people committed to individualism but who love being in groups, socializing and undertaking communal projects. Conversely, there are many socialists who prefer being alone, find socializing tedious and group projects low brow. This does not mean necessarily that they must revise their ideas in accordance with their experience. Both may feel that they themselves in their tendencies do not live up to their political ideals. But these tendencies and experiences should at least partially inform their theories. For instance, well aware of his dislike for being part of organizing groups that endlessly discuss trivialities, philosopher Slavoj Žižek claims that future society should have a kind of bureaucratic socialism in the background that takes care of all the main necessities of life while freeing up people to engage in aesthetic and philosophical pursuits. Though questions like who will watch those who run this functional background naturally arise (and some answers like radical transparency can be the answer), it is not the point here to assess the merits of this proposal, but to show that Žižek indeed tries to put his own actual experience of not wanting to participate in small democratic organizing groups into his ideas of what future socialism should be like.

It also behooves many who seem to think of themselves and others as hard-nosed economic individualists to notice just how much time and emotion they devote to interactions with others that bring no actual profit. Personal sociability or lack of sociability actually stands in a complex nontrivial relationship with normative ideas on how the political should be structured.

All this is to say that man is a symbolic animal, believing his ears more than his eyes, privileging the concepts he or she was provided with, favoring the inner monologue of thought above concrete experience. It is this susceptibility that is utilized by ruling elites to easily patch up any anomalies such as the existence of homeless people, global heating, school shootings, suicide bombers and prisoners, and keep the rest of us from fighting for a different kind of society.

Chapter Twelve

Why We Believe What We Believe

There are three sources to what we believe. We are told what to believe, we sometimes learn what to believe from experience and observation, and finally we rationalize and legitimize our actions through the situation we find ourselves in. These sources of knowledge are not neatly differentiated from one another, nor are they in any type of harmony. Let's start with the first source, being told what to believe. Being told what to believe is an overwhelming force in our lives. Humans are born the most helpless animals, we spend countless years being dependent, supported and learning from others. We are dependent not only physically but also epistemologically, that is, we need to learn things from caretakers in order to survive both in the world and in society. If our parents tell us that there are small dark holes in the wall, that if you stick something into them one might get a lethal shock, we believe them, though we have never observed such a thing. They could have told us never to try cat food since it will make us grow whiskers, and we would in all likelihood have believed them. This susceptibility to believe in almost anything, especially things that authority figures tell us are dangerous, stays with us and is used by rulers and politicians throughout history to maintain their rule.

We are told what to believe most of our lives by parents, teachers, friends and media. All of these sources are formative on two levels. First, and most crucially, what authority figures say is often the default. If we get one worldview, we don't get exposed to another. There are an infinite number of beliefs and viewpoints that are not present when certain beliefs are put forward before us. The most powerful effect of socialization is not so much what is stated but the crowding out of alternative ways of thinking and believing. Beliefs, worldviews and ideologies are presented as self-evident, normal, ordinary, commonsensical and natural when in fact they are far from all of these things. They are stated as if they are obvious in contexts that are not explicitly about convincing and persuading. A parent, for example, will talk about work, money, pleasure, nation, God, race, gender and environment in all kinds of contexts. Some of what this parent says, some of this talk, creates things that are immaterial (God), other words pick out certain aspects of reality, while other features can just as easily be highlighted. For example, trash thrown in a street can be ignored if one does not think it is important; alternatively, it can be described as people failing their duty to be tidy and clean or can be described as overconsumption leading to environmental problems. What the parent casually comments on, something as trivial as trash in the street, will first and foremost create a model of the world, a kind of spontaneous interpretation of reality. In one model, bad things happen because people neglect their duties, in another we all participate in a system that is unsustainable. Without these models that interpret reality, that both tell us what is happening and crucially describe what is good and what is bad, reality itself remains mute; the world does not speak to us on the level that most matters. For human beings, reality is not simply given, it is always mediated socially. What exists for us, our ontology, is a social ontology.

A good illustration that highlights and accentuates the way caretakers create reality is demonstrated in the film *Life Is Beautiful*. In the film, Roberto Benini plays Guido Orefice, a Jewish Italian bookshop owner who is sent with his wife and family to a concentration camp. Separated from his wife, Guido tells his son that existence in the camp in fact consists of an elaborate game, that whoever gets a thousand points wins a tank. If he complains, if he is hungry, cries or wants his mother, he loses points. At one point, when a guard comes to the barracks and asks for someone to translate to Italian, Guido, knowing no German, volunteers to help translate the guard's words. He stands next to the guard and as the sadistic guard speaks in German, he mistranslates the camp rules into rules in Italian on how to play the "game" of the concentration camp. The father thus protects his son through an elaborate fantasy. Though the two levels of reality are exaggeratedly different, game vs. concentration camp, still in a way is this not what all parents and teachers do? Their words function like augmented reality that sometimes contradicts empirical reality with an elaborate game that we play until we are 20-something if not longer. It's often the case that only in midlife do people reach a crisis in an understanding of the world created for them as children.

The sheer strength of our belief in what others tell us is evident on the historical level as well. For hundreds of years people believed in easily empirically falsifiable "local" truths. Many followed Aristotle in thinking that men and women have a different number of teeth, an easily falsifiable belief that stayed alive through the Middle Ages. Erroneous global frameworks like creationism were only slowly and partially dismantled.

Yet it is certainly not the case that people who are more resistant to socialization, who reject what is being told to them, are more prone to discovering important truths. Children who resist socialization are not more disposed to pursue meaningful alternative ideas than the ruling ones. They are usually beholden to their desires and passions, and these, in turn, are not more authentic or truthful ways to orient in life. They often follow biological scripts that frequently are used to further the status quo. For example, following your biological urge to eat lots of sweets, against your parents' and teachers' instruction, does not lead you toward meaningful autonomy but simply makes you a victim of the sugar industry.

Meaningful rejection of ruling ideas needs a very particular and rare kind of individual able to both learn and unlearn, a kind of epistemological hero. As we saw, culture offers us various epistemological heroes from early Greek philosophers to Peter Weir's *The Truman Show*. By looking at the narratives of epistemological heroism we can perhaps learn something on how to free ourselves from social ontology and the ruling ideas that come with it.

Myth vs. Science

The history of thinking, of philosophy and science, is at least partially an attempt at freeing oneself from ruling ideas. Philosophy, which has included the natural sciences in the past, has pride of place here. The ruling ideas about the universe were mythological for millions of years of human prehistory. They were anthropomorphic entities, gods, that were used to explain the origination of the physical universe, the earth, the sea, the sky and the seasons. In marked contrast, the pre-Socratic philosophers gave material and largely nonintentional explanations for the universe. Things are the way they are not because anthropomorphic gods wanted them to be this way but for largely material and structural causes. It is hard to overestimate the difficulty of making this change in how we explain the world.

Mythology, which was the ancient pagan religion, is lively, moral and deeply satisfying; it ties society together, it provides fests, moral injunctive and enjoyment. A ritual of mythological storytelling in the ancient world functions like a church, a film theater and a university classroom combined. It deeply resonates on many levels. To put all this away for the material explanation like the one that Empedocles provided in which everything is composed of the four elements not only sounds unpersuasive but is absolutely an emotional letdown. Would you like to hear about the origins of the world as an exciting story of parents killing their children and conniving sibling rivalry, or a dry discourse that states that mixing four elements in different proportions produces the universe? And yet the latter explanations were closer to the truth. Indeed, discounting particulars, these kinds of explanations are the best we have regarding our world.

Let us imagine quite anachronistically a young person responding to the critique of mythology/religion of the time, the kind that philosophers mounted together. Yes, she would say, the world is perhaps best explained materially, but at least in human affairs we have no choice but to follow mythological precepts. There is no alternative than to take instruction and inspiration from the gods and heroes, from the wisdom of Athena, or from the temperance and cunning of Odysseus. The emotional and ethical limitations of a rational picture of the world are enduring and difficult to surmount. Philosophy, the attempt at a rational worldview of the natural and social world, never became anything more than a school for the training of Greco-Roman elites. Even philosophy itself was highly distorted in its social view of the world as Aristotle, for instance, rationalized both slavery and patriarchy in terms of nature (to his credit, Plato did neither). Philosophy, in short, never caught on because it did not address deep emotional needs that arise from the experience of suffering that most people experience in the world. It is true that Plato had a practical blueprint for how to run a city-state; however, it became largely irrelevant under the age of Greek and then Roman imperialism. Under these conditions there can be no sense of a robust citizenship and ancient philosophy veered toward depoliticized doctrines of skepticism and especially stoicism. These ancient therapeutic sources of what today is called rational-behavior therapy attempt to make your beliefs about the world more rational, but making your beliefs about your situation and the world more rational is rarely uplifting enough for a suffering creature whose accurate beliefs about his or her social oppression are indeed very real and very rational. In short, Europe and ultimately most of the world yielded to the stronger opium of the monotheisms of Christianity and Islam. Till this day they remain one of the most powerful ruling ideas, and the tradition of critiquing these ideas is the most important tradition of critique in the name of emancipation.

Chapter Thirteen

Forgoing Ruling Ideas

Religions and Political Ideologies

The physical world around us, its people and institutions are filtered by our ideas of reality. It is impossible to live long in the world without some framework that tells you why the world is the way it is, how it came to be and what your place within it is. This need for an explanation is a human universal. All cultures have origin stories, stories that tell us how the world was created, who we are within this world, what orientation one should assume in one's society, how one should be and what one should do. Our framework of how to be and what to think is largely given by the ruling ideas. For those who espouse a traditional religion, the cosmic story is tied to an identity and an ethical imperative. Religion often attempts to answer all of these questions at one go and with one central narrative. God created the world, you are Christian, Muslim or Jewish, and these are the things that you should do. For many who are less traditional, religion still provides much of the framework within which they understand and answer these basic questions. Though many have ceded the story of the origin of the universe and sometimes even of life to science, they still do see themselves as having an identity and an orientation that is based on traditional religions, that is, they see themselves as Christian, Muslim, Hindu or Buddhist and follow the respective precepts of these religions.

For others, political ideologies have come to replace religion. Political ideology as a belief system of the masses of people was born in the French Revolution and continues to develop today. Liberalism, socialism and feminism have been powerful ideologies that have reshaped whole societies. They have long, complex histories that exhibit a dependency on circumstances and constant change and adaptation. Like religion, they too are a theory of the world, what is wrong with it and how these wrongs need to be addressed. However, wholly unlike religion, they do not make use of the supernatural. Like scientific theories, they are idealized in the sense that they pick certain attributes from reality and discount and ignore others. Just as in classical physics it is unnecessary to compute air resistance when calculating the acceleration of a metal ball, just so classical Marxists, for example, tend to discount the effect of personalities on history and view historical change as due to a combination of the development of the means of production (technology, knowledge, labor, etc.) and the social relations and classes that arise from the means of production.

Unlike science, ideologies are usually partisan – they embody interests. These interests may be very narrow, like legitimizing the rule of a king, or they may be wide, like emancipation of a whole nation or class. It is also true that it seems that the wider the interest, the more truthful and less distortive the ideology, since it does not need to lie to most other people. Yet regardless of how wide the interest is, ideology is always interested. It is true that science can be utilized to dominate nature; however, I claim that fundamentally science provides knowledge that is not necessarily tied to interest. Knowledge about black holes may never be utilized. In contrast, ideology is unimageable without humans and their interests.

Nevertheless, some contemporary elites in the Western world would like to think of themselves not as holding an ideology but as being consistently scientific, that is, articulating things that are merely true. Yet when one examines their take on the social world, there is nothing scientific per se in the doctrines of rights guaranteed by constitutions, nor by the cult of the superhuman entrepreneur. Rights cannot be based on science, nor are freedom of the will, personal responsibility and individualism concepts that are couched in scientific theories. Still, this amalgam of liberalism with a dash of Nietzschean capitalistic will-to-power is the belief of the ruling elites today. For the masses of human beings around the world, certainly in the whole of the Middle East, South America, North America and Africa, religion still functions as the ruling ideology. Religious belief functions as a coping mechanism for dealing with the world as well as a main orientation. Christianity, for example, helps one cope emotionally in various ways. God has a plan, he cares and watches over us, and guarantees that we are wanted in the world. The injunction for brotherly love simplifies our lives emotionally and gives us a whole array of positive emotions to handle a world that puts us down and exploits us. Instead of having a whole host of negative emotions for the people around us, resentment to those above us, anger to those who seem to stand in our way, fear of competitors and those who will usurp us, the injunction for brotherly love simplifies the response to social situations and heightens well-being. The concept of Heaven and Hell first and foremost overcomes death and incentivizes both ethical behavior and our attachment to God. It also assures us that our life on Earth is but a temporary abode. All religions deny the contingency of existence, ascribing purpose to the world and one's existence in it. The injunction for brotherly love might be a good heuristic for our lives together; it may, however, lead one to self-victimization as well as lack of realism regarding other people and the repression of the complex, both negative and positive feelings, that animate us in our interactions. However, whatever our thoughts on the injunction for brotherly love, the idea of some heavenly father watching over us and another existence, a "Heaven" awaiting us, are clearly comforting illusions.

Living without Ruling Ideas

What happens, however, when one loses these beliefs? One is

suddenly confronted with the world with its finitude and its ugliness. For Marx, capitalism and the bourgeoisie have begun this process all by themselves; in the communist manifesto, he and Engels write this deservedly famous passage:

> The bourgeoisie, wherever it has got the upper hand, has put an end to all feudal, patriarchal, idyllic relations. It has pitilessly torn asunder the motley feudal ties that bound man to his "natural superiors," and has left remaining no other nexus between man and man than naked self-interest, than callous "cash payment." It has drowned the most heavenly ecstasies of religious fervor, of chivalrous enthusiasm, of philistine sentimentalism, in the icy water of egotistical calculation. It has resolved personal worth into exchange value, and in place of the numberless indefeasible chartered freedoms, has set up that single, unconscionable freedom – Free Trade. In one word, for exploitation, veiled by religious and political illusions, it has substituted naked, shameless, direct, brutal exploitation.

Though the passage may deeply resonate within us, clearly Marx was wrong in thinking that illusions are disappearing. The passage is almost a kind of wishful thinking that illusions are being eroded by capitalism. The wishful thinking is precisely Marx's belief that disillusionment and disenchantment will ultimately lead the majority of humanity, the workers, to understand their own subjugation and exploitation and to emancipate themselves. What Marx underestimated is that capitalism is a social system that creates new illusions; it does not simply rely solely on the old feudal religious fervor and chivalrous enthusiasm.

Capitalism has invented new illusions and revitalized old ones. Among the most pernicious ones are the illusion that race exists as a kind of essential entity, and that one's race is superior to others. The related illusion is that your nation accrues various privileges as a result of its singular, exceptional history. Central to these illusions is the doctrine that competition and trade themselves are necessarily beneficial for society, that the individual is the fountainhead of all value, and that possessive individualism leads to the greater good. All of these come to prevent an unpleasant rift between man and his world, but also a great rift inside each person.

Forgoing illusions is painful. One becomes alienated from the world – angered, disgusted, estranged and hurt. One is also in conflict with oneself. One suddenly sees that things one does every day contribute to the inequities of the world. One's education and job are often seen in a new light as supporting and more crucially reproducing this world. One's family, one's friends and lovers very likely partake and express ruling ideas repeatedly. They may express views that one's nation or race stands above others, or that other nations or religious communities are natural enemies, and they seek your approval for their beliefs. They may show disdain for others and be self-assured that their way of life is good for the world and for humanity. They may view the poor as responsible for their own plight. You are then faced with the choice of either getting into intractable and alienating arguments or remaining inwardly distant from people who are close to you. One's self and personal history have also become foreign. One has spent years being socialized and domesticated by a system that lies to you. Habits, states of mind, and most importantly, enjoyments and pleasures are intimately related to a world that you now reject. Seeing the world as it is is necessarily seeing how these enjoyments, pleasures and habits contribute to keeping most of humanity oppressed and endanger the planet. There is a painful process of devaluation of the self as ruling ideas are shed; they not only propped up the world, they propped up the self with it as well. As one feels the effects of shedding the ruling ideas, one realizes the importance of belief today. When one drops the ruling ideas, one is left "naked" – angry, suffering, afraid, lacking self-worth and isolated. The world becomes ominous – violent, arbitrary and controlling at the same time. One is disoriented and alone, estranged from family, exploited and humiliated at work, and lacking in a clear sense of direction. With the desire for money, professional advancement and fame undermined, there seems little with which to orient oneself.

Cultural Narratives of Discovery

Philosophers in the West have sometimes tried to describe what happens when the frameworks that we usually understand as reality break down. Plato describes a person yoked free from the cave who feels the pain of the dazzling natural daylight after being forced to contend only with shadows. Daylight and truth, he tells us, need getting used to. The prisoner can only look at shadows on the ground and then at people's reflection in the water. He contemplates the heavens more easily at night, and only after lots of practice is able to look at the sun and recognize that it is the source of light. Descartes notices that from his earliest youth he has amassed many false beliefs and would like to "seriously undertake to rid myself of all the opinions which I had formerly accepted, and commend to build anew from the foundation." Descartes's doubts make him feel radically uncertain; he says that it is as if "I have fallen into very deep water, I am so disconcerted that I can neither make certain of setting my feet on the bottom, nor can I swim and so support myself on the surface."

Breakdown of belief is represented even more viscerally in history, fiction and biography. A dramatic change in beliefs has been a staple of dramatic literature from the beginning, though it is usually quickly followed by a recognition of the way things really are. Aristotle already commented on moments of anagnorisis in tragedy. For Aristotle, it was a "change from

331

ignorance to knowledge, producing love or hate between the person destined by the poet for good or bad fortune," but it would be more precise to say that it was not ignorance but a false sense of reality that is suddenly changed. In classic and Shakespearean drama as well as in the Bible, what we usually find out is that our identity is not what we thought it was. Classic examples include Oedipus discovering he killed his father and slept with his mother; Iphigenis, who realizes just in time that the strangers she is supposed to sacrifice are her brother and his friend; or Joseph's brothers discovering who he is.

Nor is this type of critical discovery absent from modern fiction, for example, Luke Skywalker discovering that Darth Vader is his father. In science fiction, implanted memory has often become a focus of discovery, leading protagonists to completely overhaul their sense of the world and of self-identity. *Ghost in the Shell*, for example, tells the story of a counter-intelligence agent who has a human brain with a synthetic body put together by Hanke robotics. She believes she was born of refugee parents who were killed in a terrorist act. Ultimately, she learns that she – her brain – was one of several brains taken from anti-augmentation political radicals who were abducted by Hanka robotics and used as test subjects. Discovering who you are in this case entails a totally different political orientation toward the world. The transition that is portrayed in the film is, in fact, a dramatization of an everyday occurrence. It is the transition from being a loyal agent of a corporation to understanding the crimes committed by it and ultimately going against it. Both *Blade Runner* films, loosely based on Philip K. Dick's novella *Do Androids Dream of Electric Sheep?* use a similar trope. In the first 1982 film, Rachel discovers late in life that she has been implanted with the human memories of her creator Dr Eldon Tyrell's niece that serve as an emotional cushion, when in fact she is a replicant; in *Blade Runner 2049*, the main hero is a replicant who for a certain duration of the film believes that he is a human being because he discovers his memories were real, that they have happened. *Total Recall*, also based on a Philip K. Dick story, has identity and essentially reality itself hinge on the truth or falsity of memories. A construction worker opts for memory implants of a trip to Mars as a secret agent instead of a costly real vacation. While trying to implant the memory, something goes wrong and the company decides to drug him, erase his visit, and put him in a cab. On the way, some people try to kill him, he kills them and goes home to discover that his whole life has been false, that his memory of his life with his wife has been implanted.

In general, false memory reveals that our sense of reality depends just as much on identity as on our senses. Realizing that you are not who you thought you were has the same effect as undermining your known reality. Meaningful reality itself is supported by your memories, which are not just memories but memories that are structured by ruling ideas. For example, in *Total Recall*, they are memories of normative marriage and work, etc.; in *Ghost in the Shell*, they are the idea that the state legitimately uses violence only in order to protect from violence and restore law and order. When these memories are undermined as false, the ideas themselves come under challenge. This is especially clear in *Ghost in the Shell*, in which the protagonist comes to understand (just as many minorities and natives know well) that the state is there to protect only one group of people, but regularly exercises its violence on other groups of people. Without the memories and the ruling ideas that structure them, one is left as an incoherent subjectivity that is unable to make sense of itself and the world. This is always a moment of vulnerability, possibility, ontological confusion, shock and possibly rage – a dark realization of what it means to be a person.

Such a classic discovery scene is when Neo from the Matrix wakes up to find himself connected to the Matrix, a kind of electronic womb that provides him with his "reality" and is used to exploit his energy. In the scene, he is flushed down what looks like a birth channel but is, in fact, a toilet for recalcitrant humans who have woken up from the Matrix; he is born again into a confusing buzzing world. This is, of course, Plato's cave in its modern inverse; instead of ascending to the sun from the cave, one descends from the unreal ordinary world to the hell of a cave, which itself is the reality of the situation. This discovery aligns itself with Marx, who is a Plato in reverse. To see this transition, we merely need to look at how reality presents itself in a mall with its ambience of luxury, choice, modernity and enjoyment. But as Marx argued, seeing the world in this way is a form of commodity fetishism; we look at the commodity, what is being sold, without knowing how it was produced. If we trace its origin, we will quickly descend like Neo in the Matrix to hellish scenes of work in Africa and Latin America, where raw materials are extracted, and then to a Chinese factory, where workers are exploited and air is cancerogenic. Just like the Matrix, our own reality is itself always bifurcated or doubled. We have scenes of consumption separated from scenes of production.

Sometimes such moments of transformation appear not with a direct waking into the real reality but with various confrontations directed to those who are complicit in structuring our own reality. This sometimes appears as breaking the fourth wall. A scene from the film *The Truman Show* reveals this well. Truman, who unbeknown to him has been from the day of his birth the star of a television reality show, is having an altercation with his wife; he asks her why she would want to have a baby with him when she obviously cannot stand him. Distressed and neurotic, she starts addressing the audience with a product placement for hot chocolate milk. She threatens him with peelers to which he in turn threatens her, at which point she breaks character completely and addresses the camera directly and screams, "Do something!" breaking the fourth wall, to which he asks, "Who are you talking to?" For the first time Truman suspects that there is an entity directing his world. This, however, is but one point in the mythic narrative of Enlightenment. What *The Truman Show* reveals is the painful journey of disconnecting and freeing oneself from the world as it is presented. Truman is like a detective who finds out more and more things that stick out of the ontological fabric of his universe, things that don't make sense: a spotlight falling from the sky, radio frequency that describes his movements, elevators that don't go anywhere, rain that falls only on one spot. Most of these things are explained away and normalized. For instance, the spotlight falling is normalized by discourse on the radio that tells him that planes have begun to shed parts – which also serves the purpose of scaring him from flying. This is indeed the way in which power works when there are states of exception.

A telling episode is when Truman sees his television father (who was drowned early in the show in order to make Truman fear water) as a homeless man. This is explained away by his mother, yet in many ways the scene is isomorphic to people in middle-class America whose normative model of the world was periodically challenged by things that seem inexplicable from their perspective, for instance, social problems like crime and homelessness and social protests. Indeed, anyone interested in the truth must, similarly to Truman, notice the exceptions to the social rule, give them importance and attention in a society that marginalizes them, and discount the explanations given to such occurrences.

It is important to notice how seemingly small and marginal are these clues. If you lived in Nazi Germany in the late 1930s, you might have noticed that your neighbor is not there one day. In the Second World War when millions of soldiers, workers, engineers and whole families were moving around, one needed to pay special attention to the fact that communists and Jews were being moved as well. On a plantation in the US South, one needed to read and inflate subtle cues that showed one that black people are, in fact, equal human beings. They did not behave, speak or act as your equals; it would take an effort to see them as such. Consumers in the West need to be positively inquisitive, really detectives, to learn how the stuff they buy is made and how it is disposed of. People in the global north need to look at very specific, often technical information in order to understand the devastation that their way of life is causing the planet. Using the cues as well as overcoming the resistance of ruling ideas that are imbedded not only in your head but in your family, friends and your physical surrounding is extremely difficult. You are likely to doubt yourself since what truth itself is, is a minority position. Truth and especially truth about one's society is very rare.

Decolonizing – Decarbonizing

A good example is the situation in any colony or former colony in the long 500-year history of colonialism. Colonists in North America, South America, Australia, South Africa, North Africa and the Middle East as well as India have always had to tell all of their members false stories about what they were doing. Growing up in a colony, one is necessarily preview to a kind of socialization that is not only patently false, but that relates the exact opposite characteristics of the nature of the endeavor itself. One, for instance, is regularly taught that the colony is morally exemplary and that it helps the natives. Puritan John Winthrop delivered a sermon on March 21, 1630, in which he told his fellow Puritans that their new community would be "as a city upon a hill, the eyes of all people are upon us," a morally superior "beacon of hope" for the world. Indeed, from the start of colonization in 1492, religion has played an important role in creating an alternate reality in which colonizers claim that they are moral people doing God's work while simultaneously hiding from sight the very brutality, injustice and violence that colonization entails. Hugo Grotius, the great Dutch humanist, in his support of colonization, wrote the following on how to deal with the American Indians' "rebellion" of not worshiping Christ:

> Some indeed are weak enough to imagine, that God, as a being of infinite goodness, will never be provoked to punish this rebellion; a spirit of revenge, say they, is wholly incompatible with the attribute of perfect goodness. A fatal and absurd idea this! The powers of Mercy must be limited, that her actions may be just; and when wickedness becomes excessive, punishment as it were unavoidably arises out of justice.

Another good example from a different continent belongs to Afrikaner Calvinism in South Africa. Calvinists believed that God has judged it fitting for the Gospel to be taught to the natives' children and heard by the natives themselves. Thus, Christians as God's chosen people in South Africa have a unique responsibility to be pure in faith and just and protect the land that has been claimed in the name of God. A related sense of legitimization comes from religious persecution experienced in Europe that adds a layer of self-righteousness and lack of ability to see the political reality of the colony. These two ruling ideas have stayed with us since the sixteenth century.

However, after the Enlightenment, colonists sometimes persuaded themselves and their children that they were in the colonies for the betterment of the natives. For example, in 1899, Rudyard Kipling, beloved writer of *The Jungle Book*, wrote the poem The White Man's Burden that exhorts the United States to grab power over the Filipino people and their country in the Philippine-American War. The poem begins:

Take up the White Man's burden –
Send forth the best ye breed –
Go bind your sons to exile
To serve your captives' need;

Colonies need to mask their violent, illegitimate existence, always creating an alternative reality in which their endeavor is justified. This alternative reality is one of the most brilliant tools of elites in their control and exploitation of the masses, since they can count on poor or working-class colonizers to believe in their reality over and against the resistance of natives. In this, their view of the world wins new adherents that would be enemies in the mother country.

Colonization is one of the most effective means of preventing class conflict in the interests of the rich and powerful. For colonizers, living without the ruling ideas associated with colonization means viewing one's own existence and one's place in the world as essentially illegitimate. Given the natural feelings of familiarity and affection to one's place of birth, this is a particularly troubling feeling of emotional and cognitive disorientation. One does not know where one belongs and consequently in many ways who one is. The decolonization of the mind and personality is a painful process. The colonized themselves are often attached to the ruling ideas of elite colonizers, especially to the idea that the colonizer is in some ways superior to themselves and that they must mimic his culture and behavior. If the colonizer believes in small business like he does in the US, then displaced and colonized blacks and Native Americans will ask themselves where their own small businesses are, etc. If colonizers wear imperial Western clothes, then the Japanese in 1870 begin wearing Western imperial clothes. If Europeans have round eyes and light skin, then you can be sure that many in the Third World will aspire to both.

While colonization has affected most of the world, many

places are on their way to figuring out their own path to modernity. This is especially true in Asia. China, India, Japan, India and South Korea are on track to becoming not autonomous in the strict sense, but important players who will not forever be beholden to the West in terms of their economy, power and ultimate autonomy. However, on a deeper level, most of the world has failed to develop alternatives to Western political ideas and culture; it has sometimes hybridized its own traditions with the worst that the West offers. Thus, authoritarian nationalism is often a very strong political force among the formerly colonized in Asia, Africa and the Middle East. Yet at the same time on a societal level, people the world over belong increasingly more to their class than to their nation. Professional classes across the world, for instance, are becoming similar in many respects as are the precariat and working classes.

Nevertheless, we have yet to see the invention of a new truly post-Western culture. Around the mid-twentieth century, the high time of decolonization, the original cultural project of the former colonies was to take the most progressive aspects of European realism and modernism and infuse them both with the tradition and situation of the colonized creating a new culture. Indeed, the heights of anti-colonial and postcolonial literature of that time deliver on this promise, and yet since the 1980s this literature has been co-opted by the West. Its writers are more likely to circuit lecture in elite colleges and universities in the US than to create a new culture for the formerly colonized.

Another development that precluded creative autonomy is the way that commodified popular culture, both American and local variants, has flooded the market. "High" culture itself, with its aspirations for creating transformative and challenging experiences, was beat back by global capitalism and now exists in small "islands" that cultivate it in European and American academia. Aside from small bits of progressive or rebellious hip-hop, popular culture presents little that can transform or edify. All over the world it presents reactionary ideas of individualism, fame and money. These values are not being rethought; they are simply copy-pasted from the West to the rest of the world.

But perhaps even more disturbing to the fate of the planet is the way that the value of rapid unsustainable economic growth has spread to the whole world. Asking those who have been subjugated and exploited by the West to renounce their plans in the name of planetary health that has been predominantly ravaged by the West is adding insult to injury. Yet it is also clear that decarbonization is intertwined with decolonization from Western style capitalism, and while it's true that the West bears responsibility and should be the first and most radical to transform itself, ultimately everybody will be needing to partake in this change. This means freeing oneself from many ruling ideas that are so much ingrained in us as to seem unalterable.

For example, the idea that more is better than less appears hardwired into us biologically; hunter-gatherers, who for 99 percent of human history were the only humans in existence, would have found the idea of accumulation strange. Even agricultural societies with their surplus stocks of wheat or rice revered ideas of ascetism that appear in all religious and philosophical traditions of the premodern world, including Hinduism, Buddhism, Christianity and Islam as well as Platonism. Freeing oneself from the thought of "more" is difficult; again, without it there is much disorientation. "More" is seemingly inscribed on our psyche like nothing else is. If one asks what people desire, they are most likely to describe it with "more." Not only the obvious more money, more fame, more sex, more travel and more house desires instilled as children and teenagers, but even anti-consumerist, anti-capitalist virtues express themselves in "more" – more time, more relationships and more fulfillment. Again, without the thought of "more," we are largely disoriented and demotivated. We can try to describe this new self-emptying state using concepts like the Christian kenosis or emptying out, the Buddhist state of desirelessness, or the Sufi state of fana, passing away or annihilation of the self. However, if we do not change the culture, the ecologically induced state of "less" will not feel like exultation and unification with God or cosmos, nor will it be an individual experience. It will be mostly seen as a troubling or even devastating loss. We will see more and more climate anxiety, depression, grief as we move into the future; we will reach a point in which we are radically unsure of ourselves and ruling ideas will be largely emptied of content; God, individualism, freedom, technology, progress or feminism will no longer seem like viable ideas.

Even sustainable development will not present itself as a good alternative idea. Sustainable development is an oxymoron. As philosopher William Ophuls eloquently put it, "Industrial Man has used the found wealth of the New World and the stocks of fossil hydrocarbons to create an anti-ecological *Titanic*. Making the deck chairs recyclable, feeding the boilers with biofuels, installing hybrid winches and windlasses, and every other effort to 'green' the Titanic will ultimately fail. In the end, the ship is doomed by the laws of thermodynamics and by implacable biological and geological limits that are already beginning to bite."

We really need to start the work of finding alternative ideas.

Chapter Fourteen

Alternatives to Ruling Ideas

As we have seen in several chapters, ruling ideas are tricky and can be used for a variety of purposes. Christianity is a good case in point. Its message of love, turning the other cheek, of non-calculating generosity and forgiveness of sins has been used to justify genocide in the New World as well as to legitimize slavery. Buddhism with its call for compassion and ceasing of desire has been used to legitimize theocracy as well as instill a sense of equanimity in Japanese soldiers who brutally colonized China and flew kamikaze airplanes in World War Two. The American Constitution, one of the most progressive pieces of legislation in the modern world, set on providing freedom and equality for all men, regulated an outstandingly cruel slave-holding society where women and poor people have no say. Communism committed to ending the exploitation of workers, peasants and those who were brutally colonized (together forming 99 percent of humanity!); an ideology that promised a new society and a new man in which all will be equal and share together in the common good is today used to legitimize an authoritarian regime in China that crushes independent unionizing by workers, where industrial workers who work for Western capitalist firms commit suicide because of their terrible working conditions.

This is something that should give us reason to pause and think. One could think, well, why then deal with ideas? Since any idea, no matter how good, can legitimate any action or any type of inequality, why not do away with ideas altogether and just look at actions and behaviors that are good or bad?

I think this is largely impossible. Actions are motivated by our ideas, and we orient ourselves with ideas like with a map.

A map is a simplified, idealized representation of how the world is and where we want to go. The ideas of Christianity, Buddhism, nationalism, liberalism, capitalism and socialism give us precisely this. They are narratives of how the world is and what we should do in it. They are maps that alert us to what is valuable, and they provide a narrative that explains where the world is going and points to opportunities and perils that exist in it. They create some of our most valued feelings – the inward warmth of love of Christianity, the compassion and equanimity of Buddhism, the freedom from coercion of liberalism, and the moving solidarity in the face of oppression and exploitation of socialism. At the same time, these ideas and their associated emotions are often used by elites to legitimize their rule. How are we to deal with this situation?

There are two options. One is making elites accountable for the ideals that they seem to promote; the second is using ideas that have not yet been co-opted by elites themselves. If we start with the first, can we pressure the Buddhist elite to be truly selfless? Or the Christian elite to be loving? Or the US elite to treat people like it says in the Declaration of Independence, "We hold these truths to be self-evident, that all men are created equal..." and to truly promote "Life, Liberty and the Pursuit of Happiness"? We can ask the communist regime in China to provide ownership of the means of production to the workers just like Marx says they should. Dramatic transformations can happen when the people suddenly stop being cynical about the claims of the elites and forcefully take the elites at their own word. This option is not easy, but it's always an option. A second option is to posit new ideas that will dislodge or challenge elites in unsuspected ways. This is always a good thing almost regardless of ideology. Let's take an example. A classic case is the revolutionary ideas of the Enlightenment.

A small class of bourgeoisie, originally merchants and craftsmen of European cities (the boroughs), used ideas as their tool in order to open up and change an extraordinarily repressive society: a society in which Catholic Christianity is the only belief system allowed, and most value is siphoned off from those who produce on the land and given to the church and nobility; a traditional society in which there is no recognition of human beings as having any kind of autonomy, where everyone is both a subject and a Christian, subordinate to both church and nobility. A flurry of Enlightenment ideas such as humanism, liberalism, nationalism and democracy were effective weapons of revolution that ultimately did away with the authority of church and the nobles and kings around much of the world. We should, however, not overestimate the progress that these ideas brought. Now let's say my interlocutor is an American slave in 1830. She can say, "What does it matter if one is a serf in Europe under a king and church or if one is a slave like myself suffering under the plantation owners who wrote the Declaration of Independence?" There is little one can answer to her. One can only say that most of the human population were either slaves and serfs for thousands of years, and the ruling idea of divine right of kings ruled them with no ability to contest this rule. Indeed, contesting it in a systemic way was inconceivable. For example, in the feudal world depicted by Shakespeare and, as a matter of fact, the one portrayed frequently by Disney, one can change an unjust king by what was perceived as a just one, but one cannot contest the rule of kings. In contrast, under the effect of ideas of liberalism, contesting slavery seems inevitable. The Thirteenth Amendment to the United States Constitution abolished slavery in 1865, only 75 years after the Constitution came into force in 1789. Considering that slavery existed since the Neolithic revolution 11,000 years ago, 75 years is not a lot. This shows us the truly revolutionary spirit of Enlightenment ideas, ideas that we otherwise can regard with much cynicism. One can concede that, originally, they were meant as a weapon of the rising bourgeoisie against those above them. But it is important to stress that these ideas had unforeseen consequences for all the world. Our very sense of what is now a human and citizen flows from them. Many feminists, anti-colonialists and even socialists, while critiquing the hypocrisy that inheres in implementation of Enlightenment ideals, and even when they argue more fundamentally against them, rely on the bedrock of these ideas. For example, without the Enlightenment, the creation of a public sphere, with its newspapers, journals and associations of feminism and anti-colonialism, is unimaginable. Spaces in which people of different ranks in society intermingle over various causes is an invention of the Enlightenment.

Nonetheless, it is also clear that the emancipatory potential of the Enlightenment has exhausted itself, especially in the West. Enlightenment values are mainly used to reaffirm the status quo. Witness any kind of global elite gathering in the world – the G8 summit, Davos, TED, or any one of a myriad of tech conferences – and one will hear classic notions of the Enlightenment like progress (now couched as disruption), efficacy and technical wonders bandied about. The philosophy of the Enlightenment is the ruling ideology. To challenge ruling ideas, one needs to create a space of freedom from them. How are we to do this?

Negation and True Contrarian Thinking

In the famous Monty Python "Argument Sketch," Michael Palin walks into an office and asks a receptionist for an argument. She tells him how much an argument costs and directs him to Room 12. Eventually he reaches the right room in which John Cleese tells him upon entry, "I've told you once," to which he answers, "No, you haven't." After countless "No, you didn't!", "Yes, I did!" exchanges, the man complains that this is not an argument, merely a contradiction. He further explains:

M: An argument isn't just contradiction.

C: Well! it CAN be!

M: No, it can't! An argument is a connected series of statements intended to establish a proposition.

C: No, it isn't!

M: Yes, it is! 'Tisn't just contradiction.

Indeed, contradiction looks childish. Even debates, from high school to presidential, are largely superficial. They tend to regress to a kind of sophistry and have little to do with creative intellectual work or even with persuasion. They are a kind of self-validating entertainment with roots in competitive sports mentality. Yet contradiction is important; a skillful thinker like Nietzsche can develop a wholly creative philosophy simply by attempting to contradict Platonism and Christianity. Contradiction and negation are especially important when we consider freedom from ruling ideas. Ruling ideas are so encompassing, so deeply embedded in us, that to immediately find alternatives to them is difficult. A humbler start for shaking off their hold upon us would be to contradict them with their opposite. So, let's contradict some of the ruling ideas and see what kinds of freedoms that affords us. What would contradicting individualism mean?

In the film *Fight Club*, Tyler Durden, the charismatic revolutionary alter ego of the main character, is putting together an anti-consumerist, anti-corporate militant group, Project Mayhem. While training them he says, "You are not special. You're not a beautiful and unique snowflake. You're the same decaying organic matter as everything else. We're all part of the same compost heap. We're all singing, all dancing crap of the world." Interestingly, the designation snowflake in this context has migrated from a left-wing anti-corporate context and become a term used by conservatives to typify liberal college students. In any case, Tyler Durden's original message is where we should start. His statement "You are not special" is a fitting contradiction to *Life of Brian*'s "You are all special." While Brian's message of specialness mixes anti-authoritarianism with a seventies kind of depolitization (the film appeared in 1979), he is essentially dispersing this crowd, each to find his own solution to life's problems; the message of being *not* special, just "decaying organic matter" is revolutionary. In our time, any intellectual tradition or practice that negates the individual wins us some degree of freedom from the tyranny of ruling ideas. Buddhism, for example, teaches the doctrine of Anattā, a Pali word consisting of "an" (not, without) and "attā" (self). More precisely, since exacting Buddhist philosophers did not want to state something (self) and then negate it, they have claimed that "self exists" is a false premise. Everything is impermanent. Consciousness presents itself often as a self that "grasps" an object. For example, on my morning walks in the park I can enjoy nature or being out; however, sometimes I start ruminating on some behavior of a departmental colleague and I start flaring up emotionally. Like masochistically playing with a wound, I start thinking of how greedy and fearful this person is, how he tries to manipulate the institution instead of concentrating on teaching and research, how I am forced to be nice and accommodating since he is above me in the department, etc. This wave of mental "dirt" affirms a strong sense of self, a self that is prideful and wants recognition. If one, however, closely pays attention, one sees that as this mental wave of negativity subsides, so does the sense of self. There are points in time when both disappear, my sense of self as well as the object that it is grasping. Buddhism teaches that if we pay attention to experience, we always find this pair of subjects grasping for an object. However, both are illusionary because they are impermanent.

Monotheistic traditions too have played down the special individual. In contrast to Greek mythology, with its strong or cunning heroes, Old Testament protagonists have no special gifts; they are largely arbitrarily chosen by the will of God.

While I stressed before that this being God-chosen is a great way to be legitimated as ruler, I would like to stress that from the perspective of a contemporary reader, this humble self is useful to counter individualism. In many of its traditions, the various monotheisms stress that one is a small part of creation. At the same time, one ought to be careful and selective in using these traditions to contradict the modern self. In many instances, especially in Protestant Christianity, religious doctrine lives side by side or even contributed to possessive individualism. In fact, one of the most influential accounts of the contemporary self-aggrandizing individual, described by sociologist Max Weber, sees his origins precisely in the Protestant Reformation. Nevertheless, we can learn much from these traditions. For example, consider voluntary simplicity or as it was better known in the Christian tradition, voluntary poverty. It is important to distinguish voluntary simplicity from destitution, which means having less than one needs, and from poverty that is enforced on one. Both of these are bad things that should be eradicated. Voluntary poverty is for all intents and purposes the opposite of today's individualism. Individualism today means wanting wealth. Instead of looking for being a lone individual on the new frontier, in finding new ways to hustle and make a buck on Mars, why not reconnect to humanity and nature? Living in voluntary simplicity connects you with the way that most of humanity lives; it deindividuates you from false specialness. It means practical solidarity and unity with other people, in the sense that you live like others and are likely to need help and to help other people as well. Voluntary simplicity is more likely to lead to a life of service to others rather than to a self-interested and self-aggrandizing life. Voluntary simplicity connects one with nature and teaches one to be part of nature. Apart from the very wealthy, middle-class people have to work extremely hard to sustain their lifestyle. This work often stresses individualistic career making that comes at the cost of connection with lovers, reading, friends and nature, helping others, etc., all things that cause people to move beyond themselves into concerns that are outside of themselves.

Voluntary poverty is part of ascetic strategies that belong to all religions. These types of practices are actually a strategy of anyone who resists mainstream society. At the core of ascetic self-negation is the desire to become a new person in a community that is different from mainstream society. Asceticism allows one to deconstruct behavior, opinions and emotions and rebuild them into a new kind of person.

Besides classical religions, Marxism, anthropology and modernism can also be of use in countering individualism. Marx and Engels have tried to provide a more scientific account of history. This account should be seen in its context of radical revolution in self-understanding what happened in the middle of the nineteenth century. The biblical view of history and of man was overturned completely by Charles Darwin; the discovery of the ancient civilization of Sumer by archeologists such as William Kennet Loftus (1820-1858), George Smith (1840-1876) and Henry Creswicke Rawlinson (1810-1895); the discovery of the cell and cell biology; and more. Similar to these discoveries, Marxism attempted to provide a more scientific approach to history. Until that point in time, history was often told as stories of great men and their decisions. Marx and Engels saw the fundamental changes in history as changes in material production from hunting-gathering to agriculture and from agriculture to industry. In this they were fundamentally correct; any world history that attempts to be objective in relating the most significant and sweeping changes the human race has undergone, will largely recapitulate the same transitions. The import of Marxism in countering individualism is twofold. First, it stresses the fact that production is social activity, that whatever we have is a result of the complex work of many. Second, it sees individualism itself as resulting from distorting ideology whose roots are in the rise of the commercial classes and their stress on individual property rights. What is important for our purposes here is to be aware that the world around us is a collective creation and that some of the things that we most pride about ourselves are false and distortive ideology. Marxism humbles us and makes us realize that alone we are not much of a historical force, that we usually live out our lives according to our historical epoch and our class and that we do not strictly have individually authored lives.

While Marxism stresses our deep dependence on historical and economic substructure, anthropology stresses the culture around us as largely decisive to what we do and who we are. When we go to another culture, especially a foreign one, we are always met with the overwhelming need to explain actions and behaviors in terms of culture and not as individual preference. For example, if one visits the Azande people of north-central Africa and on a particular day sees someone poisoning a little chicken and another waiting to see if the little chick dies or not, it would be absurd to view these actions as individual preferences. These actions get their meaning from the belief in magic and witchcraft that permeates every aspect of that society. The oracle is feeding poison to the chicken in order to determine guilt or non-guilt around adultery, theft, etc. If this African oracle was transported to France and saw an 80-year-old fussing over little square papers that are then put carefully into albums, this person will need to understand the institute of stamp collecting; it is not some mad idea of an individual. When I myself saw older people in China slapping their own arms and legs forcefully when they exercised, I was forced to view this behavior as systematic (not individual) and as ultimately explained in terms of traditional Chinese medicine discourse. Human individual behavior by itself usually does not make sense. Like the cloud that follows the Pink Panther around and rains on him wherever he goes, in the same way our actions are meaningful only because a cloud of discourse hovers above us and this cloud is linguistic-social, not individual. It is the discourse that we internalize that gives meaning and controls what we do. We should remember this when we think that we are autonomous human beings making our own decisions.

Modernism might seem a strange inspiration to counter individualism. Are not the great masters of modernism, for example, Picasso, the quintessential individualists, magically expressing themselves in a variety of styles? Not quite. The main tradition in modernism is largely depersonalized. If we take this seminal modernist work, Marcel Duchamp's urinal, it is clear that it is not personal expression but a provocation to its audience to examine and think about the power of the artist and the museum itself to confer the state of art on anything no matter how degraded. However, an even more direct counter to individualism is Kazimir Malevich's work *Black Square*. Here is a picture of a woman looking at it in a museum:

In his manifesto, Malevich wrote, "When, in the year 1913, in my desperate attempt to free art from the ballast of objectivity, I took refuge in the square form and exhibited a picture which consisted of nothing more than a black square on a white field, the critics and, along with them, the public sighed, "Everything which we loved is lost. We are in a desert...Before us is nothing but a black square on a white background!" Malevich viewed the square as an expression of the desert of inner reality against a white background. Malevich writes:

> It is from zero, in zero, that the true movement of being begins.
>
> I transformed myself in the zero of form and emerged from nothing to creation, that is, to Suprematism, to the new realism in painting – to non-objective creation.
>
> [Black Square is meant to evoke] the experience of pure non-objectivity in the white emptiness of a liberated nothing.

It is only by starting with personal zero, by negating ourselves and our "figure" that we can hope to fashion something new and worthwhile. It is only by disruption and divestment that we can help create a new kind of subjectivity. Only by becoming black like a closed television set that we can hope to generate new images.

In the twentieth century, one way of countering individualism was through self-sacrifice in the name of nation or class. While self-satisfied liberals look back at this eager participation in bloodbath in a kind of self-satisfied "look at how those stupid young people went to kill and be killed enthusiastically" way, perhaps one should turn the look toward those same liberals and ask what precisely is the middle-class liberal willing to risk their lives for? If the answer is nothing, if safety *always* comes first, then we are facing a certain diminution of man. Scientists, artists, revolutionaries, spiritual leaders and lovers have always taken the furthering of their cause beyond their safety.

As we saw, since the 1960s, individualism is tightly connected with free sexual expression. From that point in time, the right to express yourself sexually became celebrated in market societies. In fact, homosexual sexuality together with gender nonconforming behavior has become the most significant active demonstration of Western freedoms. They are strictly about the individual's expression and are an important part of the ruling ideas. It is clear that one should not go back to sex negativity of traditional cultures, a negativity whose main motive was controlling women's sexuality in the name of patriarchy. Nor of course should one go back to heteronormativity and obligatory gender conformity. Nevertheless, one should contradict their individualism. Sexual individualism has reached such an extreme, in which instead of mutual sexual collaboration and mutual sexual transformation, in which people take on and transform each other's fantasies, we have solipsistic masturbating and a hooking-up culture in which people play out their fantasies irrespective of other people, both in porn and via the webcam. In real life, people are conceived of as a market and are looking to find a fitting person to fulfill their fantasies. The problem with viewing the world as an opportunity for meeting individualist preferences is first that these preferences are not authentic and are created by capitalistic society, and second is that meeting personal preference discourages growth. The evolution of our preferences themselves often occurs when our own desires are frustrated by the world, often by doing things with other people.

In the first chapter we dealt quite a lot with the way in which our attention is fixated on a dozen world leaders, business tycoons and celebrities. What would the negation or contradiction of this be? There are several options. One option is to create our own cannon of people that we would like to be interested in, thus moving away from the most important figures to lesser known but nonetheless impressive achievers. Both in history and today one might gain much from getting to know the achievement of lesser-known people in any kind of area that one is interested in. Why not get to know Dorothy Height instead of just Martin Luther King Jr.? Perhaps get to know Ferdinand Lassalle, Edward Bernstein, Freydun Atturaya or Sylvia Pankhurst instead of just Marx and Lenin; how about José Clemente Orozco and not just Picasso? To complement lesser-known figures, one might reexamine regular people's lives. In France following the 1848 revolution in which people demanded the right to work, artists began seeing working-class people in day-to-day scenes and events as worthy topics for literature and art. This movement begins with Gustave Courbet in painting and Stendhal in literature and reaches well into the twenty-first century with the films of Ken Loach.

If the reader remembers, the adulation of the famous and the rich is one of the ways that the wealth and abundance of society is privatized, while the creation of villains is the way in which its problems and evils are privatized and externalized. To contrast this process, we must move away from presenting good and evil through charismatic individuals and see both of them spread out throughout our societies. Hard work, ingenuity and empathy are spread out in the lives of billions, while the evils of inequality and environmental and personal degradation are scattered out as well. We must learn to see the good and the bad in thousands of little things around us. A nurse or teacher who does their job well, a polluted "cloud" above us, the noise of our urban dwellings, the trees of our parks, the ingenuity of our tools, the good and the bad are interspersed and interconnected throughout our world. The most falsifying picture of our world is the picture that Hollywood gives us at the end of an action film in which the good hero fights the bad villain and once he wins, the world is restored to its basic goodness.

Another form of the individualism that we encounter is the calculating agent, an agent who tries to measure and compare utilities and outcomes for himself or herself. How would we counter this type of individualism? First is to reach an understanding that anything that is quantifiable is usually not worth much. Our life is made from experiences and events. Most of the things that really make life worth living – love and sexuality, being in nature, music, political or religious meaning – are not things that can be made into quantities. We have to be coerced with rigorous education, with mathematics and algebra, which are resented by most students, in order to instill in us a sense that the world is to be evaluated according to quantities. And yet even after this long education spanning years and years and thousands of hours, most of us "stupid" human beings would rather engage in music, sports, religion, travel, literature and history and not mathematics or quantitative science. Measuring is a certain kind of pernicious abstraction. It marks the coalition of technology, science and capitalism, between exchange value and calculation. It allows us great power as a society, but translated into individuals trying to calculate their way to happiness and meaning, it is much less satisfying.

Chapter three dealt with ruling values and virtues. What would be the meaning of contradicting values and virtues? There are several options here. One option already invoked by Socrates is instead of looking at amorphous virtues, one should look at concrete procedures that generate value, what Socrates exemplified as *techne* or crafts and praxis itself. However, we must look beyond just the utility of production and technology and look at the way goods and bads are created and distributed throughout the whole process of the creation of value. This, however, leaves out much that is related to the original function of values and virtues – to orient and motivate the individual. Contradicting values and virtues might mean looking at what is known as situational ethics, that is, thinking what the best action is in this particular situation. For example, instead of developing biomedical ethics, a doctor should do all in his power with the resources available to help someone who does not have medical coverage or who is an illegal alien, regardless of legal and other consequences.

As we saw, one of the most important ruling virtues is the virtue of work. Negating it is already well underway. Automation has made even high-tech billionaires call for universal basic income. More importantly, countering work means developing a sense of value that is outside of one's career. It also entails telling the *truth* about work, that many professional and middle-class jobs are either useless or actively sustain and further the "bads" of the world, and that millions are employed in creating violence within "defense" and army industries. Others are employed in creating illusions and lies in the entertainment, religion and advertisement industries, conformity and arbitrary reproduction of class hierarchy in the education industry, mass incarceration in the legal industry, and creation of poverty and debt in the financial industry. In fact, if someone is doing something that is truly harmful for society on a grand scale, you can be sure that he or she will be well remunerated, while if someone does something truly beneficial, things like taking care of the young and old, cooking, cleaning, taking care of the sick, or farming, you can be sure they will be among the poorest in society. Perhaps the strong public relations dependence of universities and other institutions in the medical profession is due to the fact that today few professionals outside this field are actually doing things that are unambiguously beneficial for society.

Subjectively, and especially for men, a sense of self-worth has been bound with being a provider. With financial crisis, mass migration, pandemics, automation and other crises, employment is no longer secure for an increasing percentage of the population. It is crucial in such a world to develop a post-work identity and culture. Meaning and purpose can easily be generated by participating and organizing activities such as those that involve music and other arts, social engagement, sports, religion/spirituality, sexuality, education and various ways of connecting with nature. All of these activities are self-rewarding, that is, people do them for their intrinsic worth.

Knowledge is another ruling idea. Knowledge, as we saw, is one of the virtues that ruling elites pride themselves with the most. As we saw, technical knowledge is promoted while true knowledge of society is discouraged. Nevertheless, the virtue of knowledge always flirts with substantial social reform. First and foremost, current knowledge needs to be democratized, freed from serving the interests of a small minority. We must uncouple knowledge and our understanding of it from anthropocentrism, imperialism and class domination. Just like there was Nazi racial science, there is capitalist economic and political science, and there are area sciences that are devoted solely to extending the power of the West over the rest. Our knowledge is intimately imbricated in a society that creates various "bads" like extreme inequality and destruction of the environment. Technology as well needs to serve humanity and indeed the planet at large and not a small elite. Letting techno-capitalism dictate society and environment will simply lead to its devastation. We must contradict any ruling ideas that put techno-capitalism as the first priority. One needs to think of our priorities first and see what arrangement of the economy and technology serves them best. Agricultural, industrial and postindustrial society have been superstructures constructed inadvertently from their techno-economic base. It is both immature and destructive to determine one's society from its techno-economic base. There is little warrant to uncritically celebrate technological innovation; in our current society it is one of the main ways of sucking value from regular people toward a tiny elite. Its benefits are definitely not universal. The flush toilet invented in 1596 is still to make its way to one billion people who do not have access to it. The Industrial Revolution and its new technologies and the colonization that came in its wake have truly worsened life for millions of workers and non-Western peoples, and have devastated nature. In the daytime, our corporations and our press worship ruthless business tycoons and the "progress" they have created, while at night our real feelings are revealed by Hollywood that makes more and more dystopian fiction, or represents us with fantasies of people having solidarity and friendship. Negating the ruling idea of technological innovation means that you don't think that some technical solution would solve fundamental human and environmental problems, but that political and cultural solutions come first.

We should reverse economy and technology to suit what we believe to be a good society. We should no longer be disrupted by the economic-tech system but let actual human needs and capabilities disrupt the economic-technological system.

Imagine our mainstream discourse of technological innovation through the eyes of a mother living in the great world slums (one in eight people in the world live in slums). Cutting-edge knowledge and technology are not only not useful for her but surveillance software and armed bulldozers are used regularly by soldiers and policemen to terrorize her and threaten her children. If she is part of an indigenous people, technology and "progress" are even more ominous, as they are used to decimate her habitat and identify, torture or kill her children who are resisting the land grab. In fact, what appears as an exciting technological "frontier" for those living in the core is a kind of violent chaos to those living beyond the frontier. For every person raving at a TED talk about new technology, there are thousands working in industrial plants and living in slums. For every bland talk of putting people together, there is the practice of pulling people apart. In fact, the main trajectory of technology, from the television to virtual reality, is toward isolation, not connection. Technology and knowledge can often exacerbate isolation and inequality.

How do we negate the ruling idea of simple progress, a

golden past, or a simple dystopian future? First, we should reject the idea that there is some "good" point in time in the past that it is worthy to return to. Fundamentally, there is no going back in time. Causality flows forward, and the world is always profoundly changing. The cyclical view of time adopted by "timeless" agricultural societies was both an illusion and a ruling idea in itself. Ecclesiastes 1:9 demonstrates this ruling idea well: "The thing that hath been, it is that which shall be; and that which is done is that which shall be done: and there is no new thing under the sun." Rulers always want to say, "What is, will always be." Agricultural societies were not timeless but began only 12,000 years ago, in some places 4,000 years ago, a split of a second in the timescale of the Earth and even of life itself. Another conservative ruling idea attempt was not timelessness but the end of history, first promulgated by Hegel and then by Francis Fukuyama. As we currently see, history did not stop with the Prussian state nor with the collapse of the Soviet Union. It is always changing.

Even when there is a collapse of civilization, like the fall of Rome, things never go back to what they were before. Trying to return to the past is always a dangerous illusion. We are always faced with new values, new cultures and new ways of doing things that make going back impossible. Negating the idea of a "glorious" past means looking at the present for opportunities for a break for a better future. Contradicting the present is much harder than contradicting the past. Its immersive and captivating power is unparalleled. Yet all of us have felt how our captivation by the present is false. We all remember being extremely worried, anxious or fearful about things that very quickly lose meaning. We also notice that changing place and culture easily releases us from presentism. Technology and events are very likely to change relatively quickly the most fundamental aspects of how life is lived. For example, for many years, people's physical location was determined by their job. This has been seen as one of the most solid and present aspects of human beings. People choose to live a manageable commute from their work. Post COVID-19, we will see that this will no longer be strictly the case, especially for white collar workers. In the future living arrangements are likely to change as people will decide where to live according to their hobbies, their children and their health. We might be seeing the end of working physically together. This is a tremendous historical change. Hunting, sowing and reaping, working machines in industrial plants, office work – all of these were always done physically together. People's main physical social interaction was work related. It will soon be unrelated to work. Perhaps we are witnessing the end of the city as a center for work, and we should think about new ways of sociability and physicality. On the shorter timescale, the COVID-19 and economic crisis has made libertarian positions untenable; the Reagan era is over and everyone will be demanding more government. In short, the present is always changing; it should not determine what we want to do.

Being free from the ruling ideas regarding the future is tricky. Ruling ideas of optimistic industry leaders, billionaires and their academic acolytes are less and less persuasive; we know that the future holds both predictable dangers such as unemployment due to AI and global warming as well as unpredictable fears such as war, epidemics, disasters, etc. Contradicting our own current presentation of the future means forgoing helplessness, our ever-incessant imagination of various catastrophes, and mobilizing and organizing to create the future that is desirable.

Though negating the ideas of God, nation and family has been done extensively before, by the Enlightenment as well as by all forms of socialism, we are faced with the need to do so again given that these old ruling ideas have been in resurgence for the past 40 years, starting with the Iranian revolution in 1979, the fall of Soviet Russia in 1991, and the rise of European and American populism since 2016. Negating God needs to be done in two different stages. First and most importantly is separating God from politics and political rule. Privatizing God is essential since as an emotional prothesis this idea creates much less damage than as a political idea of God used to legitimize authority. This has already partially happened in the American and French Revolutions, but it needs to be implemented worldwide. The idea of God should not figure in state affairs in any way. Any religious intuition needs to be translated into a common nonreligious language when it steps into the public sphere. One needs to demonstrate that the fetus experiences pain or consciousness, that the territories of the West Bank are important strategically, etc., without invoking God. This allows a discussion to form in which people can argue on grounds of experience and thought. If one invokes God, then it becomes an argument regarding the will of God and an exegesis of the Bible in which both unbelievers and believers of other faiths cannot truly take part on the same levels. This means that in any modern heterogenous state (which is currently all states), some have more authority than others. God should never be used as a ruling idea. The private God, the God as emotional prothesis, separated from politics, is less problematic. Nevertheless, there are problems here too as the idea of God often detracts from assessing the situations and their possibilities. God may energize people to do certain things ("in the name of God") as well as make people more passive ("God has a plan for you"), but both are distortive because they do not follow strictly from what exists and what is possible.

The nation should be negated with a strenuous anti-nationalism. Even when nationalism is at its most just, a nationalism that originates in opposition to colonialism, it very quickly becomes unjust after decolonization and independence. After decolonization, the interests of nationalist elites become very different from those of the masses of humanity. Nationalist elites soon form a new predatory upper class. A look at South Africa, Algeria and India confirms this. It is needless to say that the nationalism of the strong core countries (Germany, England, US, Japan, etc.) immediately turns into violent imperialism as these countries conquer and decimate various populations. Though in popular presentation we are led to believe these countries are very different from one another, in actual fact, each of these countries instigated racist genocides and forced labor. Spain, England and the US may have started with the genocide of Native Americans, the colonization of the world, and slavery, but the model was exported so that by 1910, Japan subjugated Korean peasants to forced labor and took over their land, and in the 1930s, Germany followed suit in the policies toward their policy toward

When thinking about nationalism, it is important *not* to view it from the perspective of those who largely benefit from the nation-state, that is, the upper and middle classes, but from the perspective of minorities. The pattern of violence toward marginalized communities of the nation-state is unmistakable, as it has been stable and global. Everyone's imagination is, of course, captivated by short-term events like the Nazi Holocaust. In negating nationalism, we should rather concentrate on more low-key violence that is exercised constantly and relentlessly. Waterfront communities of Otodo Gambe in Lagos Nigeria, or of Colombia's Pacific city of Beunaventura are being forcibly evicted; Arabs in East Jerusalem, and natives have been evicted from their lands since the nineteenth century in both North and South America. The capitalist world system always expresses itself in types of colonization and displacement. Afraid of displacement and competition themselves, and needing to generate returns on investments, capitalist firms have to look for new things to commodify, new resources to get a hold of. Grabbing land, evicting tenants and so on is always both a nationalist mission as well as good for strong real estate players.

In contrast to libertarian propaganda, capital always works with the state first and foremost to get the land it needs for everything else to happen. This happened in the great enclosure of seventeenth-century England and is happening in the West Bank today.

Going against nationalism means looking at your own country and other countries and recognizing that you are largely in a similar ugly ship. Your respective working-class minorities are in the same violent ship and your middle-class reader is in the same trivial and anxious ship, worrying if your kids will make it to the middle class, trivially enjoying food and television, buying stuff from Amazon, etc., believing in many of the same ruling ideas, including, for example, nationalism. There is really no "us" and "them."

Negating the ruling idea of the family can take various forms. But certainly it is not to be done in the way that our competitive society is currently "negating" the family, creating socially withdrawn individuals like the Hikikomori of Japan. Negating the family simply means unburdening it from all the different things that it is now supposed to do and by letting other institutions and relationships do some of the work. For instance, should spouses and children provide you with what friendship provided back when people had friends? Should food be prepared at home? Why not release men and women from this inefficient drudgery and have them eat in a cafeteria or canteen? Do children need to spend so much time with their nuclear family on long vacations and weekends? Why not free caretakers as well as make life more joyous for children by having them spend more time with one another? Is lifelong monogamy really realistic for most relationships? Most importantly, why not focus on political or artistic goals together with like-minded groups, groups centered around ideas, rather than spending so much time in a group ultimately based on biological reproduction?

Negating the ruling idea of the eighteenth-century Enlightenment does not mean going back to tribalism and traditionalism. It also does not mean simply reforming eighteenth-century Enlightenment ideals that simply had a little problem with women and slaves. The eighteenth-century Enlightenment was an abstract unhistorical doctrine. Being most purely implemented in the US, it at the same time claimed to espouse freedom from coercion in the abstract while driving natives from their lands, subjugating nature and women, owning slaves, and exploiting workers. It falsely claimed that the economic realm is free from coercion, pretended that companies and corporations do not need the state to guarantee property rights, is able to provide a literate workforce through public education, and create infrastructure for the transport of resources. Additionally, the state has always helped secure various monopolies. The biggest companies, from the East India Company through to United Fruit and Google, have always relied on the power of an imperialist state to overcome resistance to their highly exploitative operations abroad. While eighteenth-century Enlighteners and their contemporary libertarian avatars lie about the role of government, they absolutely deny the degradation of nature and global heating. In fact, from the very beginning, the Enlightenment has desacralized nature and presented it as following a set of mathematical laws and existing as raw materials to be used at will.

Alternative Ideas

A fire in California, a drought in Cape Town or India, a hurricane off the coast of Florida: the weather is becoming more extreme. Forests are being cut down and the extinction rate of animals makes our period the great sixth extinction. We seem to be bombarded with this message every day. Environmentalism might seem like a ruling idea, but it is not. A ruling idea is not defined by its prevalence (although most ruling ideas are very prevalent), but whether it is used to legitimize hierarchy, by its support for the status quo, and there seems to be no idea in our time that threatens the status quo today more than environmentalism. As Al Gore called it many years ago (when only half of today's emissions were in the air) – an inconvenient truth. What he meant was a truth that was inconvenient for elites. I don't expect that those who have suffered under capitalism (workers, slaves, etc.) would be much surprised by its violence toward the natural world; after all, it was very violent toward them. And yet it is hard for everyone irrespective of class, gender or race to accept the new situation. Most of us are using various defenses in order not to truly internalize the threat that humanity is facing. This knowing something and yet not fully acknowledging its implications is a rather common thing.

Undergoing transformation is usually not a result of new knowledge but of something that has made this knowledge emotionally salient enough to affect life. We all know many things: that half of the world's population lives on less than 2.50 dollars a day; that the way we grow, wear, experiment and eat animals is cruel; that the spread of novel viruses is increasingly dangerous; that natives have been either killed or displaced from their lands and are kept on reservations, in open air prisons or real prisons by the millions; that workers find it difficult to sustain families and need to work at two or more jobs or cannot find regular work. Knowing something does not entail truly internalizing it on an emotional level and acting upon it. Che Guevara knew that there was abject poverty in South America – but to experience it firsthand caused him to take a revolutionary path. Likewise, people in psychotherapy often hear things that they already know; however, in a new context, laden with emotion in a relationship with a certified professional-stranger, these words make a difference.

It is difficult to get people to be truly responsive to the environmental crisis, especially in the global north in which it is felt much less. Today we know, for example, that the Permian extinction, also known as the "great dying," happened 251 million years ago. It occurred precisely because of the rather slow release (compared to today) of CO_2 and methane. This acidified the ocean, killing up to 96 percent of marine life. On land, a third of animal species died, and nearly all the forests died as well. Many of the possible causes are familiar to us: extensive CO_2 in the atmosphere that results in acidic oceans, while hotter temperatures and melting ice caps cause the stagnation of the world's oceans. Though we are not as worried as we should be, our horizon is changing. The environmental crisis is undermining all ruling ideas. Since the French and American Revolutions, we have been telling heroic narratives about humanity. We have had fierce political battles about which precise stories to tell and the exact meaning of those narratives. However, they have much in common.

For the sake of illustration, let's take two very different, even opposing, stories from the twentieth century, the story of Henry Ford and the story of Vladimir Lenin. Though there could not be more mortal enemies than these two, they agreed on many things. They both believed in the revolution of modernity, narratives of "more." Lenin wanted the redistribution of power and its intensification: "All power to the workers councils plus electrification of the whole country." Henry Ford said, "I will build a car for the great multitude." He believed that with mass mobility comes freedom and progress. Though Lenin lived a very modest life while Ford gave his son a birthday gift of what would be today 120 million dollars in pure gold, they both agreed on the positive potential of technology, factories, big industry, the importance of rationality, the authority of science and the value of hard work. Like older religious doctrines, they agreed that people should bring more children into the world. They both believed in progress, though they differed in how each one of them interpreted this concept. They were bitter enemies, of course, as well. Lenin saw someone like Ford as a capitalist who ruthlessly exploits workers. Ford, of course, saw Lenin as a dangerous communist, unchristian and immoral. They embody well the face-off between the right and the left in the twentieth century.

Enter the environmental crisis. This crisis undermines all the stories that we have been telling ourselves, not only the right and left ones but also monotheistic ones. Be fruitful and multiply, work hard, become independent, gain power and success, expand your control over nature, but most importantly, grow! There are several kinds of responses to the challenge to the ruling orientation that climate change poses.

The first and most simple is a kind of denial: it's not serious, we can ignore it, nature will return to some equilibrium. It is, however, noteworthy that elites who claim that we should not be worried about the environment are themselves preparing for the results of climate change. Oil drilling rigs are planned to be built with consideration to raising sea levels, for example, while the ultra-rich are preparing in various ways for "the event," buying apartments in fortified underground complexes that were built in the past to withstand atomic war, or large houses in remote New Zealand where supposedly social unrest will not reach.

The second way in which the environmental crisis is reacted to is to propose that capitalism will solve it through pollution rights, markets and green consumption. The right to pollute will have to be purchased. This will have the effect of internalizing pollution in costs instead of making it just an externality, something that does not affect profit. On the consumer side, there is buying eco brands, garbage sorting, not eating meat and not flying. Of course, all these proposals are too little too late; they cannot hope to reverse the juggernaut of the fossil fuel industry, an extractive economy, or a society and culture based on consumption.

A third related response is the technological fix. This can take a variety of forms from simple and minimalist to highly ambitious. On the basic level, improving technology of sustainable wind and solar energy will make it irresistibly efficient and simply replace the fossil fuels industry. More ambitious is geo-engineering, various currently only imagined ways of sucking carbon out of the air, reflecting sunlight away from Earth in order to cool it, reengineering crops to make them heat resistant, building giant seawalls to mitigate the rise in the oceans, etc. The most ambitious proposals include genetically modifying humans to be more resistant to heat, creating hybrid humans or colonizing dead planets. These exaggerated forms of techno-optimism are broadcast loudly by the elite both for legitimizing its rule and also for self-promotion (e.g., Elon Musk, who said he wants to die on Mars). One can say that our political imagination is indeed caught between visions of trying to minimize our disturbance to the Earth by reconnecting to nature and minimizing our carbon footprint with various maximalist versions of relocating ourselves to other planets or uploading ourselves to the cloud.

Futurist and sociologist Steve Fuller says that our political ideas have made a 90-degree turn. Instead of left and right, we have today what he calls up and down. Left and right were originally designated by the seating arrangement of the French National Assembly of the French Revolution. On the right of the assembly sat supporters of the king and church, to the left sat various factions devoted to changing the status quo, from business class liberalism to communism. The deciding factor was whether to go back to the legitimization and institutions of the past (king and church) or stake out new ways of organizing society in the future. The right claimed that history had already revealed the basic characteristics of human behavior and the social institutions that are congruent with it. Legitimacy comes from tradition; we should trust what has worked. The right sees social arrangements and governing patterns as arising from solving local problems, custom-made for the place. The left, mobilized by inequality and exploitation, highlights the variability in social arrangements that signal the human potential for yet untold kinds of societies. The left wants reason to adjudicate the best kind of social arrangement, the most viable institutions. The right thinks of our place and affirms hierarchy; the left thinks of time and possibility.

Fuller suggests that the division between left and right has lost much of its salience. He thinks that politics will be divided into people who believe that we are bound to our earthlike current existence, the downwingers, a prime example being environmentalists; and those who think we should be able to go beyond the earthly existence either by uploading ourselves into the cloud or by traveling into space – upwingers. Upwingers want us to leave our default biological patterns by genetic modification or by uploading consciousness into machines. Downwingers see human beings as part of the planet, part of the ecosystem that sets limits to growth. There are rigid and final constraints to human development and human growth. Fuller identifies with the upwingers, adopting what he calls the proactionary principle, the opposite of precautionary principle.

Though I think he is correct in his analysis of the shift in politics, I would argue that upwingers are a conservative reaction to the environmental crisis and for demands for environmental justice. As we have seen, positing a new frontier is simply a well-proven strategy of displacing demands for redistribution of wealth. Reaching for the stars is a way of saying that we can continue the political way we are doing things on Earth. It is also true that the proactionary principle appeals to our feelings of courage and progress, but I think that the techno-optimism espoused by his proactionary principle is wrong. Many technologies such as nuclear bombs and biological weapons are dangerous to everybody. Other technologies like the car and television have come at deep costs to society and the natural world. A thinker like Fuller is indeed a great symptom of our time. Under the guise of upholding the values of risk, innovation and disruption, he marks a conservative denial of the environmental crisis. We can see a similar kind of response in other intellectuals like Jordan Peterson, Steven Pinker and Jonathan Haidt who represent conservative Enlightenment responses to feminism and socialism.

The climate crisis truly undermines many of our most cherished ruling ideas. All of the ways of dealing with it mentioned above – carbon trading, green consumption, carbon sequestering or modification of humans – are various forms of evading the need to transform both values and ways of life. The climate crisis ultimately undermines the most important ruling ideas that we have. Increasing material productivity, for instance, has been a staple of ruling ideas since at least the Protestant Reformation. It has been central to all ideologies in the nineteenth and twentieth centuries. Both capitalism and communism sang the praises of productivity though they argued about who was truly productive. Capitalism ruled by a business elite tries as best it can to present those on top as the most productive. Papers like the *Wall Street Journal* sing the praises of the tireless efforts of heroic single-minded businessmen and entrepreneurs.

Communism recognizes that production comes from the people who design and produce the work itself; it knows that an iPhone does not come from the head of Steve Jobs but from thousands of hours of tireless toil of thousands of workers and hundreds of engineers. However, aside from some comments of Marx on nature and its appropriation, the culture of real existing communism itself was hyper-productionist. The USSR made productivity of workers themselves into a cultural ideal. It regularly honored and promoted those who found ways to produce more, a good example being the labor hero Alexey

Stakanov. Stakanov was born to a poor family in 1906. He started working in a coal mine in Kadievka. On August 31, 1935, it was reported that in five hours Stakanov mined 102 tonnes of coal, 14 times his quota. Later on he set a new record by mining 227 tonnes of coal in a shift. Stakanov went on to receive two Orders of Lenin and the order of the Red Banner of Labor, and a town was named after him. At the time, coal was the fuel of modernization. It was used for electricity and presented deep kinds of progress as the whole country fought to overcome hunger, illiteracy and superstition. Today we may think that it was good of the government to recognize the efforts of workers (what today's societies still fundamentally deny), yet at the same time we know what they could not have known, that it would have been better to leave the coal in the ground.

In an age in which global heating looms above humanity like a kind of death sentence, the values of productivity and growth are bound to be challenged. Production of any material thing will inevitably look more and more like extraction. Extraction is highly ineffective and harmful. Indeed, coal is a good example. When we use coal to make electricity, only 40 percent of the energy gets used; the rest results in sulfuric acid, low-grade heat and carbon dioxide. Work itself becomes less important while we continually take valuable resources from nature and then dump them back as harmful nondegradable garbage. Productivity and growth rest on false premises that resources are infinite or nondegradable.

The belief in growth was essentially created in the West by the "discovery" of America. Europeans who had depleted the resources in their own land, having chopped down most of their forests, killed all of their wild animals and depleted their soil, had unexpectedly found a place with a seemingly endless supply of land, fur, trees, gold and silver. The huge availability of land plus the labor of imported slaves produced sugar, cotton, coffee and tea that enabled plantation owners to live like minor royalty in Europe. It was this discovery that prompted the idea of boundless riches, efficiency, productivity and endless growth. Christian ideals that used to critique and suppress those desires in the population were overturned by the Reformation. The Reformation created an incentive to become rich as a way of showing that you were chosen. It ultimately reoriented people to no longer fight over religion and the sacred but to devote themselves to the conquest of nature and the amassment of riches. With the new focus on wealth came a host of other values that include responsibility, prudence, calculative rationality, hard work and efficiency. Capital flows from the Americas to Europe reaffirmed these ideas. The search for power and efficiency led the pioneers of industrialization in England to promote experiments using the combination of engines and fossil fuels that mechanized and automated labor.

In the nineteenth century, industrialization took place at a record pace among competing European powers and then non-European powers. Industrialization first started in England in the 1780s, and then about 60 years later it developed in Germany, France, Austria and the Scandinavian countries, spreading to the US, Japan and then Slovakia, Poland, Hungary, and then Russia in the 1890s. Industrialization presents a radically new era in human history. We really should set our global time not to the birth of Jesus (who in any case represents but just one religious tradition) but to the birth of modern industry since it is this time and this process that shall determine whether humanity survives or not. It is industrialization that has led to the quick colonization of what remained of the uncolonized world. It forms the necessary backdrop that led to World War One and World War Two, from the scramble for Africa to Hitler's Lebensraum. Industrialization leads to the treatment of every natural resource as fit for expropriation and aggressive expansion.

The praxis was rationalized by the greatest thinkers of the

time. Property rights – the appropriation of land and its use – were defended by Locke as secured by labor on the land itself. What one takes from nature essentially does not harm anyone "since there was still enough, and as good left: and more than the yet unprovided could use." The theory was always wrong both because the world is finite and because property rights were a result of violent conquest and displacement of natives. A political regime was formed whose monopoly of violence was mainly used to guarantee property rights. Adam Smith added another layer to ruling ideas that had important consequences. Smith argued that dogged pursuit of self-interest guarantees the best outcome for society: "It is not from the benevolence of the butcher, the brewer, or the baker, that we expect our dinner, but from their regard to their own interest." By the 1980s, this was taken to say that greed is good.

The politics of Locke and Smith, that of hedonism, materialism and individualism, demand that nature continues to provide for humanity unabated. It was the Marquis de Sade who drew the most radical and consistent conclusions from liberalism. All is just self-interest and pleasure. There is no justice in the world, only the ability to follow one's desire. If this pleasure comes at the expense of the suffering of others, so be it. Better yet, one can even derive pleasure from the suffering of others. Classical liberalism was more hypocritical than the marquis. As we saw with Adam Smith, it argued that seeking individual pleasure, wealth and power is consistent with the general good. However, today and due to the environmental crisis, the plausibility of such pretense is eroding fast. Seeking individual pleasure, wealth and profit is consistent with the collapse of agriculture, the flooding of coastal cities and the civil wars that arise as millions of refugees will attempt to move north from island nations that have flooded, as well as from large swaths of Africa and the Middle East that will become uninhabitable.

In reality, nothing taken from nature is without cost.

Becoming rich has meant getting something now while keeping its costs off our books and consciousness. Getting cheap land comes at the price of displacing indigenous populations and the slashing and burning of forests, and getting cheap energy comes with the price of global warming and toxic fuels, and polluted air. Even for those who most benefit from this system, an orientation toward profit has meant a significant diminishing in the ability to feel beauty, goodness, spirituality, and the joy of direct connection with other people, as well as a loss of connection with nature. It also causes ethical blindness, a condition in which one lives in a kind of denial of the pain and suffering that is happening in one's world, ignoring in the name of economic "rationality" not only the destruction of nature but the poverty, racism, sexism and state violence in human societies themselves.

Philosopher Val Plumwood argues that the "dominant forms of reason – economic, political, scientific and ethical/prudential – are failing us."[1] These forms, she argues, do not allow us to see the blind spots of the way we understand our relationship to nature. They have identified the biospheric other as an invitation for endless exploitation. Our conception of rationality has become the way in which we legitimize and reinforce privilege. The reason/nature dichotomy and polarization neutralizes inequality and justifies privilege; the class associated with reason is seen as deserving of control and power. Losers such as the unemployed, shanty town Muslims and Christians, and Indian subsistence farmers are viewed as rationally deficient just like slaves and women were in the past. The great heroes of capitalism are indeed the "sado-dispassionate"; they are usually impassive males who lack basic empathy to any kind of other. The heroes of the screen, from Clint Eastwood to Tom Cruise, embody this ideal for us. Plumwood empathizes that maybe the last scene of the world could be imagined as a hero of reason choking "the life from his planetary partner in a final sadistic act of mastery."[2]

The motivation to use this kind of instrumental reason in the West has always been that it produces growth; however, ultimately and sooner than we know it the environmental crisis will challenge all ideas related to growth. It is not the case that the negative effects of subordinating society to instrumental reason, profit and growth have been overlooked by poets, thinkers and writers in the past. The critique of profit and growth include thinkers such as Plato, Jean-Jacques Rousseau, Thomas Malthus, Friedrich Engels, the Luddites, Henry David Thoreau, John Stuart Mill, William Wordsworth, Tolstoy and Gandhi. From the 1970s until quite recently, these thinkers and their ideas were mocked by the techno-elites – they were viewed as passé; now they will be reexamined by the masses as blueprints for the world that necessarily must come. Such a reexamination deserves a book of its own. Still, it would be good here to give the skeleton of such a reevaluation.

Plato was most concerned with the way in which the market economy effects virtue. He looked at his own society and the desires of people within it for "cakes and prostitutes" with distaste. Plato describes people who desire as bottomless barrels or leaky jars. In contrast to desiring ever more, Plato suggested contemplation of the forms of the beautiful and the good as a kind of "sustainable" preoccupation that allows society to settle down and people to live simply and be content with their lives.

Jean-Jacques Rousseau presents us with an early prototype of a critique of modernity. He looks back at the state of nature as that in which:

Abandoned to its natural fertility and covered by immense forests that the ax had never mutilated, the earth offers at every step food and shelter to animals of every species. Men dispersed among them, observe and imitate their industry and thus raise themselves to the instinct of beasts, with the advantage that each species has merely its own instincts, while man, having perhaps none that are his own, appropriates them all, nourishing himself equally on a wide selection of foods that other animals share, consequently finding his sustenance with greater ease than any of the others.[3]

In his account of man's natural state, Rousseau makes use of travel literature from the Americas and the first European accounts of the Native American culture and way of life. He notices that natives are less ill than the civilized and that they do not die earlier, and that civilization has brought new illnesses of their own. He also finds excess of work with some and idleness in others, that the food that the rich eat "inflames humors and triggers indigestion; the bad food of the poor, who often have no food at all." He notices that the first humans who have become sedentary and have built themselves lodgings "provided himself with things that he did not particularly need, since until then he had done without them." Rousseau thinks that man in the state of nature has a heightened sense of vision, scent and hearing and yet in the state of nature humans do not desire more than they have.

Human ability to learn and improve, the very basis of the accumulation of knowledge, is a kind of mixed blessing. In contrast to animals, human babies are helpless while the old become imbecilic and in terms of self-sufficiency become less than animals. For Rousseau, this faculty of adoptive learning, of getting more knowledge and more ability, is the source of many human misfortunes, not least the knowledge of death and creation of endless desire. It is civilization that plants many of the vices and desires. Unlike Hobbes who imagined people with the same endless desires in the state of nature only without a sovereign to keep them in line, people in the actual state of nature do not possess these desires of endless accumulation and power. Rousseau is one of the first critics of possessive individualism. He famously begins the second part of the origins of inequality with:

> The first man who fenced in a plot of land and dared to say, "This is mine," and found people who were sufficiently simple to believe him, was the true founder of civil society. How many crimes, wars, murders, how much misery and horror, could have been spared the human race if someone would have pulled out the stakes or filled in the ditch and called out to his fellow men: "Beware! Do not listen to this imposter! You will be lost if you forget that the fruits of the earth belong to all, and that the land belongs to no one."

It is private ownership of land that is the root cause of inequality as well as all the methods and ideas needed to justify it. Experiencing a place like the United States as well as visiting newly privatized places like China, one realizes the truth of Rousseau that so much of organized violence is created to defend the institution of private property. Rousseau describes well the way that hunter-gatherers go down the path of civilization; he depicts the increasing conveniences and comforts that man possesses and the problems associated with them:

> ...but the conveniences they had invented soon became habitual, losing their appeal almost entirely, while at the same time deteriorating into commodities men could no longer do without. Being deprived of them becomes crueler than possessing them had been pleasant, and men were unhappy at losing them without ever having been happy to possess them.

It was already clear to Rousseau that "iron and wheat," metallurgy and agriculture, made the human condition worse:

"vast forests turned into sunny fields that had to be watered with men's sweat, and in which one soon saw slavery and poverty sprouting and growing along with the harvest."

For Friedrich Engels, the agricultural revolution brought with it the birth of exploitation and patriarchy. On the level of the family, it has institutionalized private property and inheritance, which reinforced misogyny as fathers wanted to make sure that their inheritance would go to their biological offspring. Engels, who one would think (as a Marxist) would celebrate the development of forces of production, is far from doing this unproblematically. Forces of production brought with them all the evils of institutionalized hierarchy into this world, hierarchies that continue to torment and plague us. This is seen most significantly in the terrorizing power of the state to kill, punish, tax and conscript the young, and the power of the workplace to exploit, control and threaten with unemployment. Engels was no simple believer in progress; in the story he tells, humanity goes forward in its ability to control nature and produce but goes backward in terms of the way humanity treats itself. It is a story of a downfall from primitive "communism" of hunter-gatherers to the ugliness of warrior and priestly led agricultural serfdom and then to the even worse conditions of industrialism.

Engels first book, *The Condition of the Working Class in England*, is a detailed study of how moving into the cities and factory work has worsened the lives of workers who came from the country. Engels demonstrates how scarlet fever, whooping cough, measles and tuberculosis increased substantially and how the death rate of both children and adults has gone up substantially in towns that have gone through industrialization. He exposes the crowding, the lack of clean water, the dangerous and planless building of apartments and houses that keeps the streets damp with feces and contributes to disease. Workers' apartments do not have beds or tables; in fact, workers have very little property, and usually a whole family lives in one small room, often in a basement that is dark, damp and without light or air. Parents who work all day neglect their children. Children wear cheap woolen clothing that is not fit for English weather and quickly disintegrates and is patched up. Adults and children feed on what is left from the market after a whole week and is sold at the lowest prices; often this means eating rotting flesh and cheese. Coffee is sold diluted with earth, or black pepper with dust.

Employees work up to 16 hours a day and sometimes work nights as well. Working conditions are despotic; workers must do precisely what is required of them or else they are punished severely. They stand for hours on end, which causes problems with their backs and knees and conditions such as varicose veins, ulcers and deformed pelvises for women. Engels demonstrates throughout the book that these life conditions are significantly worse than they had been in agricultural villages before. In the short run at least, Engels is very weary of teleological narratives of progress. Given that factories in China today, more than 180 years into Engels's future, have some of the same characteristics, we too should be weary of notions of progress and always ask, "Progress for whom?"

Another type of critique of progress follows a wholly different logic. In his *Essay on the Principle of Population*, Thomas Malthus points out to those who believe in the perfectibility of society and of progress that there are limits to growth. Malthus assumes two postulates, that men eat and that they procreate; however, these grow at different rates: "Population when unchecked increases in a geometrical ratio. Subsistence increases only in an arithmetical ratio." For Malthus, this is the main reason why a society in which all members live in ease and happiness is impossible; poverty is a result of reproduction. Malthus backed up his argument with countless examples both from the natural world and from human society and history. These examples show how growth proceeds exponentially when there are ample resources (for example, the population in the back settlements in America that did not receive new immigrants) and how this expansion is ultimately checked by war, famine and epidemics:

> The power of population is so superior to the power of the earth to produce subsistence for man, that premature death must in some shape or other visit the human race. The vices of mankind are active and able ministers of depopulation. They are the precursors in the great army of destruction, and often finish the dreadful work themselves. But should they fail in this war of extermination, sickly seasons, epidemics, pestilence, and plague advance in terrific array, and sweep off their thousands and tens of thousands. Should success be still incomplete, gigantic inevitable famine stalks in the rear, and with one mighty blow levels the population with the food of the world.

Though Malthus believed in technological improvement, he did not believe that this improvement is without limit. There is a limit to the way in which we can improve food production. He sums up that the power of population growth is widely greater than the power of the Earth to provide food for man.

It is not easy to disentangle what is correct and what is not in Malthus. On the most obvious level, Malthus rationalized the poverty of his society. According to Malthus, poverty does not stem from an elite expropriation of most of the produce of peasants and laborers but from their own vices – they have too much sex and procreate to an extent that makes the Earth unable to feed them. In a way, this is the old and continuing refrain, that the poor are poor because of their lack of morality. Today, we have the variation that claims that poverty and crime arise from the lax morals of the working class (fathers don't stay with families, etc.). This is clearly wrong, a classic ruling idea, an idea used by elites in class warfare against those who are most disadvantaged.

Though elites still use the idea of the lax morals of the working class, they do not actively promote active population control for several reasons. First, procreation provides cheap labor that would become dearer without it, although there are ways to circumvent this through immigration or "guest" workers. Second, population control goes against the idea of freedom as well as the idea that the West is virtuous precisely because it fought against those who would control populations, the Nazis and then the communists.

There is obviously also something right about Malthus's idea, but the question remains, how do we separate it from its use as a weapon of class war? We do this by advocating redistribution not only between classes but between humans and the Earth. Redistribution must happen between the rich and poor but also between all of humanity and the biosphere. The Earth and its resources cannot be distributed only with the thought of man; otherwise, eventually even man will not exist.

Malthus expresses a contrast between the wishes of the Enlightenment and what the Earth can sustain. For those who believe in deep kinds of progress, there is something discouraging here. The vast majority of humanity has waited patiently, so to speak, to live the quality of life enjoyed post-World War Two by the Western middle class. On the present trajectory, they will never get there; their condition will only worsen. Still, perhaps there is an opportunity with Malthus's thought. The realization of the limits of growth can move societies away from the ideals of material growth to those that stress quality of life.

Research affirms what is intuitively well known – that people thrive with contact and cooperation with other people; that being in nature puts them at ease; that music, sex, play and storytelling are beneficial to their mental and physical health, etc. All of these desires can be fulfilled in a sustainable way. Fundamentally, most of these desires arose and were fulfilled in hunter-gatherer societies. There is an understandable yearning for a more materially simple life, one that is connected to local nature that repeats itself throughout history whether it is found in Rousseau or in Thoreau. Connection with nature reminds us of things that we appreciate, such as our very simple fascination with animals, with storms and with stars; the way people enjoy growing plants and food; and the way we like to feel embodied in the world, to live in bodies and emotions, not just being mediatized.

Alternatives to Ruling Ideas II: Revolutionary Ideas

Of course, everyone talks of revolution today and also of the revolutions of the past. The American and French Revolutions are the foundation of many democracies around the world, and naturally our business culture talks about revolution and disruption all the time. Revolution might look like a ruling idea rather than an alternative to ruling ideas. Yet modern-day political elites have been very actively repressing many attempts at revolutions since the Russian Revolution of October 1917. These include the repressions and coups against leftist politics in South America, the Vietnam War, and the strong repression of movements inside the West like the students' movement in France and the Black Panthers in the US. Business elites want to own a technical innovation that will disrupt other industries and that will sell their product, service or platform rather than theirs; they sometimes use the word revolution, but essentially, they want everything else to stay the same. This is, of course, not a revolution.

A revolution is a wholly new arrangement of society and culture. One only needs to think of the French Revolution to see this. A culture and society in which power was based on nobility and the church changed to a society in which power is based on the middle class and industrialists. This is a change in law (constitutions), in political arrangements (parliaments, political parties, congress, judiciary, etc.), in culture (realism) and in economics (industrialism), etc. All of these changes happened in a relatively short time frame. The American Revolution between 1765 and 1783, the French Revolution, 1789-1799, and the Industrial Revolution from 1780 to 1820. These three events fundamentally changed the world; we all still live with their accomplishments, costs and dangers: basic political rights and political representation, the start of a rise in the standard of living for the population, but also the much-accelerated decimation of nature and what can only be described as the gassing and heating of the world.

True revolutions entail so many novel ideas and practices that they create a new way of life. Past revolutions were prepared by destroying previous ideas and introducing new ones. In continental Europe, the Enlightenment fought a long and hard battle against established religion and introduced a new notion of human equality and freedom. These were such new ideas that much of history since then can be well described as a fight between groups regarding what precisely they mean.

Today we need new ideas, for a new kind of revolution. Unlike the situation in France and America in the eighteenth century, we face two developments that cannot be addressed within the existing political system. The first is the heating of the biosphere and the second, automation and AI. Within the existing political economic coordinates, both will lead to a world of interlinked global elites ruling over masses of "superfluous" human beings including climate refugees, the unemployed, the poor and the old. In order to avert this future, we need many ideas, ideas that precisely counter the ruling ideas. Some of them will be creative opposites of ruling ideas, some will be entirely novel.

Counter-hegemonic ideas that are already articulated today

are, for example, localism and the gift-economy. These ideas attempt to find alternatives to the globally integrated capitalist economy. Localism is a revolution on many levels. One can start with local perception and local truth. Perception of locality and local politics instills many truths that counter ruling ideas by themselves. A good look at any city will offer one a whole array of important truths about today's world. One is likely to see various very distinct spaces. Literally on top is the corporate space with its tall large glass buildings, offices and cafes; today, every city in the world is dominated by this corporate space. It is the global network between these urban centers that rules the world.

Right next to this corporate downtown, we see the dilapidated neighborhoods of the "superfluous" people who are hustling to make a living. Any large city in the West will have these very sad spaces, where people try to make a living simply buying and selling bad food or degraded products, along with those who are on welfare or engaged in petty crime. In the global south, of course, conditions are much worse. For example, only four kilometers from the busy downtown of Mumbai, with its banks and high-tech firms, there is Dharavi, a slum in which families support themselves on 84 dollars a month, where warm-hearted people, beaming with hospitality, will invite you into their tiny home, feed you and give you tea, show you their tiny kitchen and unsanitary water, and how a family of five sleeps on the floor. Localism reveals truth.

Have an extended conversation with a local person, a taxi driver, a secretary or a small shopkeeper and you will often get a fresh and truthful perspective. Globalism in its neoliberal variety is likely to be much more divorced from any kind of truth. Global conferences are a good pointer to the way globalism lies. Take TED conferences or the economic forum at Davos, or South by Southwest or any one of the myriad conferences that feature pitches for new products or technologies or personal development. Such places will be filled with ruling ideas and their distortions.

Localism counters globalization in other ways as well, particularly as it relates to our relationship with the way we live, eat and socialize. These include autonomous buildings (buildings that don't need infrastructural support), local food, organic farming, simple living, etc. Becoming local is a different kind of orientation. It means discovering people around you and organizing with them. However, we must also remember that globalization today is largely monopolized by capitalism and that there were and are alter-globalization movements such as socialism, and anti-imperialist and global environmental activism.

The gift-economy was first theorized by Marcel Mauss. Mauss noticed the obligatory nature of gift giving in "primitive" societies and the way in which it involved participants in a moral economy that creates a moral bond between people and builds communities. Giving a gift, like hosting a dinner, essentially puts the other in a kind of social debt that needs to be reciprocated within a certain period of time. Giving a gift usually involves the expectation of reciprocity over time; this contrasts with exchange in the market where we expect immediate exchange of value, often at the expense of the other. A market exchange usually leaves zero goodwill after the exchange has been done. Gifts provide joy to the giver as well as recognition for tailoring the gift to the enjoyment of the receiver. Gift-giving culture is also possible only between equals, as the giving of something to someone who is significantly poorer becomes a donation or charity. Localism and gifting are clearly counterhegemonic ideas.

There are also more sinister counter-hegemonic ideas such as a return to ethno-nationalism and the threat of a neofascist counter revolution. Such a neofascism does not look like the old fascism; it will fit today's world, it will be hip, and networked and apped and trendy and probably consumerist, but it will attempt to reassert existing and past hierarchies. While the original fascism was mainly anti-socialist (this was the revolution that threatened it), the future fascism will be anti-environmental. While fascism took many things from socialism (mass political participation, anti-bourgeois rhetoric, political youth groups, mass rallies, etc.) and subverted them against socialism, a future fascism might take elements from the environmentalist movement and use them in order to act in unexpected ways against environmentalism. These are dangerous counter-hegemonic ideas and trends that will support a counterrevolution.

On the more promising side, there will be new ideas that do not articulate themselves around what is known as a new form of politics. Probably, these will be new ideas that combine the democratic urge that has been with us for the past 300 years together with new technologies as well as creative adaptation to environmental constraints. What will radically democratic, green, technological and local ideas look like? What strange political networks of coalitions will form between "superfluous" humans, animals, plants and technology? What kinds of transfiguration of values will occur? It is hard to say. The past offers us only one such long-lasting transfiguration from an otherworldly transcendent orientation around God to an immanent transformation around humanity and productivity.

Transfiguration of values fundamentally changes the discussion. In the sixteenth and seventeenth centuries, Catholics and Protestants fought a Thirty Years' War in which eight million people were killed; in terms of percentage of death of the population, it was deadlier than World War Two. For many of us, that conflict is unclear today, and needs to be explained by teachers and professors for a long time just to make sense, let alone to animate us significantly. Though we are still suffering and are likely to suffer even more in the future under

386

capitalism, some of the factionalism among different socialist and communist groups in the beginning and middle of the twentieth century is quickly becoming distant; relatively few people know the difference between Maoism and Trotskyism. In many ways, we could have had a third transformation of values if time was not constantly being "pulled back" by conservatives around the world.

Skeptics would say that history does not show a discernable progressive or moral trend. In the expanded circle of moral concern, Jesus included our enemies while Buddhists included the suffering of all sentient beings, while 2,000 years later, we witness people with an extreme form of moral concern so constricted that they care only for their very own material pleasures. Nevertheless, there are long-range reasons for optimism regarding the expanding circle of moral concern. One such reason has to do with democracy; the other with growing interdependence.

Democracy is very much an unfinished project that has vacillated in the past 300 years. Still broadly, the principle of some form of popular sovereignty has expanded to the whole world in the past 300 years. In reality, most states are different types of oligarchies; the US is an oligarchy just as much as China is. Both countries have a small ruling elite that determines most of the decisions made. Nevertheless, both countries invoke the will of the people as their proper legitimization. This makes them vulnerable to the people in various ways, and presents an advance in comparison to feudalism. Democratic projects have, for example, largely enfranchised women and minorities. Again, though very different in many ways, the US, Russia, India, Europe and China have all opened public office to everyone irrespective of gender, class and race. Of course, there are glaring material inequalities in gender and certainly in race, but we must not forget that millions of women, for example, are financially independent of men, something that would have been unimaginable only a hundred years before. In places like China, 300 million people who were largely destitute made it to the middle class. These advances should not be taken for granted and they might be reversed, yet they might be a long-term trend. The second reason that the circle of moral concern will widen has to do simply with our interdependence. Fantasies of independence are increasingly implausible, as we become more and more aware of our dependence on biodiversity for food security, for medical research and for health. This awareness is likely to be heightened in the future as well.

These are long-term trends that are unlikely to be reversed. They signal that we should have the courage to discard ruling ideas whose time has passed and bravely change our values and our orientation. In this book, I have tried to outline the main ideas that have come to rule and largely to ruin our lives. It is my hope that their negation will help us all on a path of emancipation.

Endnotes

Chapter One: Individualism Part I

1. Louis Althusser, *Lenin and Philosophy and Other Essays* (NYU Press, 2001), 117–20.
2. Jacques Lacan, *On the Names-of-the-Father* (Polity, 2013).
3. Norman Nelson, "Individualism as a Criterion of the Renaissance," *The Journal of English and Germanic Philology* 32, no. 3 (1933): 317.
4. Wilhelm Reich, *The Mass Psychology of Fascism* (Macmillan, 1970), vii.
5. Abraham H. Maslow, *Motivation and Personality*, 3rd Edition, ed. Robert Frager et al., 3rd edition (New York: Longman, 1987).

Chapter Two: Individualism Part II

1. James Holmes, "Resume submitted to University of Illinois Urbana-Champaign" (PDF). Reuters. p. 11. Retrieved August 11, 2012.
2. Keith Coffman (June 29, 2015), "Coworker recalls Colorado movie massacre gunman acting 'spaced out'". Yahoo! News. Retrieved June 29, 2015.
3. Read more: http://www.dailymail.co.uk/tvshowbiz/article-3193027/Documentary-Heath-Ledger-s-father-reveals-journal-actor-kept-prepared-role-Joker-resurfaces.html#ixzz4HZXFC43E.
4. Joseph A. Schumpeter, "The Creative Response in Economic History," *The Journal of Economic History* 7, no. 2 (1947): 149–159; David Harvey, *Seventeen Contradictions and the End of Capitalism*, Reprint edition (Oxford: Oxford University Press, 2015).
5. Domenico Losurdo, *Liberalism: A Counter-History*, trans. Gregory Elliott (London ; New York: Verso, 2014).

6. Losurdo, p.100.
7. Alan Brinkley, *American History: Connecting with the Past*, 15th edition (New York, NY: McGraw-Hill Education, 2014), 333.
8. Henry David Thoreau, W. S. Merwin, and William Howarth, *Walden and Civil Disobedience*, Reissue edition (New York: Signet, 2012), 4.

Chapter Three: The New Commandments
1. St Jerome, Against Jovinianus, Book 1, Section 20, 40, A.D. 39.
2. Omri Gillath, Gery C. Karantzas, and R. Chris Fraley, *Adult Attachment: A Concise Introduction to Theory and Research*, 1st edition (Amsterdam: Academic Press, 2016).

Chapter Four: Values and Virtues
1. "Our Culture," *HUAWEI* (blog), May 8, 2014, https://huaweico.wordpress.com/our-culture/.
2. Brian Daizen Victoria, *Zen at War*, 2nd edition (Lanham, Md: Rowman & Littlefield Publishers, Inc., 2006).
3. Franco Moretti, *The Bourgeois: Between History and Literature*, Reprint edition (London New York: Verso, 2014), 30.

Chapter Five: Knowledge
1. Carl Sagan, *Cosmos*, 1st edition (Carl Sagan Productions, Inc., 2010), 2.

Chapter Six: Technology and Disruption
1. Xenophon, *The Economist of Xenophon* (Ellis and White, 1876), 22–23.
2. We have two opposite takes on Socrates and the mechanical arts. The one cited above by Xenophon and Plato's early dialogs where Socrates sees the mechanical arts as a worthy model of both knowledge and utility so much so

that he compares every virtue to those barrel makers and shoemakers. Indeed, sometimes he is being made fun of by his young aristocratic companions for appreciating these sorts of people and what they do. Thus we have one account in which Socrates has an untypical worldview that goes against the norm (in Plato) and one version in which he says what is usually acceptable. From the two, I believe Plato's version since it is unlikely that the aristocratic Plato invented such a thing. It is simply Xenophon putting reasons in Socrates' mouth for the normal way in which different trades are appreciated in Athens.

3. James B. Pritchard, *Ancient Near Eastern Texts Relating to the Old Testament with Supplement* (Princeton University Press, 2016), 432–34.

Chapter Seven: Neo-Nietzscheans

1. Friedrich Nietzsche, *Nietzsche: Beyond Good and Evil: Prelude to a Philosophy of the Future*, ed. Rolf-Peter Horstmann and Judith Norman, trans. Judith Norman, Cambridge Texts in the History of Philosophy (Cambridge: Cambridge University Press, 2001), 151, https://doi.org/10.1017/CBO9780511812033.

2. Oscar Levy, *The Complete Works of Friedrich Nietzsche* (RareBooksClub.com, 2013), 275.

3. Friedrich Nietzsche, *On the Genealogy of Morals and Ecce Homo*, ed. Walter Kaufmann, Reissue edition (New York: Vintage, 1989), 35–36.

4. If one just exchanges the term Enlightenment with the economic system of the Enlightenment – capitalism – one can see here the root of Max Weber's famous thesis that capitalism originates from the incentive structure of certain Protestant sects.

5. An important precursor is the Marquis de Sade, who negated both Christianity and what he thought of as

Christianized forms of the Enlightenment in the name of egotistical pleasures. Of course, he predated socialism and could not critique it.

6. Levy, *The Complete Works of Friedrich Nietzsche*, 4294–379.

7. Levy, 218.

8. Levy, 3948.-style-language/schema/raw/master/csl-citation. json"}

9. Levy, 3700–01.

10. Friedrich Nietzsche, *Nietzsche: The Anti-Christ, Ecce Homo, Twilight of the Idols: And Other Writings*, ed. Aaron Ridley, trans. Judith Norman (New York: Cambridge University Press, 2005), 60.

11. Levy, *The Complete Works of Friedrich Nietzsche*, 1456.

12. Charles A. Beard, *An Economic Interpretation of the Constitution of the United States*, Edition unstated (Mineola, N.Y: Dover Publications, 2004).

13. Ayn Rand, *Atlas Shrugged* (Paw Prints, 2008), 1065.

14. Joseph A. Schumpeter, *Capitalism, Socialism and Democracy* (Routledge, 2013), 83.201.

Chapter Eight: Ruling Ideas: The Past, Present and Future

1. Joseph A. Schumpeter, *Capitalism, Socialism and Democracy* (Routledge, 2013), 83.

Chapter Nine: The Holy Trinity of Conservative Thought: God – Nation – Family

1. Of course, private worship took place in the home as well; it was not deemed as effective but it let people remember the importance of the gods and therefore reaffirmed the need for public worship.

2. *Renaud Camus (English)*, accessed August 9, 2020, https://www.youtube.com/watch?v=CMxhMtv1qvE.

3. Douglas Murray and Robert Davies, *The Strange Death of*

444

444

Europe, Unabridged edition (Audible Studios on Brilliance Audio, 2017).

4. Daniel Boyarin, *Border Lines: The Partition of Judaeo-Christianity* (University of Pennsylvania Press, 2010).

Chapter Ten: A Short History of the Modern Critique of the Ruling Ideas

1. "2020 World Press Freedom Index | Reporters Without Borders," RSF, accessed August 20, 2020, https://rsf.org/en/ranking.
2. Hubert Cieslik, "The Case of Christovão Ferreira," *Monumenta Nipponica* 29, no. 1 (1974): 35, https://doi.org/10.2307/2383462.
3. Louis-Armand de Lom D'Arce de Lahontan, *New Voyages to North-America,* Vol. 2 (Place of publication not identified: Forgotten Books, 2018), 420.
4. Lahontan, 420.
5. Lahontan, 439–40.
6. Lahontan, 443.
7. Lahontan, 452–53.
8. Lahontan, 454.
9. Lahontan, 454.
10. Lahontan, 463.
11. Lahontan, 464.
12. Lahontan, 462.
13. "The Dark Side of Thomas Jefferson," *Smithsonian Magazine,* accessed October 8, 2020, https://www.smithsonianmag.com/history/the-dark-side-of-thomas-jefferson-35976004/.
14. Althusser, *Lenin and Philosophy and Other Essays,* 117–20.
15. Given that Althusser was a believing Catholic for most of his childhood and young adulthood, it is likely that this example formed the inspiration for his concept of interpellation.

Chapter 11: The Work of Patching Up

1. David Graeber, *Bullshit Jobs: A Theory* (New York: Simon & Schuster, 2018).
2. P. Pignarre and I. Stengers, *Capitalist Sorcery: Breaking the Spell*, trans. Andrew Goffey, 2011 edition (Houndmills, Basingstoke, Hampshire ; New York: Palgrave Macmillan, 2011), 32.

Chapter 14: Alternatives to Ruling Ideas

1. Val Plumwood, *Environmental Culture: The Ecological Crisis of Reason*, 1st edition (London; New York: Routledge, 2001), 16.
2. Plumwood, 22.
3. Jean-Jacques Rousseau, *The Essential Writings of Rousseau* (Modern Library, 2013), 17.

Bibliography

Althusser, Louis. *Lenin and Philosophy and Other Essays*. NYU Press, 2001.

Bataille, Georges. *The Accursed Share: An Essay on General Economy, Vol. 1: Consumption*. Translated by Robert Hurley. 1st edition. New York: Zone Books, 1991.

Beard, Charles A. *An Economic Interpretation of the Constitution of the United States*. Edition unstated. Mineola, N.Y: Dover Publications, 2004.

Boyarin, Daniel. *Border Lines: The Partition of Judaeo-Christianity*. University of Pennsylvania Press, 2010.

Brinkley, Alan. *American History: Connecting with the Past*. 15th edition. New York, NY: McGraw-Hill Education, 2014.

Cieslik, Hubert. "The Case of Christovão Ferreira." *Monumenta Nipponica* 29, no. 1 (1974): 1–54. https://doi.org/10.2307/2383462.

Gillath, Omri, Gery C. Karantzas, and R. Chris Fraley. *Adult Attachment: A Concise Introduction to Theory and Research*. 1st edition. Amsterdam: Academic Press, 2016.

Graeber, David. *Bullshit Jobs: A Theory*. New York: Simon & Schuster, 2018.

Harvey, David. *Seventeen Contradictions and the End of Capitalism*. Reprint edition. Oxford: Oxford University Press, 2015.

HUAWEI. "Our Culture," May 8, 2014. https://huaweico.wordpress.com/our-culture/.

Lacan, Jacques. *On the Names-of-the-Father*. Polity, 2013.

Lahontan, Louis Armand de Lom D'Arce de. *New Voyages to North-America, Vol. 2: Giving a Full Account of the Customs, Commerce, Religion, and Strange Opinions of the Savages of That Country;...and the Present State of the Commerce of T*. Place of publication not identified: Forgotten Books, 2018.

Levy, Oscar. *The Complete Works of Friedrich Nietzsche*.

RareBooksClub.com, 2013.

Losurdo, Domenico. *Liberalism: A Counter-History*. Translated by Gregory Elliott. London; New York: Verso, 2014.

Maslow, Abraham H. *Motivation and Personality*, 3rd edition. Edited by Robert Frager, James Fadiman, Cynthia McReynolds, and Ruth Cox. New York: Longman, 1987.

Moretti, Franco. *The Bourgeois: Between History and Literature*. Reprint edition. London New York: Verso, 2014.

Murray, Douglas, and Robert Davies. *The Strange Death of Europe*. Unabridged edition. Audible Studios on Brilliance Audio, 2017.

Nelson, Norman. "Individualism as a Criterion of the Renaissance." *The Journal of English and Germanic Philology* 32, no. 3 (1933): 316–34.

Nietzsche, Friedrich. *Nietzsche: Beyond Good and Evil: Prelude to a Philosophy of the Future*. Edited by Rolf-Peter Horstmann and Judith Norman. Translated by Judith Norman. Cambridge Texts in the History of Philosophy. Cambridge: Cambridge University Press, 2001. https://doi.org/10.1017/CBO9780511812033.

— — —. *Nietzsche: The Anti-Christ, Ecce Homo, Twilight of the Idols: And Other Writings*. Edited by Aaron Ridley. Translated by Judith Norman. New York: Cambridge University Press, 2005.

— — —. *On the Genealogy of Morals and Ecce Homo*. Edited by Walter Kaufmann. Reissue edition. New York: Vintage, 1989.

Pignarre, P., and I. Stengers. *Capitalist Sorcery: Breaking the Spell*. Translated by Andrew Goffey. 2011 edition. Houndmills, Basingstoke, Hampshire; New York: Palgrave Macmillan, 2011.

Plumwood, Val. *Environmental Culture: The Ecological Crisis of Reason*. 1st edition. London; New York: Routledge, 2001.

Pritchard, James B. *Ancient Near Eastern Texts Relating to the Old Testament with Supplement*. Princeton University Press, 2016.

Rand, Ayn. *Atlas Shrugged*. Paw Prints, 2008.

Reich, Wilhelm. *The Mass Psychology of Fascism*. Macmillan, 1970.

Renaud Camus (English). Accessed August 9, 2020. https://www. youtube.com/watch?v=CMxhMtv1qvE.

Rousseau, Jean Jacques. *The Essential Writings of Rousseau*. Modern Library, 2013.

RSF. "2020 World Press Freedom Index | Reporters Without Borders." Accessed August 20, 2020. https://rsf.org/en/ ranking.

Sagan, Carl. *Cosmos*. 1st edition. Carl Sagan Productions, Inc., 2010.

Schumpeter, Joseph A. *Capitalism, Socialism and Democracy*. Routledge, 2013.

— — —. "The Creative Response in Economic History." *The Journal of Economic History* 7, no. 2 (1947): 149–59.

Smithsonian Magazine. "The Dark Side of Thomas Jefferson." Accessed October 8, 2020. https://www.smithsonianmag. com/history/the-dark-side-of-thomas-jefferson-35976004/.

Thoreau, Henry David, W. S. Merwin, and William Howarth. *Walden and Civil Disobedience*. Reissue edition. New York: Signet, 2012.

Turgot, Anne-Robert-Jacques. *Turgot Collection Pocket Edition*. Auburn, Ala: Ludwig von Mises Institute, 2011.

Victoria, Brian Daizen. *Zen at War*. 2nd edition. Lanham, Md: Rowman & Littlefield Publishers, Inc., 2006.

Wu, Tim. *The Attention Merchants: The Epic Scramble to Get Inside Our Heads*. 1st edition. New York: Knopf, 2016.

Xenophon. *The Economist of Xenophon*. Ellis and White, 1876.

From the Author

If you would like to learn more about my new thinking on the Ruling Ideas as well as hear podcasts with scholars and activists about these issues, please look into my channel on YouTube called the Ruling Ideas:

https://www.youtube.com/channel/
UCs9TQiRM4TslYM7KnSkBPGw

If you would like to contact me personally, my email is:
ariofengen@gmail.com

Sincerely, Ari Ofengenden

CULTURE, SOCIETY & POLITICS

The modern world is at an impasse. Disasters scroll across our smartphone screens and we're invited to like, follow or upvote, but critical thinking is harder and harder to find. Rather than connecting us in common struggle and debate, the internet has sped up and deepened a long-standing process of alienation and atomization. Zer0 Books wants to work against this trend. With critical theory as our jumping off point, we aim to publish books that make our readers uncomfortable. We want to move beyond received opinions.

Zer0 Books is on the left and wants to reinvent the left. We are sick of the injustice, the suffering and the stupidity that defines both our political and cultural world, and we aim to find a new foundation for a new struggle.

If this book has helped you to clarify an idea, solve a problem or extend your knowledge, you may want to check out our online content as well. Look for Zer0 Books: Advancing Conversations in the iTunes directory and for our Zer0 Books YouTube channel.

Popular videos include:

Žižek and the Double Blackmain
The Intellectual Dark Web is a Bad Sign
Can there be an Anti-SJW Left?
Answering Jordan Peterson on Marxism

Follow us on Facebook
at https://www.facebook.com/ZeroBooks and Twitter at https://twitter.com/Zer0Books

Bestsellers from Zer0 Books include:

Give Them An Argument
Logic for the Left
Ben Burgis
Many serious leftists have learned to distrust talk of logic. This is
a serious mistake.
Paperback: 978-1-78904-210-8 ebook: 978-1-78904-211-5

Poor but Sexy
Culture Clashes in Europe East and West
Agata Pyzik
How the East stayed East and the West stayed West.
Paperback: 978-1-78099-394-2 ebook: 978-1-78099-395-9

An Anthropology of Nothing in Particular
Martin Demant Frederiksen
A journey into the social lives of meaninglessness.
Paperback: 978-1-78535-699-5 ebook: 978-1-78535-700-8

In the Dust of This Planet
Horror of Philosophy vol. 1
Eugene Thacker
In the first of a series of three books on the Horror of Philosophy,
In the Dust of This Planet offers the genre of horror as a way of
thinking about the unthinkable.
Paperback: 978-1-84694-676-9 ebook: 978-1-78099-010-1

The End of Oulipo?
An Attempt to Exhaust a Movement
Lauren Elkin, Veronica Esposito
Paperback: 978-1-78099-655-4 ebook: 978-1-78099-656-1

Meat Market
Female Flesh under Capitalism
Laurie Penny
A feminist dissection of women's bodies as the fleshy fulcrum of
capitalist cannibalism, whereby women are both consumers and
consumed.
Paperback: 978-1-84694-521-2 ebook: 978-1-84694-782-7

Babbling Corpse
Vaporwave and the Commodification of Ghosts
Grafton Tanner
Paperback: 978-1-78279-759-3 ebook: 978-1-78279-760-9

New Work New Culture
Work we want and a culture that strengthens us
Frithjof Bergmann
A serious alternative for mankind and the planet.
Paperback: 978-1-78904-064-7 ebook: 978-1-78904-065-4

Romeo and Juliet in Palestine
Teaching Under Occupation
Tom Sperlinger
Life in the West Bank, the nature of pedagogy and the role of a
university under occupation.
Paperback: 978-1-78279-637-4 ebook: 978-1-78279-636-7

Ghosts of My Life
Writings on Depression, Hauntology and Lost Futures
Mark Fisher
Paperback: 978-1-78099-226-6 ebook: 978-1-78279-624-4

Sweetening the Pill
or How We Got Hooked on Hormonal Birth Control
Holly Grigg-Spall
Has contraception liberated or oppressed women?
Sweetening the Pill breaks the silence on the dark side of hormonal contraception.
Paperback: 978-1-78099-607-3 ebook: 978-1-78099-608-0

Why Are We The Good Guys?
Reclaiming Your Mind from the Delusions of Propaganda
David Cromwell
A provocative challenge to the standard ideology that Western power is a benevolent force in the world.
Paperback: 978-1-78099-365-2 ebook: 978-1-78099-366-9

The Writing on the Wall
On the Decomposition of Capitalism and its Critics
Anselm Jappe, Alastair Hemmens
A new approach to the meaning of social emancipation.
Paperback: 978-1-78535-581-3 ebook: 978-1-78535-582-0

Enjoying It
Candy Crush and Capitalism
Alfie Bown
A study of enjoyment and of the enjoyment of studying. Bown asks what enjoyment says about us and what we say about enjoyment, and why.
Paperback: 978-1-78535-155-6 ebook: 978-1-78535-156-3

Color, Facture, Art and Design
Iona Singh
This materialist definition of fine-art develops guidelines for architecture, design, cultural-studies and ultimately social change.
Paperback: 978-1-78099-629-5 ebook: 978-1-78099-630-1

Neglected or Misunderstood
The Radical Feminism of Shulamith Firestone
Victoria Margree
An interrogation of issues surrounding gender, biology,
sexuality, work and technology, and the ways in which our
imaginations continue to be in thrall to ideologies of maternity
and the nuclear family.
Paperback: 978-1-78535-539-4 ebook: 978-1-78535-540-0

How to Dismantle the NHS in 10 Easy Steps (Second Edition)
Youssef El-Gingihy
The story of how your NHS was sold off and why you will have
to buy private health insurance soon. A new expanded second
edition with chapters on junior doctors' strikes and government
blueprints for US-style healthcare.
Paperback: 978-1-78904-178-1 ebook: 978-1-78904-179-8

Digesting Recipes
The Art of Culinary Notation
Susannah Worth
A recipe is an instruction, the imperative tone of the expert, but
this constraint can offer its own kind of potential. A recipe need
not be a domestic trap but might instead offer escape – something
to fantasise about or aspire to.
Paperback: 978-1-78279-860-6 ebook: 978-1-78279-859-0